The Gathering

The Gathering

A Story of the First Buddhist Women

VANESSA R. SASSON

SHEFFIELD UK   BRISTOL CT

Published by Equinox Publishing Ltd.
UK: Office 415, The Workstation, 15 Paternoster Row, Sheffield, South
Yorkshire S1 2BX
USA: ISD, 70 Enterprise Drive, Bristol, CT 06010
www.equinoxpub.com

First published 2023

British Library Cataloguing-in-Publication Data
A catalogue record for this book is available from the British Library.

ISBN-13 978 1 80050 339 7 (hardback)
         978 1 80050 340 3 (paperback)
         978 1 80050 341 0 (ePDF)
         978 1 80050 362 5 (ePub)

Library of Congress Cataloging-in-Publication Data

Names: Sasson, Vanessa R., author.
Title: The gathering : a story of the first Buddhist women / Vanessa R. Sasson.
Description: Bristol : Equinox Publishing Ltd, 2023. | Includes bibliographical
    references and index. | Summary: "This book is a retelling of the story of
    the women's request for ordination"-- Provided by publisher.
Identifiers: LCCN 2022055064 (print) | LCCN 2022055065 (ebook) |
    ISBN 9781800503397 (hardback) | ISBN 9781800503403 (paperback) |
    ISBN 9781800503410 (pdf) | ISBN 9781800503625 (epub)
Subjects: LCSH: Women in Buddhism. | Ordination of women--Buddhism--
    History. | Women--Religious aspects--Buddhism. | Buddhist nuns in
    literature.
Classification: LCC BQ4570.W6 S27 2023 (print) | LCC BQ4570.W6
    (ebook) | DDC 294.3082--dc23/eng/20230130
LC record available at https://lccn.loc.gov/2022055064
LC ebook record available at https://lccn.loc.gov/2022055065

Typeset by Scribe Inc.

Printed and bound by CPI Group (UK) Ltd, Croydon, CR0 4YY

For the women of the *Therīgāthā*

Contents

Introduction

Reference to the first Buddhist women can be found in several early sources. These tell us that, about twenty-five hundred years ago, the prince of a small kingdom left home to pursue his quest for spiritual awakening. He wandered through the forests of Northern India for six years trying out various techniques until he finally achieved what he had set out to achieve and became the one we now know as the Buddha—a perfectly awakened being.

Word soon spread of his accomplishment and men followed. Like him, they left their homes, their obligations, their families, with idealistic hopefulness. They approached the Buddha reverently with palms pressed together and asked for ordination. The Buddha's response in most cases was simply, "come." And the men became monks.

The monks built a community among themselves, working together but individually in the hopes of achieving what the Buddha had achieved. There were skirmishes, of course, and many misunderstandings, but, overall, the community was harmonious. Men from all kinds of backgrounds learned to live together in the forest, each one steadily developing themselves as they followed the path the Buddha had set out for them.

So far so good, right?

The next part is where things get tricky.

One day, women showed up and asked to be let in. They too had heard about the Buddha and all he had achieved. They had heard that he was living in the forest, that he was showing the way to the end of suffering, that monks were there with him, learning to live the life he was living. The women wanted a chance to try the path for themselves, so they too asked for ordination. Like many women before them, at other times, in other circumstances, in the face of other institutions, the first Buddhist women were asking for access.

This book is a story of those first Buddhist women and what happened when they made their request. The first Buddhist women were probably not naïve. They must have seen the barriers they were attempting to cross, the glass ceilings they were trying to break. They must have known that they would not be immediately welcomed with open arms. But they asked anyway, because the cost of not asking was worse than the risk.

The most obvious place to look for the story of the women's quest for ordination is in the Vinaya, the Buddhist monastic code. While there are a few versions of the Vinaya, these collections are for the most part similar. Monastic rules are often prefaced with an introductory story that explains what led to the rule's creation, and the rule is eventually followed with a discussion of how to remedy the offence if the rule is broken. In the Pali version of the Vinaya, the story of the nuns' request for ordination serves as the introductory story that prefaces the list of rules nuns are expected to follow.

I have relied on the Vinaya (in its many recensions) for the outline of this book, but the Vinaya does not tell us everything. The women's request for ordination is neatly packaged and quickly delivered in what is otherwise a lengthy discussion about monastic life. The Vinaya provides us with the story of the women's first attempt, the Buddha's obscure rejection (best not to ask, he said), and then describes the women pursuing the Buddha to ask again. The outline of the story therefore belongs to these monastic codes and many details are worth noting (I have made reference to some of these in the notes that the reader will find at the end of the book), but these codes are not the heart and soul of my retelling. My inspiration comes from elsewhere. In particular, it comes from the *Therigatha*.

While most early Buddhist texts are attributed to men, and most were probably preserved by men, the *Therigatha* is a book that stands as a precious gem apart. It is believed to be about two thousand years old and it is attributed to women—specifically those first monastic women. The *Therigatha* is a collection of seventy-three poems by some of the first Buddhist women who joined the monastic community. It may be the oldest collection of women's voices we have in the world.

Unlike the monastic codes, the poems of the *Therigatha* do not tell us much about the women's journey towards ordination. Instead, the focus is on each author, her life circumstances, her existential yearnings, and her unequivocal success in becoming free. Vimala, for example, the main character in the story recounted in this book, declares at the end of her poem in the *Therigatha*, "I have thrown away all that fouls the heart, I am cool, free" (76).[1] The nun Vijaya says that she split open the mass of mental darkness and then stretched out her feet (174). The nun Chala addresses Mara (the rough equivalent of the devil) and tells him, "know this evil one, you are defeated, you are finished" (188). These women have set themselves free. And they never apologize for it, diminish it, or pretend it was no big deal.

What is particularly moving about these poems is not just that they are songs of women's accomplishments, but that their accomplishments often arrive on the heels of great suffering. The *Therigatha* does not gloss over women's experiences. It does not idealize their circumstances or try to soften the blow. On the contrary, the stories preserved in the *Therigatha* are often devastating. Some of the women are prostitutes; others have horrible husbands. Siha tries to kill herself (she achieves awakening just as she places a noose around her neck). Many have lost their children and their loved ones.

Of course, not all the women struggle so much. Gotami is a queen who leads the women with regal dignity. Sundarinanda is a princess who joins their ranks because everyone else had too. She does not appear to join out of hardship, but because she had nothing better to do. But for many others, the stories are steeped in suffering, and this is not because the *Therigatha* is an especially dark text, but because suffering is quite simply a feature of human life in general. And perhaps of women's lives in particular.

The women of the *Therigatha* are, however, not limited by their suffering, nor are they defined by it. The wonder of it all is that, despite the pain (and perhaps in part because of it), these women tried for something more. They shook themselves free of their circumstances, walked into the forest to ask for what they needed and thought they could receive.

---

1. I rely here on Charles Hallisey's translation of the *Therigatha* (2015).

And, like so many other women, they did it together. One of the most impressive features of the *Therigatha* is the fact that it holds poems of all kinds of women at once: prostitutes and queens, beggars and ascetics. The mad and the dignified. Everyone is welcome in the *Therigatha*, so long as she strives for awakening. In a world that was deeply stratified and hierarchical, where caste divisions had begun to take root and communities were pulling apart, the *Therigatha* is a miracle of collaboration. Women of all different stations share the pages of this text. Prostitutes and queens walk together through the forest, and prostitutes and queens share their songs.

The story of these first Buddhist women is not confined to ancient history. It is not an academic tidbit, or a random curiosity. The story of these first Buddhist women is, on the contrary, the bedrock upon which so many practitioners depend. Buddhist nuns the world over carry this story, embody it, and live it in their everyday lives. In every nunnery I have had the privilege of visiting over the years, every woman monastic I have had the opportunity to sit with has tackled this story with me (in part because I have asked). Why did the Buddha initially say no? Did he *actually* not want women around? Or was he just being cautious? Maybe he thought he had no choice. Whatever his reasons (insofar as the texts recount the scene), the Buddha did not at first say yes, and Buddhist monastic communities have been wrestling with these questions ever since.

The first time one learns this story, it can be shocking. How could the Buddha say no? How could an awakened being discriminate that way? The second and the third time one reads the story, it might remain shocking. The Buddha did not only reject the women (albeit with obscure wording). When he finally did accept women into the Order, his acceptance proved devastatingly conditional. The women had to accept eight "heavy" rules (known as the *garudhammas*) before ordination would be granted. I don't want to say too much about these rules here (it would spoil the story ahead), but suffice to say that the rules did not usher in an era of idealistic monastic equality. The *garudhammas* challenge monastic communities to this day.

The point, though, is not that women's ordination had strings attached. That is important, to be sure, but the story is bigger than that. The point (for me at least) is that those first Buddhist women did not take no for an answer. And according to the *Therigatha*, those first Buddhist women soon became free. Their accomplishments are sung and recited, taught and invoked, painted on nunnery walls. Patachara, for example, faced an onslaught of suffering, but she overcame it. Vimala was a prostitute. Chanda was a homeless widow. Mahapajapati was a queen. These women achieved awakening according to the tradition. Each one became free. How we tell their stories, what their stories mean, what is carried over (and by extension, what is left behind) shapes so much of the experience of what it means to be a Buddhist practitioner today. Those women did not get everything they wanted, but they fought for their place in the community and they became teachers in their own rights. With strings or without them, the women of the *Therigatha* are heroic ancestors of the Buddhist story.

I cannot close this short introduction without recognizing one other source of inspiration for this book: the many monastic women I have had the privilege of spending time with over the years. While the texts may be my intellectual home, people matter more. I cannot sufficiently express my gratitude for all the teachers I have had the honor of meeting, all the women in robes who have challenged me, inspired me, and sometimes even frustrated me. The monastic friends, the colleagues, and the monastic strangers that I sometimes find myself watching from afar. Each one of these women made a choice that I cannot help but admire. Monastic life is not perfect, monastic history for women even less so, but to live a life of renunciation in a world dedicated to accumulation is something I have always looked up to.

The story of the first Buddhist women is not easy. For the reader unfamiliar with it, consider yourself warned. This is a challenging narrative that does not end as many of us might hope. Like so many other gatherings women have organized, the women's gathering to ask the Buddha for ordination was not an unconditional success. The women were initially rejected and dismissed. When they *were* finally accepted into the community as fellow monastics, it was with heavy conditions attached. Men may have been welcomed into the community with open arms, but women had hoops to jump through that kept them apart. If this sounds familiar to a contemporary reader . . . well, it should. The more things change, the more things stay the same.

But the women of this story persevered. They did not collapse with despair. They brushed themselves off and asked for ordination again, because they wanted more than their world was offering them. Like so many great women after them, probably like so many women before them too, these first Buddhist monastic women did not accept no for an answer. They persevered, however imperfectly, in an imperfect world.

Many Years Later:
Vimala Remembers the Gathering Women

"Aunty, Aunty! Are you awake?"

Young hands were nudging my shoulder. I knew she was trying to be gentle, but her exuberance always seemed to get the better of her. She paused after a few moments. My eyes were still closed, but I could sense her hovering.

I smiled.

"You're awake!" she declared victoriously.

"How could I possibly be asleep after all that?" I replied, opening my eyes. My little mischief maker, Darshani, was standing over me with a great big grin. What a delight to see that young face first thing in the morning.

Suddenly, the sound of rushing feet came barrelling towards us.

"Darshani, you've been told not to disturb Venerable while she's sleeping! What are you doing here?"

Venerable Sundarinanda reached my doorway, huffing with frustration. With one hand on her hip, she stared down at Darshani with imperial disdain. She had flung a rag over her shoulder. She had probably been supervising the morning meal before she came tearing in.

"It's all right," I whispered. "Darshani is welcome to stay."

"But you need your rest, Venerable Vimala," Sundarinanda replied defensively. "And Darshani must learn better behavior. She can't just race into your room this way without decorum. We are responsible for teaching her."

The irony of the situation seemed to escape her, flying through the nunnery as she just did with her own lack of decorum. After all these years, Sundarinanda still rushed about like a storm in a jar. She did try to temper herself, but her habits were deeply ingrained. The transi-tion from palace princess to Buddhist nun had not been an easy one for her. Learning to adapt had not been easy for any of us, no matter what our origins, but it always seemed more challenging for those who came from illustrious stations in life; they had a much higher podium from which to fall. I remembered what our teacher Gotami always said: that while we must have compassion for all beings, it was particularly important not to forget the imperial ones. Their suffering was too easily dismissed.

I tried to prop myself up in bed, lifting myself onto my elbows. Dar-shani hurried to help me and tugged at my arm too quickly, trying too hard to be of service and almost toppling me sideways in the pro-cess. "Whoa, child, go easy on me! I'm not much more than a raggedy old doll nowadays," I chuckled. "I can barely keep myself from falling apart." Sundarinanda frowned and seemed on the verge of launching another accusation at Darshani for the way she handled me, but I raised my palm in a gesture of reassurance before she could get a word out.

"Darshani is doing fine, Venerable," I said, trying to catch my breath. "She's still young."

"She's not that young, Vimala. She must be ten years old by now. She's a novice in training and you're spoiling her."

I sighed.

She was probably right. Sundarinanda used to be the one ignor-ing the rules when we first started out. Back then, she was convinced that they did not apply to her, haughty as she always was. But these days, she had become quite strict; I was the one letting go.

"Venerable Sundarinanda is right, Darshani," I offered in a more conciliatory tone. "You are here for your training and must learn to behave accordingly. Your parents entrusted you to us for that very reason. Venerable is only thinking of your own good."

Sundarinanda's entire body had been rigid with accusation when she first arrived at my door, but the moment I praised her, she soft-ened. The arguments she was preparing were dissolving as I shifted to take her side.

"You are most attentive, Venerable," I added. "But the fault here is my own. I was the one who asked Darshani to wake me. Do you think she might be excused from her duties today?"

Venerable Sundarinanda flushed with embarrassment.

"Of course, Vimala, if that's what you prefer."

"It would give me great pleasure."

I could sense Darshani's excitement, but I did not dare look at her. She sat herself down on the bed beside me (yet another mistake where monastic decorum was concerned), trying to hold her tongue. We both waited with bated breath for Sundarinanda's permission.

She granted it. She then bowed lightly, her prickly bald head aimed at the two of us, and walked away with as much dignity as she could muster.

Darshani waited for the sound of footsteps to recede. When she was convinced she was safe, she let out a sigh of relief.

"Great Goddess, is she mean!" she declared. "Why is she always after me?"

In another time, many years earlier, I would have scolded her for such impertinence. Or worse—I would have joined her in the easy accusation. There was nothing I used to love more than pointing out other people's faults.

But that time was long ago.

"She's not mean, Little One. She's your teacher."

"You're my teacher," she replied emphatically. "She just likes being mad all the time."

I shook my head, but I knew better than to argue. Darshani would learn in time, just as we all do. Monastic life does not transform any-one quickly. Bhadda Kundalakesa, my dear friend and steady com-panion many years ago, once described nuns living together as being like a bag full of rocks. The rocks begin with jagged edges, but if you shake the bag around long enough, the rocks rub against each other and smooth one another out. Monastic life is like that. In time, we all lose our hard edges.

"Shall we go greet Surya the Sun God?" I asked, changing the sub-ject. "He must be expecting us."

Darshani clapped her hands with glee as she leapt off the bed.

I once told Darshani that to miss a sunrise was to miss the greatest show on earth. She, of course, responded with authority that she had seen the sun rise many times. She was no amateur when it came to the Sun God's trajectory. Nevertheless, Darshani had been coming into my room almost every morning since then, jostling me awake in

*time for the show. It was a wonder Sundarinanda had never caught us
doing this before now.*

*I leaned on Darshani's young body as we limped out the door, every
step carefully calculated, slowly maneuvering towards our goal. We
eventually reached our favorite spot, right at the edge of our small hill.
She helped me into a seated position, then sat down beside me.*

*"We made it!" she declared. "The Sun God is just about to get
started!"*

*The sky's darkness was brightening, bit by bit. A light breeze rus-
tled, announcing the tender day ahead. It was the end of the long
summer months, my favorite time of year, when the heat evaporates
and the promise of cooler days is just around the corner. Winter here
is always so dry and cold and Monsoon so very wet and muggy, but
in between the extremes, the Earth Goddess provides a moment of
respite. The air lands lightly, the sun offers just enough warmth, and the
sky is crisp and bright.*

*"You promised to tell me the story, Aunty. You said when I was old
enough, you would tell me. And I'm definitely old enough now! I do
my chores, attend to my studies, and I don't even fight with the other
novices anymore."*

*The sky was a magnificent shade of orange. Birds were bursting
into song.*

"Quiet, now. Watch the sky. It's what we have come to see."

"I know, but I see it every morning. I want to hear your story!"

I turned to look at her.

"You are frightfully impatient, you know?"

*"You said the young are always impatient, so it's not my fault. I'm
made this way!"*

I laughed. Who could resist such an impish little creature?

But I knew she was right.

*My body was wasting away, more every day. I was ageing at an
almost hurried pace. Soon even the short walk out of my room would
prove to be too much. I looked down at my hands that were resting in
hers. Mine were so old and knotted now. Spotted, with swollen joints,
every tiny bone clearly defined beneath my skin. I must look as old as
Neelima, I thought. When I was young, I was convinced no one could
ever be older than her. She was as ancient as the Earth Goddess, but
she dragged herself around on those little legs of hers, undeterred by
the fatigue she must have felt with every step.*

My, how I had loved her.

Most of the Gathering Women had passed away. I was one of the last ones left. Me and Sundarinanda, in fact. All the others had taken their leave when their bodies were finished with them.

Some of them left behind songs of accomplishment just before they died, and each one of these I carefully transcribed when it was time. As one of the only literate women in the community, the role of preserving the songs was entrusted to me. When a woman felt ready, I was summoned to her bedside. I would bring my jar of ink and a piece of dried out birch bark and wait for the words to emerge.

It was an intimate experience to hear a woman's final song. Sometimes the words soared out triumphantly; at other times, they were soft whispers of grace. I always wanted to close my eyes, to savour the experience the way the others could, but as the community archivist, I could not allow myself such a privilege. I kept my eyes open, transcribing each word as it was sung. When the song was over and the ink was dry, I would roll up the birch bark and store it in a clay jar, already painted and prepared for the occasion. We now had dozens of these jars in the nunnery. It was the beginning of our very own library.

I had, however, become responsible for more than the songs over the years. I also had to deliver the story of the Gathering Women to ensure it would be cared for by others after I was gone. This task seemed even more daunting to me than the songs, the weight of it constantly on my mind. How would I tell the story of the Gathering Women on my own? It was a story we had all lived out differently, each one of us in our own way. Who was I to be the one to tell it?

"Will you really not share the story with me, Aunty?" Darshani asked again. "I've gotten so good at remembering. I can recite dozens of teachings now without even asking for a reminder! I won't forget any of it if you teach it to me."

The story was not an easy one to tell. Most women were content to follow the status quo, to keep their heads down, slave for their husbands, their taskmasters, the temple priests. Most women never attempted the lofty heights of liberation. They did not break the rules of requirement in the hope of becoming more than was prescribed by their sex.

But we Gathering Women refused to limit ourselves. We wanted more from our circumstances, we wanted more from the lives we had been given to live. So, we charged forward, daring to ask for the moon *and the stars and everything else we dreamt might be ours. We wanted to become free like the Teacher, and all the Teachers before him, to soar inside ourselves with wings as wide as our minds. The smallness of the outside world, with all of its rules and limitations and petty thieveries . . . these did not suit any of us. We refused to shrink ourselves to fit to the world's demands.*

But our bid for freedom did not go according to plan. If I told Darshani the story of the Gathering Women, as I had lived it all those years ago, what would she say?

We did not become as free as we hoped we might be. Or as free as I thought we should be. All Darshani knew was the safe haven we had built for her and the other young ones. She did not recognize the boundaries that still lay just outside our gate. But if I told her the story . . . she would see those walls where before she had seen none. Would she be disappointed?

"I suppose it is time . . ." I reasoned, more with myself than with her. She clapped her hands with a cry of joy.

"I knew it would be today, Aunty! I just knew it!"

"If you really think you're old enough to hear this story, and old enough for the responsibility of remembering it, the least you can do is stop calling me Aunty. You should know better than that by now."

"Oh yes, Aunty! . . . I mean, Venerable. Yes, yes, yes! I am old enough. I am ready! I promise!"

I looked at her a while longer, studying her expression; and, I suppose, preparing myself as well.

I closed my eyes and lifted my face to the sun's nourishing rays. A kingfisher was whistling on a branch right above me and I could hear monkeys scampering along the trunk. I knew that if I waited long enough, a herd of elephants would appear and saunter across the field toward the mud banks on the other side. The kitchen pots were clanging in the nunnery and the goatherders were whistling further away. Life was erupting in all directions. I needed to find my inner stillness before I could begin.

Gotami, Bhadda Kundalakesa, Patachara, Gathering Women all, I whispered quietly, stay with me.

Our story was not as pretty as some tellers like to pretend. It was messy and complicated, each of us making the journey with our own reasons, in our own way. One look at Sundarinanda confirmed that

fact: she did not join us with wings ready to fly. She was still strug-
gling, all these years later, old habits still proving difficult to shed.

But it was our story, our great adventure. It gave us the opportu-
nity to reach for something most did not believe could be ours to try.

Some of us became great scholars. Others great teachers. Some of
us eventually left. But some made it to the furthest reaches of their
minds. Darshani represented the next generation. It was time she inher-
ited our story, so that she might continue what we began.

I opened my eyes and I began to speak.

1

The Buddha Said No

She walked into the grove alone.

It was quiet. The early morning fog was thick and wet. The grass licked at her ankles and the banyan trees folded over her from above. Their roots fell out of the sky and dropped all around, some lodging themselves into the earth, others hovering in the air, hanging precariously. She walked through the layers as though parting curtains. She tried to dry her palms with her white cotton scarf, but everything was damp. A black crow screeched overhead. She looked up, her heart palpitating, and watched as he swept through the air.

"Greetings, Gotami."

For a moment, she thought the tree was the one to have spoken. The fog had become so thick, she could not see anyone. It was rising up from the ground and swirling with an almost seductive quality, like a spirit-creature trying to entice her away.

"I am right in front of you," the voice said.

It was not the tree.

She closed her eyes, trying to steady herself. Then she opened them. The fog that had a moment ago covered the grove like a heavy grey blanket was gone. It had swiftly evaporated as if by magical command, leaving behind the beginnings of a sparkling sunrise in its place. Colors were flooding the landscape, one beautiful hue after another. The sun was smiling and the damp wetness was dry. And right there in front of her, seated with his back against the tree, was the one she had been looking for.

"Teacher," she whispered with a surge of emotion. She lowered herself to the ground and touched his feet with the top of her head.

She could not even begin to describe the love that she felt flooding through every part of her.

"Please sit, Gotami."

He pointed to the soft grass in front of him, but she, deeply mindful of their new relationship, chose to sit to the right side. No one sat directly in front of him anymore.

"What can I do for you?" he asked.

She was certain he knew the answer to his own question. He could read minds, fly through the air, even chase the fog away when he wanted to. He knew why she had come. He probably knew everything.

He was wearing the same simple ochre-colored robe he had worn the last time she saw him. It was draped over one shoulder, leaving the other one bare—so different from the royal wardrobe he had been forced to contend with most of his life. He was raised in silks embroidered with jewels, sandals that chimed as he walked. And yet here he was with virtually nothing on him at all. Not even a ring on his finger or a protective amulet around his neck. No evidence left of the crown prince he used to be, except perhaps for the long holes that stretched out of his earlobes—the scarred remains of heavy jewels worn long ago.

He was not as young as he once was. His hair was cut short to the scalp, but she could see that the roots were starting to grey. Thin lines were beginning to form around his eyes too. He was aging. *She* was ancient. How had so much time passed them by? It seemed as though it was only yesterday that she was holding him in her arms, singing sweet lullabies, rocking his little body to sleep. Maya would have been so proud of her son.

But Maya never got to see him as Gotami saw him now. Maya died almost immediately after giving birth to him. She was granted only seven days with him and then she died, leaving Mahapajapati Gotami, her younger sister, to raise her son in her stead. She would never forget the moment the request was made.

"Please, Little Sister," she had begged. *"Take my son and raise him as your own."*

Mahapajapati Gotami had raced to Lumbini Garden the moment she heard that her sister was in labor. She had not approved of Maya's decision to travel all the way to Lumbini so close to her delivery date, but there was no arguing with her at the time. She packed a few things and asked one of the stable boys to drive a chariot to the garden as quickly as possible. She had a feeling something was not quite right, but she could not put her finger on it, so she begged the stable boy to hurry. She held her breath the entire way.

Mahapajapati Gotami arrived to find her sister standing in the middle of the garden, one hand above her head as she held onto a tree branch. Women normally gave birth squatting, usually leaning against another for support, but here was her sister, standing like a goddess with just a slim branch in her hand. She was not screaming. There was no blood. She just stood there, softly and at ease, and waited as her son slid out.

Legends about the birth began to swirl before it had even come to an end. Gods were said to have descended from the heavens, ready to catch the newborn into their celestial arms. Flowers rained over them—some so wide, you could barely reach your arms around them—and heavenly guardians banged on the clouds like drums. So many things were said about that day. So many things are said still. Everywhere and in every way, the spirits of the ten-thousand universes were described as celebrating the birth of Maya's son.

Mahapajapati Gotami had spent a long time wrestling with the stories over the years. She had been so distracted at the time, she had lost track of the difference between truth and fiction. Perhaps the heavenly guardians really did bang on the clouds. Flowers certainly seemed to be raining over them. And she could still see Lord Brahma in his brilliant regalia lowering his head to the child's feet in her mind's eye. The image was as clear to her now as it had been on that blessed, painful day. Had it all happened as they said it had? She was not sure—she never had been—but the question no longer seemed to matter. The distinction between the real and the imagined, once so absolute in her mind, was not important anymore. Age covers memory with a thin veil of mystery. Everything changes. She was no longer sure what the difference was between what she saw with her own eyes and what became the story she had learned to hold, but she had long stopped worrying about it. There was wisdom in fluidity, she now realized. Truth was not as static as she once believed it to be. Were those flowers as big as she remembered them? She did not know and it no longer mattered. The birthing was miraculous. Because birthing always is.

"What a magnificent boy, Elder Sister," she had said to Maya as she held the little bundle in her arms. She touched his forehead with the tip of her finger, a sign of protection, and whispered a prayer under her breath.

Maya smiled as she watched her sister coo over her newborn son. They were sitting together under the tree, its tremendous branches providing them with cover from the sun. The birds were chirping, the wind was rustling the leaves.

"Are you really not in any pain?" Mahapajapati Gotami asked.

Maya shook her head.

They leaned against each other, savoring the experience that a new birth always brings. They both knew that the bubble would eventually have to burst. They could not hide in Lumbini Garden forever. The shuffling sounds of nearby servants reminded them of that.

"Little Sister, I have something to ask of you," Maya said, breaking the spell.

"Of course."

Maya took a deep breath, looked up at her sister, and then, to Mahapajapati's consternation, she began to cry.

Maya never cried.

"What is it?" she asked with immediate concern. "What's wrong?"

Maya took a moment to compose herself. She wiped her tears as she looked off into the distance.

"I have seen the end of my story, sweet sister. My life is withering and soon I will be gone." Maya said. "I must ask you to take my son and raise him for me."

Mahapajapati Gotami was so surprised, she had no words with which to respond. She stared at her sister. Her story could not be over so soon. After such a glorious birthing, how could it be? Was it not evidence of the favor she had incurred with the gods? Were they not protecting her, blessing her even? How could her story be over now?

"But it is," Maya explained. "I have seen it all in a dream. Lumbinidevi summoned me here to birth my son in her embrace. But soon she will take me away."

Maya had always been able to see what would happen through her dreams. When dreaming was invoked, there was no arguing anymore. Maya's dreaming was always true.

"Please, Little Sister," Maya said, with a voice cracking with emotion, "take my son after I am gone. Hug him and hold him, nurse him, and bathe him and care for him day and night, so that he is not motherless after I am gone."

Silence was all that was left after that; the answer did not need to be voiced. The two sisters remained together under the tree until they fell asleep in a bed of giant celestial flowers. Maya's attendants hovered nearby, but they knew not to disturb them. When the sisters awoke the next morning, Maya had one last request to make.

"Go home now, Little Sister. Leave me here with my son. When it is over, you will know."

Mahapajapati Gotami had no choice. She fussed at first, taking her time to speak with each of Maya's attendants to be sure they had what they needed and knew how to care for her, and she kissed the little newborn multiple times on the top of his sweet little head, but in the end she walked away. It was the hardest thing she ever had to do. The saddest goodbye of her young life.

And then, just as her dream had ordained it would be, Maya died in that garden and the little newborn was brought back to the palace. Mahapajapati Gotami was waiting at the door to take him into her arms. She took on the role she had been asked to play and never regretted a day of it. She had loved Maya's son as though he was her own and took care of him as long as he allowed her to.

He was the man seated in front of her now. The man they called the Buddha.

"What have you come here to ask, Gotami?"

He would not call her Mother. She was not even Mahapajapati anymore, she realized. Instead, she had become Gotami. The female leader of the Gotama people. When she left the palace that morning, she had left the throne and all that it represented behind. She was not the Queen of the Sakya Kingdom anymore, but she *was* a leader bringing women forward in the hope of reaching a more illustrious goal. Those women were waiting for her at the gate of Banyan Grove, waiting to hear the outcome of the request she was about to make on their behalf. She was Gotami, a title, she recognized, that sat on her shoulders well.

"I have come here to ask for your permission to join the Order," she said. "Out there, at the edge of the grove, are dozens of women who followed me. They have all come with the same hope: to be ordained. To be given a place at your feet, to study with you and learn how to find inner freedom. Will you give us ordination so that we may live as a community of nuns beside you?"

Someone coughed behind her. She turned around to find the entire male monastic community sitting in organized rows to the side of them. She had expected them, had known they would be there, but she had forgotten about them the moment she had arrived.

"I understand what you are asking, Gotami," the Buddha said, bringing her attention back to the discussion at hand. "But I do not think you should make this request. It is not a good idea."

Not a good . . . ? *Why?*

How could he answer her that way? He had barely even considered her request before denying it. She was only asking for access to the teachings. Why would he say no, after everything she had done for him?

She chided herself an instant later. This had nothing to do with what she had done for him over the years. And this was not as simple as she was pretending it to be. She was not just asking for access to the teachings and she knew it. They both did. She was asking for everything. For the opportunity to sit beside him and practice the teachings the way he did, with her head shaved. If she was only asking for access to the teachings, that was easily remedied. People everywhere were practicing his instruction without ordination. They were doing it from home, without heads shaved, while still living the lives they had always led. But she was asking for something else. She was asking for ordination. She was asking for permission to live the life of a renunciant in a community of men. She was asking for the moon.

She asked her question again.

"Teacher, on behalf of the women who stand at the gates of this grove, please grant us ordination. We want to live a life of renunciation in your community."

This time she could hear more. Rustling movements. Coughs. Disturbance in the rows of male stillness beside her. She had a feeling they were trying to make their opinions heard. She did not give them the satisfaction of even looking their way.

The Buddha kept his eyes trained on her.

"I understand what you are asking for, Gotami, and I do not think you should make this request. It is not a good idea."

Now she knew what was happening. He was going to reject her three times in public, to ensure the message was clearly received. She had no choice but to complete the painful ritual of negotiation she herself had set in motion. With a heavy heart, she asked one more time.

"Teacher, we have come to ask for ordination. We would like to join your community to become nuns."

The Buddha remained quiet a long time. He closed his eyes and disappeared into his inner universe. A place where Gotami could not follow him. But when he opened them, he looked at her with studied concentration and replied one more time.

"I understand what you are asking, Gotami, but I do not think you should make this request. It is not a good idea."

The rows of male monastics stirred again. It sounded like a collective sigh of relief. The black crow from earlier swept overhead with another piercing call.

It was time for Gotami to walk away.

2

Vimala's Story Begins

It had been a rough night. Vimala's last customer had used her like a dirty chamber pot. She stepped outside and leaned against the wall for support. The sun was peeling itself out of the darkness. Vimala tucked her hands under her armpits. She was far from fragile, but couldn't they be a bit gentle sometimes? She lifted her robe and examined her thighs. The bruises were already beginning to show. There was a bite mark too. Red and swollen. She knew it would be worse tomorrow. She tried to rub her thighs for circulation but flinched from the pain. *Maybe I can find that healer . . .*

Then she sighed. Even with last night's shift, she still would not have enough coin to pay for it. She looked down at the bite again and wondered if it would make her sick. Some bites did.

She slid down the wall and settled onto the hard earth floor. The grass was dry and brittle. Kumari, the brothel owner, would not hire gardeners. Her focus was on the clients and the clients did not care if the grass was green.

Vimala winced as the sharp blades of grass scratched her skin. Where she came from, gardens were carefully crafted. They were tended to and loved. Grass would never be left to die this way.

"You all right?"

Vimala looked up to find Surasa standing over her.

"I thought you weren't finished," Vimala answered. "Didn't I see that tailor in the hallway?"

Surasa brushed the dust from her robe.

"Apparently, he wasn't in the mood for my type tonight. He arrived wildly drunk and slurring accusations. Something must have happened at home—probably another argument with his wife. He said he wanted to take a *real* woman this time. Not a half-breed like me."

Surasa faced those kinds of accusations regularly at the brothel. She was a *pandaka*, someone of ambiguous sex. Vimala did not know how she wound up at Kumari's, but she was certain the story was not pretty.

Truth be told, none of their stories were.

"Don't you ever wish we could run away?" Vimala asked.

"Run away? Where to?"

"Anywhere. Just run away to somewhere else."

Surasa turned towards Vimala. "Was it bad?" she asked quietly.

Vimala kept her eyes on the brittle earth between her toes.

"I could hear you fighting him," Surasa said. "Everyone could."

Vimala's toes moved the crumbs of soil around, her cracked nails now covered with brown dirt. She did not want to think about the last customer. She wanted to think of somewhere else.

"There must be another life we could live. This can't be the only version left."

"There are no other versions, Sister. You know that. Once a prostitute, always a prostitute . . ."

Vimala hated being confronted with reality.

"There's little we can do," Surasa continued. "The only alternative we might hope for is to take over the brothel one day. If we can raise enough funds to buy this place from Kumari, maybe we can get others to do the dirty work for us. Maybe that could happen."

"And become a disgruntled old hag? Miserable and frightening like her?" Vimala spit the words out in reply. Unlike Surasa, Vimala had never coveted the throne of their hovel. "Anyway, chances are slim. Kumari definitely doesn't favor me anymore. I'll probably end up a scullery maid in the kitchen once I'm used up. A shrivelled bag of bones stirring pots of stew over the fire until I die."

Vimala shivered at the thought of it. There were a few of those maids in the kitchen now. They hid in dark corners and scratched themselves indecently. It was difficult to imagine any of them having been young and beautiful once.

That being said, she was not particularly young and beautiful anymore either. Kumari used to sing Vimala's praises like a cooing lovebird when she had first taken possession of her person. "Look at these delicate arms," she would purr to wealthy clients. "So long and slim, like a creeping vine." Her fingers would trail over Vimala's skin, seducing the client without his even realizing it. "Can you imagine what lies beneath her robe?" she would whisper. The client at this point would be salivating. On cue, Vimala would let her robe slip off one shoulder and the deal would be done.

It had been that easy once.

But Kumari does not summon her for those clients anymore. Vimala's eyes had begun to crinkle. Her hair was streaked with grey. The sheen of youth was fading. She was not sure how old she was, but whatever her age, she was far from young. Maybe she was forty? Maybe thirty-five? Whatever it was, she was not a budding flower anymore.

"There are other possibilities," Vimala muttered to herself.

"*What* other possibilities? What are you dreaming up now?"

Vimala looked off into the distance, summoning up memories she rarely had the courage to face.

"I could work for Ambapali . . ."

"Who?"

"Have you never heard of Ambapali?" Vimala asked as she turned toward Surasa. "She's only the most famous courtesan in the whole world!"

Surasa scratched her dirty hair in consternation. "Vimala, you really keep your head in the clouds. A *courtesan*? You don't have the learning to be like that!"

If only Surasa knew.

"Vimala, you're not doing yourself any good," she berated her. "Stop daydreaming. This is where we live. We have no choice and no options. Even if we *could* run away, Kumari would find us. The debts we owe won't pay themselves."

Vimala turned away.

"If we got far enough, it wouldn't matter," she said. "There's only so much Kumari can do."

"Fine. So run away," Surasa replied with exasperation. "And where will you go? You think the next town will welcome a prostitute with open arms? You can try to be different, but you'll end up spreading your legs there too."

Vimala shrugged.

"I figure we're better off staying where we are than risk it being worse somewhere else," Surasa concluded reasonably.

Vimala closed her mind and turned away.

Surasa slipped back to her room, leaving Vimala to contemplate the dry earth between her toes. The brothel was on the outer edge of the town, a convenience their customers appreciated as much as everyone else. The distance from the town kept her at a distance, so that Vimala always found herself looking at it from afar. She never belonged to Kapilavatthu, even though its workings were familiar to her. The city she grew up in was bigger, but it was not significantly different from the one she watched now. Every morning, women emerged from their homes to stretch out their tired backs. Movements that were familiar, despite belonging to a past far behind.

She watched the chickens scoot about, clucking their familiar sounds, and felt homesick for the time that had been. Her childhood had not been idyllic. It was rough around the edges and broken in between, but she held onto it like stolen treasure. *I could go home*, she repeated to herself desperately. *I don't have to stay here.*

She reached out for her memories, but almost immediately retracted with shame. Too much had happened. Home was impossibly far away.

Vimala dozed off where she was, her back against the wall, her feet buried in the dusty earth. But the sun's rays grew sharp, and her hand was soon shielding her face unconsciously. She pried her eyes open.

Kapilavatthu was no longer its sleepy early morning self. The town had progressed to its daytime routine, with vendors hawking and busybodies bustling. Carts squealed their way along the rough road, a young herder hollered at her goats as she tried to get them to where she needed them to go, water-buffaloes yanked at their heavy harnesses. Everyone was occupied, because daytime was when things got done. Everyone, that is, but the women shackled to the hovel she was leaning against.

Vimala watched the town's activity with numb curiosity. Mud-brick houses lined the main road, each house just about the same as the others. Every few weeks, the walls would have to be re-plastered with a mixture of mud and cow dung to keep them from crumbling. Children were usually the ones commissioned to find the required materials. She could see a group of raggedy girls chasing cows in the field behind the houses and suspected that this was what they were up to. Sure enough, they eventually stopped and kneeled in the tall grass with their woven baskets.

Not all the homes were mud baked. If she strained her eyes, she could see past the rows toward the more elaborate ones further ahead. The nicer part of town was at the other end, by the palace where the Royal Family resided.

The king had died a few years earlier, but people still spoke of him with reverence. Unlike the kings of other territories, Suddhodana Maharaja had never terrorized his subjects, never charged exorbitant taxes, never punished with disproportionate cruelty. He had never grabbed at the village women or made obscene demands on the community for his entertainment. In most instances, kings were dangerous entities, but Suddhodana Maharaja embodied a sense of moral rectitude his subjects were proud of. They likened him to the mythical Lord Rama who always put his kingdom first.

The only blind spot the king suffered from was with regards to his son. Siddhattha had been heir to the throne and was a perfect fit in every way, but the kingdom was like a noose around the prince's neck, and as soon as the opportunity presented itself, the prince had run away. Saved himself from a role he was not interested in. Siddhattha—the heir apparent of the Sakya Kingdom, father to Prince Rahula and husband to Princess Yasodhara—had fled the kingdom on his majestic steed, tearing away as though the guardians of the hell realms were right behind. His father never saw it coming. Or maybe he did. Whatever the truth, his father was devastated.

The prince's departure was a story that had been told three hundred and thirty million times and it was still not finished its telling. For years, people repeated the story to each other. Constantly. Obsessively even. They told it with tears. They told it with sympathy. Some told it with resentment. Their prince had left them without warning or explanation. Their prince had abandoned his father—the most beloved king anyone had ever known. The prince had abandoned his son and beautiful wife.

Some people sang the story. Others performed it. But one way or another, the story of the prince's departure was wrapped around the hearts of every member of the Sakya community. It bewildered as much as it entertained. It was gossip and it was longing and it was loss. Each person wondered, in their own time, in their own way, why—in all the heavens, in all the gods' names—*why* a man would do such a thing. A man who had everything, who had known neither hardship nor hunger, who was loved with abundance, *why* he would do a thing like that. People wove the story around themselves, perhaps because they did not understand it, or perhaps because in some unspoken secret way, they did.

Vimala had heard the story dozens of times. Even though she was not native to Sakya, it had become her story too. The palace she caught glimmers of on the other side of town, the palace with dazzling towers that shimmered against the hot morning sky, was home to a story she felt connected to. To escape one's station, galloping into the unknown with unbridled freedom . . . How deeply she longed for it. She gathered the story into herself like a fisherman gathering in his net.

An old woman was approaching. Vimala lifted her head from against the wall and watched as the small creature dragged herself toward her with determination, one labored step at a time. She was wearing a blue linen robe with a matching headscarf tied around her head.

"I think I might be a bit old for this," the woman said between gasps. She then lowered herself down beside Vimala, one creaking joint at a time. She pulled a cloth out from beneath her sash and wiped her forehead with trembling fingers.

Vimala stared. No one visited the brothel during the day. Unless, of course, they were selling something. This old woman, however, had nothing but the clothes on her back.

"Can I do something for you, Old Woman?" Vimala asked.

The woman was still working to catch her breath, but she finally managed a few words. "Some fresh water would be nice."

Vimala raised an eyebrow. Then she shrugged, pulled herself off the ground and shuffled toward the kitchen for some water. The maids usually left a vessel out in case anyone woke up thirsty. She returned with a cup and handed it to the old woman who nodded silently in gratitude. She drank carefully, one tiny sip at a time.

"Would you like some more?" Vimala inquired when the cup had finally emptied.

The woman wiped her mouth. "No, I think that will do. Any more and I won't make it to the next stop before I have to relieve myself again." She giggled. "The Great Goddess knows I am not fast enough to catch up if I fall behind. And then what will become of me?"

"Fall behind who?"

The old woman turned toward Vimala and stared at her in disbelief. "Do you mean you haven't heard?"

"Heard what? What are you talking about, Old Woman?" Vimala asked with impatience. Who *was* this person?

"Oh well, I suppose you might not have heard. You *are* isolated out here, aren't you?" She took in her surroundings as though for the first time. "My goodness, you can barely see the palace, it's so far away!"

Vimala shook her head wearily and decided it was time to go to bed. She had stayed up too late already and could not be bothered with the ramblings of this maddening creature. Whoever she was and wherever she was going, it was no business of hers.

"You're welcome to sit here as long as you like, Old Woman, but I must get my rest. I wish you a safe journey." Vimala retrieved the cup and started walking back towards the door.

"Keep me company a while longer, won't you, dear?" the old woman called after her. "I think you might like to hear about this."

"Hear about what?" Vimala asked, as she turned back towards her.

The old woman smiled. She had only one tooth left, but Vimala was inexplicably drawn to her. What was this woman doing here? She must have sensed Vimala's wavering because she patted the ground beside her and smiled all over again.

"Fine," Vimala acquiesced, as she reclaimed her spot. "Just for a little while."

"Wonderful!" the old woman exclaimed as she took Vimala's hands into her own. "You have made an old woman very happy."

Each joint of the old woman's hands was knotted and swollen, with no flesh in between. Her fingers were stiff and bent; her dark skin was spotted. And her palms had been worked so hard, her calluses had morphed into cushions. These were old working hands, the product of a lifetime of labor, and she placed them into Vimala's care as though that was precisely where they belonged.

Nostalgia suddenly flooded Vimala with memories of loving elders from a distant time. She was unprepared for that.

"Let me begin with an introduction," the old woman said. She then removed her hands and used them to push against the earth to straighten herself up.

"My name is Neelima and I belong to the Royal Palace of the Sakya Kingdom. I am Princess Yasodhara's maidservant."

The old woman looked at Vimala with eager anticipation. She was obviously proud of her station, but Vimala had not registered a word of what she had said. She was staring at the vacancy left behind by the old woman's hands, caught in memories she had not invited in.

The old woman, perceptive despite failing eyesight, recognized the loneliness of the one sitting beside her and returned her hands into Vimala's care. "I am Princess Yasodhara's maidservant," she repeated more tenderly. "You may call me Neelima, but Old Woman works just as well."

Vimala nodded vacantly.

Neelima accepted the silence without another word. The last few days had been quite busy at the palace. She could use a few moments of rest. The two women sat where they were and watched the town's meanderings, hands clasped like old friends. Vimala noticed some commotion down the road, groups forming for some reason, but the hot sun created a haze that made even squinting painful.

But then Vimala finally registered the old woman's status.

"Wait, did you say that you work in the palace?"

The old woman nodded.

"But . . . what are you doing *here*?" Panic rose to the surface. "Do you know where you are?"

"Where I am? What do you mean?"

Vimala ripped her hands away and scrambled to the side. "You shouldn't be here!"

The old woman looked at her companion with curiosity, assessing the situation anew. "I know this is a brothel, if that's what you mean, dear."

"But . . . then you can't be here. It's not right for a member of the palace staff to be around something like me. You have to go!"

Vimala jumped to her feet, suddenly quite afraid for this lovely old being who had held her hands. There was a reason the brothel was at the other end of town. It was not a clean place, not an appropriate venue for respectable members of society. The old woman might be just a maidservant, but she was a maidservant *for Princess Yasodhara*. She worked in the palace and was therefore a servant of the highest caliber. If she was found out, if she was discovered sitting here with a prostitute in the dirtiest part of town, how would she recover her reputation? Concerns were flying through Vimala's mind like wild bats in a cave. She had to get the old woman away.

But the old woman had not moved. She was still sitting on the ground, in the very same position as before. "Did you say, some*thing* like you?'"

"What?"

"I believe you said that I should not be sitting here with some*thing* like you."

Vimala had not realized that the word had escaped her.

"Well . . . it's just that . . . you shouldn't be here. You work in the palace."

The old woman patted the ground beside her again. "That is very kind of you, my dear, but I am long past worrying about such things. You have nothing to fear."

"But won't you get into trouble?" Vimala asked, dismayed.

"I don't think so. Perhaps once, long ago, this would have stirred the gossip-mongers. Perhaps once I would have cared, but now? I'm perfectly content to sit with you right where we are." She dabbed at her forehead with her cloth again, new beads of sweat having formed under the sun. Then she looked up and added, "unless, that is, you have concerns about sitting with the likes of me?"

Vimala was not entirely sure she had heard correctly. She cocked her head to one side and stared at her neighbor.

Then she burst out laughing.

"No, I certainly don't have any concerns about sitting next to you, Old Woman!"

"Well, I'm relieved," Neelima answered. "I certainly wouldn't want you to get into any trouble either."

Vimala smiled.

"So where did you say you were going? What's this journey about?" Vimala finally asked as she crawled back to her seat.

"This journey is unlike any you will have ever heard about before . . ."

"Princess Yasodhara came to us as a young bride," Neelima began. "She was sixteen years old and in the prime of her life. She was, of course, not a stranger to us, having grown up around the palace, racing through the gardens with her cousins almost every single day. But it was only when she moved in that I really began to know her. Serving Princess Yasodhara has been the greatest honor of my life."

Neelima paused and turned toward Vimala, with a look as though she had just remembered something. "I wonder . . . what parts of this story have you already heard?"

Vimala reddened instantly. It was one thing for people to whisper details of royal happenings. It was something else entirely to share those whispers with someone who had actually lived them. She picked up the hem of her robe and studied the stitching while she rifled through her mind for an answer.

Neelima patted Vimala's knee in reassurance. "People are always curious about the Royal Family. You have nothing to be ashamed of, dear. Have you heard about the Choosing?"

Vimala nodded. "Parts of it . . ."

"Of course you have. The Choosing was one of the most magnificent moments in palace history." Neelima lifted her headscarf a tad to scratch her head. There seemed to be no hair underneath.

"Oh, you should have seen the palace that day!" she continued. "I don't remember it ever having been so beautiful. The ministers had called all the maidens of the land to the palace to present themselves to the prince. It was time for him to get married and he was asked to choose a bride. One woman after another appeared before him, each one dressed in the most exquisite fabrics, but Prince Siddhattha only had eyes for Yasodhara. He looked past them all, waiting for Yasodhara to make her appearance. Each maiden walked up the steps to the Royal Stage, all trembling and eager, but it was like they were not even there. He handed each one a gift but barely looked at any of them. He was waiting for Yasodhara, who was, characteristically, the last in line. She never could manage to make it on time to anything!"

Vimala closed her eyes and tried to imagine the Royal Household in all its splendor. She pictured marble walls inlaid with shiny jewels, servants lined up in rows of orchestrated obedience, giant peacock feathers fanning the guests throughout the room.

"What kinds of gifts did the prince offer the maidens?"

Neelima smiled.

"The prince had a giant treasure chest filled with jewels! He pulled something out for each maiden who presented herself—strings of pearls, sapphire nose-rings, ruby pendants. There were so many jewels in that treasure chest, it would have made your head spin."

Vimala could imagine the wealth. She could see it all with her mind's eye, despite the squalor she was surrounded by.

"Unfortunately, though," Neelima continued, "the treasure chest had no magical charms attached to it. It could not refill itself. As the parade of women continued, the treasure chest slowly emptied. And then it was Yasodhara's turn."

"Was Princess Yasodhara really the last person in line?" Vimala asked incredulously. "Was she *that* late?"

"She was indeed. The very last maiden in all the land, and by the time she presented herself, the treasure chest had nothing left to offer."

"So what happened?"

"Prince Siddhattha took one look at her, removed his personal necklace and tied it around Yasodhara's neck. She flushed, he smiled, they whispered things to each other that no one else could hear. It was all very intimate. And it was happening right there in front of everyone. No one doubted that Yasodhara was the chosen one after that."

Vimala closed her eyes and imagined.

"But then Yasodhara did something quite unexpected," Neelima added.

"What did she do?"

"She chose him right back."

Large groups of people were gathering along the road in town. The commotion Vimala had noted earlier was not dissipating. It was getting bigger. Vimala raised her hand over her eyes to try to see past the morning glare. *What is going on down there,* she wondered.

"It's time for me to go," Neelima said as she watched the crowd pulsating. "I stopped here for just a brief moment of rest, but you have enticed me into a delightful visit instead. But I really must be going."

Neelima struggled back to her feet with creaking limbs. She adjusted her clothing, tightened her sash, fixed her blue headscarf one more time. Not a single hair was peeking out from underneath.

Vimala was surprised by the sudden shift in conversation. She stood up and looked at the old woman with uncertainty. Was their interaction over already?

"I thought you were going to tell me about your journey," Vimala said, a bit sheepishly. "And what does it have to do with Princess

Yasodhara?" She did not want to let the old woman go. "Are you sure you can't stay a while longer?"

Neelima turned her attention towards the town again and seemed to calculate fragments of time in her mind.

"You're right. I have not yet told you about the journey. How did I let time pass this way? You are much too good a listener, and the Great Goddess knows how much I like to talk. But soon the others will start moving and I cannot let myself fall behind. At this age, my only hope of keeping up is to remain a few steps ahead."

Vimala was suddenly desperate not to let her go. She could not remember the last time she had been so close to kindness. She racked her brain for some way out. Some way to keep Neelima just a little longer.

"Could you at least tell me where you're going?"

The old woman stopped fiddling with her clothes and looked Vimala squarely in the eyes.

"I can . . . But it won't make much sense without explanation."

"I don't mind. I really would like to know."

"Very well," Neelima agreed. "There is no subtle way to explain it, but I do feel like you should know."

She inhaled purposefully. Steadied herself on her little legs.

"I am following the Buddha to Vesali," Neelima explained. "I am going with a whole group of women—the ones you see down there in the town. We are following him in the hopes that we might eventually join his community."

"You're following the Buddha?"

"Yes. The one who was once Princess Yasodhara's husband. The Crown Prince of the Sakya Kingdom. The one who left home, left everyone to become a teacher in the forest. It is him we are following. We are hoping he will accept us as members of his community so that we can try to become awakened like him."

"Oh . . ." Vimala muttered, almost to herself. "But you're all women . . ."

Neelima turned to face the commotion in the town, as though taking her cue from the women she knew were there.

"That does seem to present a problem," Neelima admitted. "But we decided to do it anyway."

3

The Leap

Vimala wrapped some flatbreads in a cloth and gave them to the old woman before she left. She had hoped to give more, but the kitchen was barren. A wasteland, like the rest of the house. Neelima touched the top of Vimala's head with a whispered prayer of protection and hobbled away.

The women were following the Buddha.

Vimala repeated the words to herself as she watched Neelima's figure fade into the distance. She tapped her fingers against her crossed arm and repeated the words again.

The women were following the Buddha.

She went back to her room in a daze, parted the curtains and dropped onto the straw mattress on the floor. Traces of blood were splattered on the sheet. Some old, others new, a collage of human misery.

How had her life become such a waste? Her life had had promise once. She was supposed to belong to a community, have a role and a station. But it all unraveled in the blink of an eye. She looked up at the wood slats over her head, the mold and mildew that grew in between. The smell of the last customer still permeated the room. How had she ended up here?

She could not quite comprehend the mission Neelima was on. Asking a teacher for instruction, following him into the forest in the hopes that he would actually grant it? The assumption that she was even welcome to try? Vimala circled the questions in her mind. They were like cryptic trail-markings, impossible to interpret, but pointing somewhere.

But women don't go into forests, she argued with herself. They don't attempt higher knowledge. Women were supposed to stay home, fulfill their obligations. Bow their heads to the men who lorded over them. What were these women thinking?

If only she could have asked more questions, but there had been no time. Neelima was here one moment and gone the next, like a floating forest fairy. Refusing to be caught and held onto.

Where had she said they were going?

Vesali.

The word formed slowly in a quiet corner of her mind.

Vimala sat up and shaped the word again.

Vesali.

Of all the places in Bharata, the women were traveling *there?* How long had it been since she left?

She was too afraid to count the time. Vimala stared at the dirty curtains that separated her room from the public space beyond, its edges frayed and brown. Vesali had always seemed so far out of reach. As though it had become a figment of her imagination. She was not even sure she could find her way back, but now there were women walking there together. She could go with them . . .

She could go home.

Vimala whispered the possibility aloud. *Vesali.* The word slid out of her mouth and into her hands like a prayer.

But she owed Kumari. If she left the brothel with debts unpaid, Kumari could have her arrested.

Vimala got to her feet and began to pace the length of her small room. Back and forth in front of the mattress with the stained sheet. She tapped her fingers against her crossed arm and wondered. *There must be a way.* Neelima had appeared out of nowhere and called her hometown by its name. It was a sign. It had to be.

But how to escape without detection? How to avoid something worse happening along the way?

It was then that Vimala realized how quiet the brothel had become. She pulled the curtains aside and peeked out. Sounds of the busy town filtered in, but inside the silence was like a strange echo against her ears. She stepped out and tiptoed down the hall. She looked into the rooms, one after another: the girls were sleeping. Barely even moving. One girl was flopped onto her side. Another lay on her back with her legs splayed apart. Surasa was drooling into the crook of her arm. Each one was in a different position in her isolated space, but not one of them made a sound. As though the gods had muffled them with a heavy blanket. Vimala kept going until she reached the kitchen at the back. The maids should have been busy preparing meals that would feed the customers later that evening, but the old hags were nowhere to be found.

Vimala stood still and alone on the threshold. Her eyes followed the trails of black grease that rose out of the mud baked stove. Thick layers of grime coated the walls, as though a *rakshasa* had exhaled against them with his demonic breath, the air rendered choked and suffocated. A blackened pot was tossed on its side, something thick and brown oozing out of it. Vimala wiped her hands on her robe, as though the grime was reaching her from a distance. In the corner, a pile of broken wood lay stranded. Jagged pieces were sticking out in all directions, almost taunting her with their splinters. Rat droppings speckled the floor.

Vimala turned away with disgust. She could not believe that this was where her food was prepared. She imagined slimy hands sunk into a bowl of rotten vegetables and almost retched. How had her life come to this?

Just before she turned away completely, Vimala caught one last detail: Neelima's empty cup on a ledge.

And where was Kumari? she suddenly wondered. At this hour, she should have been wide awake, screaming at the staff, tearing the quiet apart, arranging for the next evening's string of customers. Vimala looked down the hall toward the wooden door that led to Kumari's personal chambers. It was bolted. Kumari was not home.

Vimala headed back towards her room. Thoughts were swirling somewhere far below the surface, in a cavern beyond her reach. She kept tapping her fingers against her crossed arm. Kumari was away, the hags were elsewhere, and the girls were fast asleep. She recited the information to herself repeatedly, hoping it would eventually take clearer shape. Neelima had shown up out of nowhere, offering Vesali without even realizing what it meant to her. Vesali was on the other side of this battered life she had been stuck in. And Neelima had offered her a way out.

If Kumari caught her, untold miseries were sure to follow—public humiliation, perhaps even prison, some kind of violence she might not survive. But the opportunity was right there, dangling in front her. She pictured Neelima's face and she knew what she had to do. Vimala entered her room and without allowing herself a moment of hesitation, she threw open the small chest by her mattress and grabbed the treasures she had stowed inside. She took the few coins she had saved and the jewelled hairpins she had kept from an earlier time. She grabbed her comb, mirror, a small bottle of her favorite oil for when her dark skin cracked, and stuffed it all quickly into her cloth bag. She grabbed her shawl that lay crumpled on the floor, throwing it over her shoulder, threw the bag over that, and then at the last minute remembered her cloak. It was too warm to wear now, but she would not leave it behind. She draped it over her arm while she scanned the room for anything she had forgotten.

But there was nothing there.

Vimala took a deep breath, placed her hand on the amulet around her neck and closed her eyes with a prayer.

She slipped out the door and did not look back.

4

The Gathering

Vimala was walking. She was not sure where she was going, what road to take, or where the others might be. Neelima was nowhere; she seemed to have evaporated in the sun's glare. But Vimala was walking. She had to put as much distance between herself and Kapilavatthu as she could. By the time the sun set, they would know she was gone. She pulled the shawl over her head and kept going.

The brothel was at the outer edge of town, so she was certain of just one thing: the road she needed to follow was the one right under her feet, directing her away from a life she was desperate to shed. It only took a few minutes for the sounds of Kapilavatthu to fade. The familiar voices, the noises she had grown accustomed to over the years, fell away like scales off a dead fish.

The road narrowed until it became a sliver in the grass. She hoped she was going in the right direction, but she was not sure. Vesali was south-east of Kapilavatthu. She looked up at the sun, but she was not sure how to read it. Where were all the women Neelima had referred to? Where was the crowd she had seen forming earlier?

What if she had gone the wrong way? Uncertainty was brewing, weakening her resolve. Should she go back? She stopped and turned around, hoping that something would become clear, but all she saw was grass. Tall swaying grass.

Either I go back now, or I keep going. No in between, she told herself. She tightened her shawl. *If I go back, I'll never have the courage to run again.*

But what if Neelima was delusional? she argued with herself. *What if there is no journey and she was just a babbling mad woman?*

No, Vimala decided. *Neelima was not mad.*

And the journey was real. She had seen the commotion in town with her own eyes. Vimala turned around and kept going, one hand pressing against the bite mark on her thigh. A reminder of the life she was leaving behind.

She hurried, her eyes glued to her feet as they raced across the field, escaping like a wanted prisoner, her heart beating wildly beneath her chest. When she looked up again, an eternity later, she found that she had already arrived somewhere else. The swaying grass had been replaced by thick trees that bent and twisted and tied each other up into strange combinations. The branches were dark and thin and wound around themselves in layers. One tree had bent itself completely over the path, as though it had forgotten how to reach for the sun. She clambered over it to the other side. As she went further, the trees became thicker, crowding her with their hairy opulence. She felt as though she was trespassing, entering their secret world without permission. A black crow screamed at her from above.

"Are you lost?"

Vimala froze. *Had Kumari already dispatched her goons?*

"Don't be afraid," the voice said.

Vimala turned around and found herself staring at an elderly woman with a bald head, dressed in white robes.

"Are you looking for us?"

"Who are you?" Vimala mumbled, more frightened than she cared to admit.

"I am Bhadda Kundalakesa," the bald woman replied with authority. "I am going to Vesali to find the Buddha, with a community of women. I thought you might be looking for us. My apologies if I have misunderstood."

Vimala stared dumbly, trying to process the words, unhinge her fear. It took her a minute, but just as she was readying herself to respond, the woman had turned away.

"Wait!" Vimala cried.

The woman turned around.

"Are you really with the women? Are you going to Vesali?" she asked, the desperation impossible to hide.

"I most certainly am. Were you hoping to join us?"

Vimala ran up to the woman and grabbed both of her hands. "Yes, yes, yes!" she cried. "I didn't know where everyone went!"

"Well, then I'm glad I made the effort. I saw you walking so purposefully into the forest, and I was certain you were trying to find us. I could have been mistaken, but the idea of a woman fleeing into the darkness that way didn't seem right." The woman dropped Vimala's hands, apparently quite uninterested in holding them, and began walking back without further ceremony.

"Where is everybody?" Vimala asked as she scuttled to keep up. "I came out to join you as soon as I heard, but I couldn't find anyone."

"We didn't get very far. Travelling with a group of women takes time. Especially as they try to disentangle themselves from their homes." The woman walked with a deliberate gait, swiftly and with focus. She did not stumble over roots or slip on leaves. Her bare feet just walked.

"How do you mean?"

"Many of the women are from Kapilavatthu, so there are lengthy goodbyes and endless conversations at every turn. And of course, when you travel with members of the Royal Family, there are prostrations and adorations that take forever. This is not going to be the most efficient journey I have ever taken."

Vimala almost stumbled with shock.

"Did you say . . . *Royal Family?*"

Bhadda Kundalakesa glanced at Vimala with a raised eyebrow. "Do you always ask so many questions?"

Vimala stopped. Her thighs were sore from the previous night's customer and she felt the bite mark burning under her clothes. It was all suddenly too much. She had no business being in the presence of the Royal Family. She was a common whore. She was escaping bad debts and dirty sheets. She sank onto the edge of a dead tree, her cloak and shoulder bag dropping listlessly to the ground.

"Please go without me," she whispered. "I can't do this."

Bhadda Kundalakesa looked down at Vimala with sharp eyes. She did not seem to be a particularly soft character, but she was clever enough to recognize suffering when it presented itself. She lowered herself onto the ground, crossed her legs, and waited for Vimala to say more. But Vimala had closed the door.

"Why can't you do this?" Bhadda Kundalakesa finally asked. "You obviously wanted to join us. You left your home to find us. What's stopping you now?"

Vimala looked at the woman beside her, her eyes puddles of anguish. "I would rather not tell you . . ." she finally admitted. "It wouldn't be . . . polite."

Bhadda Kundalakesa's eyes rounded with surprise, and then she broke out into a big, hearty laugh. "Polite?" she repeated. "*Polite?* Dear girl, you really don't need to worry about being polite around me. I have been travelling Bharata for more than a lifetime. I have seen things that would make your head spin. You would not believe all that is out there in this wild world. I doubt you are capable of shocking me."

Vimala was taken aback. Another flippant reaction. Like Neelima, this woman appeared to have few worries where social decorum was concerned.

"Well . . ." she began uncertainly, "the thing is . . . I am not what you would call a respectable member of society."

"I figured that much," Bhadda Kundalakesa replied. "So, what is it? Are you a criminal?"

"My goodness!" Vimala replied in shock. "Certainly not!"

"Then what is it?"

Vimala looked over at her bald companion. Measuring her truths in her mind.

"I'm a prostitute."

Bhadda Kundalakesa nodded. She waited a moment, but when Vimala did not say more, she dusted the bottom edge of her robe and got back to her feet.

"We can't all be perfect. Shall we keep going?"

"But . . . I don't understand. Aren't you shocked?"

"Most certainly not."

What was with these women? First one, then the other, no one worrying about the mess her social status necessarily generated.

"Well . . . the Royal Family will be," Vimala said with growing determination. "My presence would be a stain on their honor. I cannot travel with them. The likes of me with the likes of them . . ."

"You know nothing of the Royal Family or their intentions," Bhadda Kundalakesa admonished her. "The Queen Mahapajapati and Princess Yasodhara are not on this journey to make judgments. They are going to ask the Buddha for liberation. Titles and social hierarchies are being left behind. All we are now is a group of women and we are travelling together. All of us."

"Queens and prostitutes together?" Vimala whispered. "But that's madness."

"There is worse madness in the world than that. Shall we get going?"

"But . . ." Vimala hesitated.

"But *what*? Out with it if there's more. We need to get back," Bhadda Kundalakesa seared with impatience.

"I know. I'm sorry to delay you and I really don't want to cause trouble," Vimala stammered, trying to find the edges of her confidence. "But the truth is that I'm not actually free to make this journey . . ."

"What does that mean?"

"Well . . ." she hesitated again, but then she pushed herself to the end of her sentence. "I'm indebted."

And there it was.

Vimala held her breath as Bhadda Kundalakesa took in the information.

"Let's keep going," was all she said in reply.

With no alternative, Vimala followed Bhadda Kundalakesa out of the thick forest. They passed the tree that was a bridge, passed the crow that had yelled at them, and back into the wide-open field covered in tall grass.

"You took a wrong turn here," Bhadda Kundalakesa explained. "The trail moves south from this point. The women are camping further ahead."

Sounds of celebration floated towards them. Pots clanging, songs singing, noises of exuberant congregation. They turned a small bend in the path and encountered a whole community making camp for the night. Women of all kinds were working together, setting up makeshift shelters, cooking, chatting.

At the heart of it all stood a wide round tent made of shiny golden cloth. It was open on one side. Vimala could see women moving in and out of it with folded reverence.

"Is the Royal Family in there?" Vimala asked as she pointed discreetly.

"The Royal Women are."

"You haven't said anything about the debts," Vimala whispered with increasing panic. "If I'm caught here, I'll end up in prison."

"I know."

Vimala trembled all over. Just a few hours earlier, her life had made sense. She was a common prostitute in a dirty shack on the outer edge of a small city. She owed money she could never repay and was relegated to the worst customers due to her wilting age. It was far from an enviable situation, but it was predictable. She understood it. She could watch her story unfold, one scene after the next, like the backstory of a play that had been written thirty-six thousand times before.

Now here she was, walking with a stern old bald woman, apparently about to embark on a journey with Royal Women but risking imprisonment at the same time. What had she done? Her life had been tossed to the wind and she had no idea where it would land or what to expect next. This was not a story she was familiar with.

"So, what are we doing?" Vimala asked.

"We are going to eat."

Vimala kept her head covered as they approached the Gathering Women. She did not expect to be recognized, but she did not feel like being seen. There would be plenty of time for humiliation later. All she wanted was to find a small corner where she could disappear. Bhadda Kundalakesa, however, drove through the clusters of women like a mighty elephant, aiming for a target Vimala could not see. They passed women sitting in circles, others who were by themselves. One woman was arguing with what must have been her parents. They were in a heated battle and were not embarrassed by the fact that everyone could hear them.

What Vimala did not notice was the fact that the women all seemed to be of different stations. Some were wearing elegant fabrics with gold trim, while others were dressed in more humble attire. Some had delicate sandals on their feet and others went barefoot. There were jewels glinting in the sunlight alongside simple amulets made with string like hers. All kinds of women were collected together in that strange gathering, and while they did seem to gather in small groups of familiarity, there were no barriers keeping the different categories apart. The rough linen dresses sat alongside the silk ones, the jewels alongside the string. Had Vimala only looked up for a moment, she would have noticed this, but she never did. She stared at her feet and clutched at her shawl instead.

They managed to get through the crowds with some efficiency, but when they were just a stone's throw from the Royal Tent, Vimala was overcome with curiosity and slowed down. She could not believe she was so close to the Royal Women. If she called out to them, they would hear. She stared at the open flap of the tent, wishing she could catch a glimpse, wondering what they looked like. And then she stumbled over a goat and knocked its head with her flying foot. The goat bleated angrily. Ruffled and embarrassed, Vimala pulled herself together, apologized quickly and ran to catch up with Bhadda Kundalakesa who had not—unsurprisingly—skipped a beat.

They eventually reached the cooking fire—a great conflagration with many pots teetering over the top. A handful of women were stirring warm concoctions, while another group was making flatbreads in an orchestrated line: one woman combined the flour and water, the next kneaded it into dough, the one after that parceled it out into separate balls, and the last one flattened the balls out and slapped them against the hot stone to bake. Each bread was flipped repeatedly until it was ready and then thrown onto a tray for another to serve.

When the smell of those warm flatbreads reached Vimala, she became faint with hunger. She tried to remember the last time she had eaten but could not think when it was. She leaned against a tree for support and then slowly slid to the ground. She closed her eyes and waited for the feeling to pass.

Bhadda Kundalakesa watched her ward collapse, then she shrugged and walked away.

"Here you go."

She returned a moment later and stood over Vimala with a banana leaf topped with warm food.

"Oh . . . ," Vimala responded weakly.

She accepted the meal with trembling hands. She knew she was starving but she could not summon the energy required to make herself eat. She stared at the food distantly.

"Don't just sit there," Bhadda Kundalakesa reprimanded. "Those women worked hard to make that food for you. Lift your fingers and get to work."

Vimala looked up at her newly acquired general and obeyed without argument. She picked up one of the flatbreads and nibbled at the edge. She was so hungry, it almost made her sick, but when she went for a second bite, the hunger grew. A third bite, and it was a ferocious tiger inside of her, desperate to devour, demanding to be fed. Soon she was scooping up the steaming lentils with the bread and gobbling it up as golden oil slithered down her chin.

"Much better," Bhadda Kundalakesa declared when the leaf was laid bare. "I think you might be ready for a second helping."

Vimala nodded as she tossed the leaf to the ground beside her. She licked her fingers like a greedy child, watching Bhadda Kundalakesa return to the cooking fire to ask for more.

Vimala was more capable of taking in her surroundings. What at first seemed like a cacophony of joyful women now appeared a bit more complicated. There were certainly some women chatting away happily, but she noticed quite a few solitary figures as well. One woman had skin so black it was almost blue, and a face that would have made every courtesan in the land green with envy. The woman Vimala had noticed earlier who seemed to have been arguing with her parents was now in a full-scale battle. Bits and pieces of what they said filtered through.

"I won't go back," the woman declared. "I don't want to be married anymore!"

This one was wearing a soft yellow robe and had tiny flowers in her hair. She seemed very young to Vimala, but she was apparently old enough to make her own demands. The mother seemed utterly beyond herself and was clutching at her daughter's hands. "How can you do this to us? You must go back," she pleaded.

"No," the daughter declared. "I refuse to be married anymore."

Back and forth they went, mother and daughter arguing. The mother begged for grandchildren, begged her daughter not to abandon her without at least giving her that much. When that had no effect, the father lost his temper, stamped his feet, ordered her to obey. She had no right to abandon her obligations. He even went so far as to threaten her with the authorities, but the young woman with flowers in her hair would not hear a word of it. She was determined. "I am going with the Royal Women. See if the village guards are capable to going up against *them*."

It was strange to hear the Royal Women invoked as defense this way. Vimala did not understand what it meant, but she was too tired to really think it through. Bhadda Kundalakesa arrived with a second pile of food. Vimala gobbled it up and then felt her eyes close by themselves. She did not even try to fight the sleep. She let her body drop at the foot of the tree where she had been sitting. She pulled her cloak over herself and tucked her arm under her head. She could hear the young woman arguing with sincere dedication to her cause, but the sounds faded into the background as sleep swept in.

5

The Past Comes Charging In

Vimala slept through the day and right through the night. When she woke the next morning, so many hours later, chickens were clucking, women were giggling, the goat she had fallen over was not far away, bleating to its heart's content. Vimala stretched out luxuriously as she looked up at the tree that had been her companion through her long rest. Its leaves were swaying gently in the morning breeze. What a delicious feeling to sleep for such a long time.

And through the darkness too. She usually slept through the piercing gaze of sunlight, tossing and turning as the sounds of a busy world intruded, reminding her that she did not belong. Reminding her that she was a creature of the night, not welcome to participate in the activities respectable women enjoyed. But last night, Vimala slept under the stars without the disruptions of a wakened world.

Vimala was about to drift back to sleep for just a bit more slumber when she heard a painfully familiar sound. She bolted upright.

"Ah ha!" the sound bellowed.

Vimala jumped to her feet.

"There she is!" Kumari hollered to the armed guards behind her. "I knew it!"

The dreaded brothel owner was huffing towards her, arms waving back and forth like an argument. Two guards trailed behind—one bald and the other with stringy hair. They both looked hungry.

By the time Kumari reached Vimala, she was slick with sweat. Vimala could smell the scent of jasmine that had been quickly patched over Kumari's otherwise stale body odor.

"I knew you would be here!" Kumari spat as she worked to catch her breath. "When I realized you were gone, I knew this was where I would find you. A group of women roving the forest like madwomen. Obviously, you had to run and follow!"

Kumari wiped the sweat that was slithering down her neck and fiddled with her jewelry, ensuring everything was in its proper place. She had heavy hooped earrings and a golden nose ring that dangled precariously over her lip. Each of these decorations she touched with trembling fingers, like someone looking for something in the dark. She then fingered her necklaces—layers of different colored heavy beads strung one over the other—making sure nothing had fallen or slipped in the rush. When she was done taking inventory, she returned her attention to her runaway property.

"You have not paid your debts, Daughter," Kumari declared with oozing satisfaction. "You know you cannot leave until those are settled."

Vimala hung her head. She could not believe she was defeated so soon.

"You owe me," Kumari threatened.

Kumari anticipated a well-versed argument. Some long-winded justification that Vimala had been concocting since she had stepped out the door. Or some desperate pleading, an appeal to her humanity, to life's injustices and pain. Kumari waited, tapping her sandals with impatience for the story to play out, but Vimala had nothing to say. She was far away, staring at her dust covered toes, her unadorned feet that looked as common as a peasant's. Whatever hope Vimala might have harbored the day before had proved to be as hollow as a lump of foam on Ganga's shores.

So Kumari began to pace. Back and forth, as though Vimala was not even there. Her steps clinking with the tin anklets she always wore. Every once in a while, a loose thread from her green dress would get caught in one of the chimes and she stopped to yank it out.

"I have been wondering about you for a long time, Daughter," Kumari finally said. She bent down to unravel yet another aggravating thread caught in her anklet. "You don't bring the price you used to. The clients aren't eager anymore."

Vimala did not move. Her toes did not even shift in the earth.

"Your last customer is a perfect example . . ."

Now Vimala looked up. Was she to be accused for *his* violence? Vimala felt righteous indignation for just a moment, but then it fell apart. *Of course* it was her fault. She dropped her head. Some of her tangled hair fell over her face.

"If you had more skill, you could have seduced him into quiet, but you don't seem to have that ability anymore. You disturbed everyone with your incompetence."

Vimala closed her eyes. There were dozens of women around, but somehow, she was completely alone. The world was moving on without her as it always did. She caught the sound of a bird singing in the tree above and instinctively identified it as a magpie. Without looking up, she knew it would have a black head and a long blue tail that would dip below the branch it was perched on.

"So, I have to wonder," Kumari continued. "What am I to do with you now? You know that I won't let a debt go, but I'm not sure keeping you is worth my while. You cost me more than you bring in."

Kumari stopped pacing and stared at Vimala's hunched frame.

"Your hair is turning grey," she said as she reached for some of the dirty strands that hung over Vimala's face, fingering them as though she was testing their weight.

"The thing is . . ." she continued as she let the hair drop, "you *have* been dutiful."

Was that softness in her voice? Was Kumari wavering? If there was a time for Vimala to make her case, to jump into the space between the options and push for a desired outcome, it was now.

But Vimala had climbed too far inside herself for that.

"I will admit that I had great hopes for you," she continued. "I thought I might even be able to rely on you, maybe do something more interesting with the business. But . . ." Kumari sighed dramatically, "you disappointed."

Women of the Gathering had begun to approach.

No one had bothered with Kumari and her henchmen at first. They were, after all, not the first to reclaim female property. Almost every woman in the Gathering had been accosted or accused at some point the day before. Husbands, children, parents, employers. One after another charging into the Gathering to plead with the escaping women to return. Some intruders threatened, others grabbed, but most begged. Kumari was just another proprietor attempting to reclaim what she thought was hers.

But Kumari was not like more proprietors. She was loud and her henchmen seethed with violence. The Gathering Women had stopped what they were doing, senses alert.

"I was so upset that you had run away, I had planned to have you arrested." Kumari looked at the guards behind her, as though to confirm the growing public concern. "But my anger is not what it was a few hours ago," she declared, loud enough for the spectators to hear. "I have therefore decided to forgive you. You will not go to prison."

Kumari stood with her hands on her hips triumphantly, waiting for the outpouring of gratitude she thought she deserved, but Vimala did not move. One of the henchmen—the one with stringy hair—barked at Vimala to show some respect. He grabbed her by the neck and threw her to the ground. Vimala landed by Kumari's feet with a heavy thud. A swirl of pink dust kicked up around her.

"You will return to the brothel with me," Kumari announced as she looked down at her property. "It's time to end this charade and reclaim your place. But I will be transferring you to the kitchen for the remainder of your debt. I think we can both agree that your skills in the bedroom are no longer what they once were."

Kumari nudged Vimala with her foot as a signal to rise and then summoned her guards to follow. The one with stringy hair barked at Vimala again. "You heard her. Back to the whorehouse!" He yanked her by the arm, squeezing with his fingers as he pulled.

Vimala was barely present even though she was right there, her last hopes extinguishing like a flame. She picked up her bag and cloak from the ground.

"Excuse me!" someone called out breathlessly. "Brothel Owner!"

Kumari turned to find an old woman with a blue headscarf hobbling toward her as fast as her little legs could carry her. The Gathering Women parted to let her pass.

"Can I have a word, Brothel Owner?"

The mental shackles Vimala had wrapped herself in loosened just enough to allow her to raise her head.

Neelima?

"What do you want?" Kumari barked.

Neelima caught up with them and bowed with exaggerated deference.

"If you would be so kind, Madame Brothel Owner, you have been requested at the Royal Tent."

Kumari stumbled while standing on her two ugly feet.

"The . . . Royal Tent?" she mumbled. "*Here?*" She had apparently not noticed the golden tent at the center of the Gathering.

"Yes, Madame Brothel Owner. Her Highness Princess Yasodhara would like a word before you depart."

Kumari looked around, trying to find a way out of her dilemma. When a brothel owner was summoned by the Royal Family, it usually did not bode well.

"Of course," Kumari mumbled. "But as you can see, I am conducting business. Might it be possible to delay?"

"Her Highness does not want to cause you any trouble, but she has asked to see you. So, if you don't mind, please come with me."

With no alternative at her disposal, Kumari nodded. She followed the little maidservant toward the Royal Tent, her henchmen and broken property trailing behind.

The closer they got to the tent, the more activity buzzed about them. Women were fetching jars of water, rolling up sleeping mats, folding up clothes. When they got to the entrance, they were met with a tall, muscular woman holding a spear. Her face was lined with black tattoos, identifying her as a tribeswoman from the hills. When she saw Neelima, the woman moved the spear aside to let them pass.

Vimala assumed the Royal Women would be seated on high golden thrones, decked in glittery finery. She expected celestial guardians, fluttering peacocks, radiant gems in all directions.

Instead, Vimala found herself surrounded by a bustling community of women making preparations to depart. The Royal Women did not even seem to be there, at least not in any obvious way. But then she noticed one woman who stood majestically at the center, like the calm inside a storm. She wore simple white cotton clothing and had her hair shorn, but she commanded the ranks with clear authority. "Make sure everyone outside has had something to eat," she instructed over here. "Don't forget to stamp out the fires before we leave," she instructed over there. Vimala had never seen her before, but she knew who she was. She did not wear Royal Jewels, but royalty was inscribed on her like glitter on sand. Vimala bowed instinctively.

A younger woman suddenly materialized in front of them. She too wore simple white clothing and had a shaved head.

"Your Highness," Neelima said as she bowed.

"I am Princess Yasodhara," the younger woman declared as she approached Kumari. "My maidservant here tells me that you are reclaiming this woman as your property. Is that right?"

Vimala bowed again, her entire body now trembling with fright. She could not believe she was so close to one of the Royal Women. So close that she could touch her. She kept her head down, overwhelmed by the moment, terrified of where it would lead.

Kumari stepped forward and scraped her body to the ground with theatrical obsequiousness. "Yes, Your Highness," she answered thickly. If she was intimidated by her surroundings, she did not show it.

"Why do you believe you have claims to this woman?" Princess Yasodhara asked imperiously.

"Because, Your Highness, she belongs to me."

"Do you have any proof? A deed of purchase perhaps?"

Kumari shuffled her feet a moment, as though trying to locate her response.

"Unfortunately, not with me, but I did purchase the woman you see behind me. She was a servant in a client's household. The client in question refused to pay for the services he took, so I was forced to confront him in his home and demand payment publicly. When he declared himself destitute, I took this woman in exchange."

"I see," the princess replied as she eyed Kumari.

Vimala kept her head down, trembling. She tried to follow the conversation that promised to determine her future, but the words felt like swarms of bees in her ears.

"How long has she been working for you?"

"I cannot be certain, Your Highness. I left my ledgers at home, but it has been a few years. Given how much she costs me every day with food and clothing, I am far from reimbursement."

"You sound as though you have been sorely burdened," Princess Yasodhara replied, not hiding her annoyance.

"Oh *very*, Your Highness. If only you knew the burdens I am forced to carry. The number of women I am responsible for, the difficult clients I must contend with, the dealers who try to swindle me at every pass. It's all so very difficult for a woman my age . . ."

The bustling activity kept going as the two women negotiated Vimala's person. Dust was swirling as feet stamped in all directions. Voices floated in the air. The world was moving forward while Vimala's life was caught at a standstill, as though she was not even there. As though her destiny was irrelevant in the greater scheme of things. She felt herself becoming light-headed.

"I am sure we can come to some arrangement," Princess Yasodhara stated impatiently. She obviously did not believe a word that slithered out of that snake-oil mouth. "How much does she still owe?"

Kumari looked up at the princess with undisguised appetite, recognizing as she did that a barter was underway.

"I am so sorry, Your Highness, but perhaps you have misunderstood. The truth is, I have come to love Vimala as my daughter. Even if she *could* repay her debts, I would not want to release her."

"Of course," the princess replied, preparing herself for what promised to be a lengthy negotiation. "But suppose you *could* release her . . ."

Vimala's heart suddenly cracked. She thought she could manage another bartering of her person, but she simply no longer could. She had been traded as a commodity for most of her life. From the moment she left home, she had been passed from one set of grubby hands to the next. She could not digest one more version of it.

Last night had been her first night of freedom in as long as she could remember. She had run away, made a choice for herself, taken her life into her own hands for the first time in years. She could not imagine returning to the brothel for more of the same. She had no strength for it anymore. Her knees buckled and she fell to the ground in a collapsed heap of despair.

Many Years Later:
Vimala and Darshani

I was not used to talking so much. Most of my companions had passed away and I had grown accustomed to quiet over the years. I was not alone, of course, surrounded as I was by our many novices. And Sundarinanda was still here, always grumbling about. But my own companions were gone. An entire generation of great women had faded out of existence.

I looked over at Darshani and saw that she was looking quite morose. My story must have been difficult for her to hear.

"Are you all right? Maybe you need a break?"

Darshani wiped her nose with the back of her hand but shook her head vigorously.

"I'm fine."

"Are you sure? We don't have to do the story all at once. It might be a lot for you to take."

"No, no I'm sure . . ." (she paused, here, seeming to concentrate on choosing the right term . . .) "Venerable," she articulated carefully. "I just never thought about all the suffering you came from. I didn't know. I mean, I knew a little. But not really."

"It was a long time ago, Little One. It's not suffering to me anymore."

Darshani came to our nunnery with a very different background. She knew, of course, that there were prostitutes and courtesans and widows amongst us, but her own young life was so innocent by comparison.

Her parents were dedicated practitioners; they came to our nunnery as a family every week to make offerings. Darshani especially loved coming, always eager to help wherever she could, carrying water, sweeping the perpetually dusty floors, or simply sitting beside one of us to listen to whatever it was we had to say. By the time she was seven, she was asking to stay. Eventually she begged.

And then one day, she lay down on the ground in front of the main shrine, her arms outstretched, her little legs splayed out, and she refused to budge. She made a declaration that she would stay with us. She told the shrine (in a very loud voice for all to hear) that this was where she belonged. She, little Darshani in a seven-year-old body, would not go home. Short of tearing her from the shrine and dragging her through the nunnery kicking and screaming, her parents had no choice but to accept. She had been with us ever since.

"You remember the teachings about impermanence?" I asked her.

She nodded as she wiped her nose again.

"The teachings tell us that everything is impermanent and that we must learn how to let go if we want to become free. Right?"

She nodded again.

"Well, here's the part that most people tend to forget: everything is impermanent, and this includes suffering."

She looked up at me with a quizzical expression on her face.

"I don't understand," she mumbled.

"When we talk about impermanence, we often think about all the good stuff that we have to let go of. We think of our bodies, our friendships, our loved ones, our homes. This is what most people think they have to practice letting go of, because it is what they think they are most attached to."

"But those things are impermanent," Darshani exclaimed.

"Yes, that's true, and we must learn to let go of all of it. But what we tend to forget is that the bad stuff is also impermanent. It's not just the good stuff that we have to let go of. Our bad experiences are impermanent too. They don't last forever. Nor does the suffering that comes from them."

Darshani looked up at me, almost bewildered. I could see the wheels turning in her head.

"But no one gets attached to suffering. That's ridiculous. Who holds onto that?!"

I laughed, despite myself.

"We all do, Little One. Strangely enough, one of the hardest things to let go of is our suffering. For all kinds of reasons, we hold onto our suffering the way we hold onto everything else. But our suffering is impermanent and something to let go of too."

It was a difficult lesson to learn. Perhaps the most difficult lesson of all. I patted her young hands.

"You are still at the beginning of your journey with us, Darshani. You have time to learn all of this. At every stage, the teachings become clearer. You will turn them around, see them differently, you will swim to the bottom of their truth and understand them with increasing clarity."

I could feel her growing taller as she sat next to me.

"For now, just try to remember this: the bad stuff does not last forever. It can't last forever, because forever is not in its nature. Suffering is impermanent. And we must make sure to let all of it go."

Darshani repeated the words quietly to herself as she stared at the horizon.

6

The Walking Begins

It was time to go.

Business was settled, negotiations were closed. The women of the Gathering bid farewell to the city that had been their home. The Royal Tent was ceremoniously folded and packed into its cart, the shelters were disassembled, the cooking utensils carried away.

Vimala watched the organizational acrobatics from afar. She did not know how to approach this community as her own person. Princess Yasodhara had managed to send Kumari away.

The women began to walk.

Vimala tried to lose herself in the vast collection of bodies, but her story was being whispered all around her. Everyone was curious about the one who had just been bartered free.

"The talk will die out," Bhadda Kundalakesa said in an attempt at reassurance. The two had gravitated towards each other.

"Will it?"

"People are fickle and easily distracted. Give it a day or two, and they will move on to something else."

Vimala tightened the shawl that was covering her head. Her shawl had once been shiny and new. Bright red, with yellow woven along the edges. But now it looked as old as she felt. The red had faded, the yellow looked more like a sickly shade of green.

"Do you want to walk separately?" Bhadda offered as she watched Vimala try to hide inside herself. "This group doesn't move quickly. We can wait for them to pass and pick up afterwards."

Vimala stopped walking almost instantly.

"Would you do that? I don't want to walk alone."

Bhadda Kundalakesa rubbed her bald head as she surveyed the slow-moving caravan. "It won't take much effort to catch up."

Vimala accepted the offer with visible relief. The two of them stepped back from the path and watched as dozens of women made their way onward. Heads loosely covered passed them by, some with hair, some without. Some wore silk, others wore cotton, each one covered with something different. Some heads turned towards them as they passed, wondering perhaps about Vimala's story, or just to take one more look, but no one disturbed them. Bhadda Kundalakesa's stoic presence assured them of that. When the Royal Women passed, both Vimala and Bhadda Kundalakesa bowed low to the ground. Vimala had expected a carriage or a palanquin, or anything else to declare their royal status, but there they were, walking on bare feet in widow's garb, not a strand of hair on either one of their heads.

Tattooed bodyguards followed close behind the Royal Women. One of them Vimala recognized as the one who had been standing guard by the entrance of the Royal Tent when she had gone in. She was bigger than Vimala had realized at the time, and her shoulders were unusually broad. Her sharp spear was tucked by her side. Vimala watched her march past with undisguised fascination. She had never seen a woman look so strong.

Neelima was hobbling behind the Royal Guards. She probably no longer felt the need to rush ahead. The caravan had proved slow enough even for her. Neelima's sweet face, her small form in her blue servant's dress, was a comfort. Most of the women of the Gathering were strangers to Vimala, with languages she could not decipher and histories she knew nothing about. But Neelima was like a rooted signpost, reminding her that she was going the right way.

Behind that trusted maidservant, Vimala noticed a strange figure. Walking uncertainly, eyes glancing furtively in all directions, was a woman holding what looked like a baby bundled up in her arms. She wore silk robes—bright pink fabric decorated with orange flower buds and a neckline studded with jewels. The clothing would have been beautiful once, and expensive, but it was worn and tattered now, as though she had been sleeping outdoors for weeks. The woman clutched at her child while muttering words Vimala could not hear, barely looking where she was going. It was not long before she stepped right onto Neelima's heels.

"Great Goddess," Neelima cried out, as she floundered and caught herself.

The strange woman stopped and stared at her, as though only just seeing her for the first time, but she did not apologize. Vimala was about to rush over, to make sure Neelima was all right, but Neelima pulled herself together and smiled. "No need to worry, Kisa dear," she said as she dusted herself off. She then extended her arm to the muttering woman, and the muttering woman took it. Off they went together.

What an unusual world, Vimala thought to herself.

She looked at her own companion—a bald-headed ascetic with a sharp tongue and impatient kindness. *What were all these women doing?* Never in a thousand lifetimes had Vimala expected to find herself here, in a gathering with the Royal Family, surrounded by women of every station, and apparently every measure of sanity. Moving together through the forest to find a teacher who did not even expect them. What did all these women hope to receive when they arrived? What would they do once they did? Why were so many of them taking the risk? Vimala could not wrap her mind around any of it. But she knew that she was free from Kumari's tyranny. That much, at least, made sense.

Eventually, the line petered out until it was just Vimala and Bhadda Kundalakesa, standing quietly on the edge of the path. Great trees loomed all around. Vimala closed her eyes and took in a long, deep breath as she soaked up the smell of lush greenery.

"I can't believe Kumari is really out of my life," she said, almost to herself. "I never thought I'd be free of that place."

"Your brothel owner was quite something," Bhadda Kundalakesa replied. "I've met all kinds of people over the years, but she's among the most memorable. It must have been terrible living under that roof."

It certainly was.

Vimala remembered the day Kumari charged into her life. Vimala was working as a kitchen servant for an elderly couple. She had not been raised for that kind of work, but she learned quickly how to get the job done. She tended to the vegetable garden, cooked the meals, rinsed the dishes at the well.

One evening, Kumari came stomping towards the house. Vimala was squatting on the front porch, sorting through the rice, sifting out the last bits of debris before she poured it into a clay container. She straightened up and watched as Kumari approached.

Kumari was wearing a bright red dress and she was draped in crass jewelry. She had applied thick kohl around her eyes, an oozing layer of paint on her cheeks, and she was chewing on a betel leaf which stained her teeth red. Vimala thought she looked like a parody—the kind of character that would be dreamed up for a village play. She had never seen anyone dressed that way in real life. Her mother always said that overdoing an outfit was like putting too much salt in your food. One must salt just enough to invite flavor, but not so much that you ruin the taste.

Vimala must have been staring at Kumari with blatant fascination, because when Kumari reached the porch, she barked, "Mind your own business and get back to work." Then she spit a big blob of red betel juice right at Vimala's feet.

Vimala should have dropped her eyes and scurried away, but she could not help herself. She stared just a moment longer, and it was probably one moment too much. Kumari was on the verge of barking something else, but then she retracted. She cocked her head to one side and eyed Vimala more carefully. "My, you are a pretty one, aren't you?" she whispered.

Vimala did not know what to say.

"Turn around, will you? I want to see the whole package." Vimala just stood there feeling dumb. "I said, turn around!" And instantly Vimala did. Kumari watched carefully, assessing her like a piece of merchandise, one finger tapping against her ugly chin. She then clucked her tongue and pushed open the front door without invitation, walking right in.

When Kumari emerged a few moments later, it was with the proud declaration that she had purchased Vimala as her own. Vimala would become a prostitute in her brothel because the old man had no coin left to pay for the services he had used behind his wife's back.

It still astonished Vimala, all these years later, that her person could be so easily dismissed. She had been passed around, from one proprietor to the next, since she was a young girl. Her last proprietor was Princess Yasodhara, but she claimed not to own her, despite having paid.

"You know, I wasn't always a prostitute," Vimala explained to Bhadda Kundalakesa as they began walking together. "I was born into a very different lineage."

"I'm sure most prostitutes claim as much. Do prostitutes even *have* lineages?"

Vimala reeled back from the shock of the response.

She had just taken a risk she had not risked before and tried to tell her companion a piece of the truth. She had opened herself up. Bhadda Kundalakesa's response was like a slap across her face. She had thought that Bhadda Kundalakesa would be curious about her heritage. Or at the very least, that she would be a bit kind. Did she not promise that they were all just women now, walking together? Prostitutes and queens? Social hierarchies left behind?

But Bhadda Kundalakesa had swept her story aside without even hearing it, as though it was not worth her time.

"Prostitutes have all kinds of reasons, you know," Vimala defended herself. "And all kinds of histories. You obviously don't know what you're talking about."

Bhadda looked over at Vimala with a raised eyebrow, but she did not break her stride.

"I was actually a courtesan once. I come from a long line of illustrious women that are nothing like Kumari's ugliness."

Bhadda Kundalakesa stopped in her tracks.

"You were a *courtesan*?"

I was a courtesan indeed, she thought to herself as she raised her chin. Bhadda Kundalakesa should wither in a pot of her own pride for the mistake she had made in judging her.

"But then, how did Kumari get her hands on you?" she asked, her incredulity obvious. "What happened?"

And the moment of smug satisfaction dissolved. She *had* been a courtesan once, but it all fell apart in a flash. Vimala was now barely a fraction of who she was once supposed to be.

"The lineage was broken and I had to run away."

The reasons it ended were buried deep inside her; she was not ready to voice the story of her failure yet.

"But we do have an illustrious history. My mother always said that our lineage can be traced back to the very beginnings of time—when the Primordial Man sacrificed himself for Creation. He offered himself to the gods to help shape the world we live in. His head became the priests, his arms became the warriors, his legs became the merchants. Each piece of the Primordial Man generated a piece of our world. Stitched together, these pieces created social harmony."

"I know that story," Bhadda Kundalakesa reflected. "But no one ever told me that courtesans were part of the first creation." She started walking again, but more slowly now.

"The way my mother told it, courtesans were an important part of the primordial sacrifice. Courtesans emerged from the wrist—the most beautiful part of the human body. The wrist enables a man to hold a weapon, but a woman can use it to seduce."

"Women can hold weapons," Bhadda retorted. "Didn't you see the female guards surrounding the Royal Family?"

"Women certainly *can* be warriors. We have all heard the stories of the Great Goddess who dominates the battlefield and destroys her opponents. But most of the time, women are not the ones on the front lines. The arm that flexes belongs to the men who wear armor and charge into war with wild battle cries. But the wrist . . . that is where courtesans come from. We are beautiful, intoxicating even, and we are just as essential for social welfare."

These were the words Vimala had been raised with, words that had infused her with confidence once upon a time. Courtesans belonged to the highest echelons of society. When well trained, they could advise princes, entertain the most distinguished, soothe the worried. Repair the world.

"Extraordinary," Bhadda whispered. She obviously had not realized how distinguished Vimala's heritage was. Vimala pulled back her shoulders. She had belonged to a tradition that had once meant something. Even if she now no longer did.

They continued walking together, with long stretches of silence in between. By mid-afternoon, the sun had become piercingly beautiful. Shining like a crazy diamond in the sky, rays exploding in all directions. Birds were chirping like an eager audience begging for more.

"I have been travelling a long time," Bhadda Kundalakesa eventually said. "More years than I can count."

Vimala remembered Bhadda saying something similar the day before—she had said something about all the madness she had seen in the world, that there was nothing to be surprised by. Or something to that effect.

"I have spent time with almost every type of person you can imagine, but I now realize that you are the first courtesan I have ever met. I don't know how that's possible."

Vimala shrugged.

"Courtesans spend most of their time in their secret worlds, catering to patrons who want to forget the harsh truths of life. I suppose it's not that surprising."

Bhadda considered this.

"You're probably right. Where would I have met a courtesan? Certainly not in the rest-houses I often slept in, or in the forest with teachers I studied with. I just never realized that I wasn't seeing them. I guess I didn't notice that I didn't know them." Bhadda rubbed her bald head with both hands in obvious consternation. "The thing is, I have been to every corner of our beautiful Bharata. I have walked all the way down to the tip where the ocean extends into eternity, and I have climbed up into the highest ranges of the Himalayas. I really thought I had seen it all."

Bhadda had seen the *ocean*?

"You've seen so much . . ." Vimala replied, embarrassed by her own provincial limitations.

Bhadda nodded. "I have. There is so much beauty to see out there. But . . ." she hesitated, seeming almost a bit embarrassed as she looked over at Vimala. "I have never seen the secret world of the courtesans. That is a kind of beauty I know nothing about."

The armor Vimala normally protected herself with softened like butter in the hot sun. She finally exhaled.

The day was drawing to a close. Vimala began to wonder if their walking would ever end. She was not used to walking such long distances and she was not sure how much more she could manage. The slope they were following was getting steeper and her legs were trembling with fatigue. But just as she was about to give up hope, they turned a corner and discovered a beautiful stone staircase to help ease them down. The handrail was carved into the shape of long black serpent. The workmanship took Vimala's breath away. She put her hand tentatively on the rail, convinced it would pulsate the moment she touched it, but it did not move. It was stone, even though it seemed very much alive.

When they reached the bottom, they could see the rest of the Gathering ahead, setting up camp for the night. They had chosen a clearing between tall arjuna trees, right on the banks of a gushing river.

"Do you mind if we take a short break before joining the others?" Vimala asked, her bag already slipping off her shoulder. "I am not ready for all that noise and my feet are throbbing. I can't remember the last time I walked so much."

Bhadda Kundalakesa did not argue. She was happy to avoid loud gatherings too. Vimala laid out her cloak.

"That river does look welcoming, though," Vimala said as she settled down. The women of the Gathering were splashing themselves with welcome relief. "I'm desperate to soak these swollen feet."

She looked down with dismay at the calluses already forming. Some were hardening into ugly red sores. Others were foamy white and looked ready to burst. She yearned to rub her feet, massage the heels, push her thumbs into each arch and press all the tiredness out. She was an expert at foot massage, her mother having taught her how to do it when she was very young. Every afternoon, before the patrons arrived and her mother had to dress, Vimala would sit on a low wicker stool with her mother's delicate feet on her lap. She would listen as her mother guided her in the art of foot massage, until she knew precisely where to press and how to release.

Most days, Vimala used a bit of almond oil. She would dip her fingers into the soft substance and work her mother's feet with dedicated attention. But when her mother was especially tired, Vimala was permitted to create a small concoction by adding a drop of precious camphor oil. The two of them would watch as the camphor slowly slipped out of its vial and landed with a tiny splash into the almond sea. The luxurious scent would fill the room, swirling around them like an ancestral courtesan. Vimala and her mother would inhale with eyes closed, filling their lungs until all the resistance they were holding was let out. And then when she was ready, Vimala would lift her mother's feet onto her lap, and knead the knots out, one rolling movement at a time. Hours were spent sitting together that way, infused with the smell of camphor. She at her mother's feet, where she happily belonged.

Vimala looked down at her own filthy feet. She would never touch feet in that state. She would wait until she had access to the river before she would even let herself get close.

Bhadda Kundalakesa was lowering herself to the ground when she suddenly stopped. Froze in mid-air.

"Did you hear that?"

"What?" Vimala replied, looking up.

Bhadda straightened herself back up, her face turned toward the forest behind them.

"Listen."

They waited, heads raised, eyes focused. A giant squirrel was hanging on a branch directly above. Its fur looked as though it had been painted in a swirl of bright color and its tail hung so far down, Vimala was tempted to reach up and catch it.

But she did not move. She waited for the noise that had alerted her bald companion. Waiting until . . .

There.

The faint remnant of a cry. Almost a wail. Like an animal pierced by an arrow or caught in a trap.

A second time.

A third.

"That is not an animal," Vimala reasoned, though no one had asked.

They got up and walked toward the sound, trying to find its maker. They followed it into the thickness of the forest, off the path. They had to maneuver difficult terrain, squeeze between boulders and bunches of prickly green foliage. They moved aside tall stems crowned with giant leaves; they held onto slippery moss that grew along trunks. Every once in a while, a thread of light streamed in to break up the damp darkness. Vimala caught sight of a stag scavenging for food, its head buried in the grass.

And then they saw her.

A woman, almost entirely naked, was wandering, staggering almost, without direction in the woods.

"Slowly . . ." Bhadda Kundalakesa cautioned as she crouched. Vimala lowered herself down.

The woman's hair was a nest of madness. Strips of cloth hung upon her body, the remainders of something once worn but long ago ripped away. Her dark skin was covered in welts and scratches. Bhadda Kundalakesa moved towards her like a hunter. Vimala stayed where she was.

When she was just a few steps away, Bhadda raised herself up.

"Greetings, Sister."

The woman started. She obviously had not heard them approach.

"I am not going to hurt you," Bhadda Kundalakesa said as she took another step forward with a palm raised in a gesture of fearlessness. "I am here to help."

The woman's eyes were red and puffy, as though she had cried a lifetime of tears. She seemed oblivious to her near nakedness.

"Are you hurt?" Bhadda asked, so very quietly.

Tears dripped out of the woman's eyes in heavy drops. Words seemingly buried somewhere far beneath the surface, where conversation did not reach.

"You must be hungry," Bhadda Kundalakesa said, trying a different tactic. "Have you eaten? We have food we would be happy to share with you."

At the reference to "we," Vimala showed herself. The woman stared at them both.

Eyes hollow.

The forest was filled with talkative insects, the trees were bursting with birds, the branches were like wild roadways for monkeys as they chased each other about. But the three women were stock still and silent. Waiting for the decision that would determine the direction the scene would take.

The woman wiped her cheek with her dirty hand. Her breasts hung limply and exposed. They were the empty breasts of a woman who had once been a mother.

"Come with us," Bhadda offered as she took another step. "We can take care of you."

The woman looked at Bhadda Kundalakesa, as though trying to make sense of the words she was hearing.

But still, the woman did not move.

Vimala began to worry that they had made a mistake. What if the woman was dangerous? She could even be sick. Why did they intervene? Vimala stepped back instinctively, one hand on her amulet.

But a moment later, the woman crumpled. Bhadda closed the distance and caught the woman as she fell into her arms. The woman looked as if she had been carrying a mountain of pain on her back and somebody had finally offered to help share the burden.

She was not mad, Vimala realized. She was exhausted.

Vimala rushed forward too. Together, Bhadda Kundalakesa and Vimala carried the wild woman forward. One step at a time, they built a bridge of female strength. When they reached the edge of the path, Vimala stopped to pick up her cloak from the ground.

"You might feel better this way," she suggested, as she draped it over the wild one's shoulders.

The woman looked down at herself, apparently registering her appearance for the first time. Then she nodded and slipped her arms through the openings. She pulled the neck closed with her dirty hand.

Vimala and Bhadda Kundalakesa settled their new ward by the cooking fire and then went off to the side, to sit apart. It was becoming increasingly clear that the Gathering was summoning all kinds of women into its circle. Some of the women arrived with ideals, hopes, and dreams. They were the ones walking towards something. But for many others, it was more a matter of walking away.

Vimala noticed Neelima coming towards her. She got up as the old woman approached.

"How are you faring, friend?" Vimala asked.

"I am well, Little One. A bit tired, but that is to be expected."

"Can I get you something to drink?"

A sweet toothless smile.

"Nothing would have given me greater pleasure than to share a cup with you," she said tenderly. "But I am on an errand and must therefore decline. Her Highness, the Queen of Sakya, heard about the woman you found in the woods. She would like you to bring her to the tent."

At this, Bhadda Kundalakesa rose to her feet, her body language visibly protective. "Is something wrong?"

"Not at all, dear," Neelima answered brightly. "The Royal Women try to meet with every new arrival. The Queen wants to be certain all needs are met and that everyone is comfortable. You need not worry."

Vimala looked over at the Royal Tent. The muscular tattooed guards stood at attention. The tent fabric glittered in the fading light of the setting sun. Everything about the tent spoke of its Royal Status. *But was it still a royal space?* Vimala suddenly wondered, for the first time. *Was the Queen still really the Queen?* She had abandoned her kingdom, become a wandering renunciant, the day she left home. She was walking towards Vesali with all kinds of unusual companions, eating communal food. Could she still be the Queen after all that?

But could the Queen really be anyone else?

The Queen obviously still felt responsible for the women in her care. She was meeting with each new recruit, checking in on every situation. When Kumari threatened to reclaim her property, the Royal Women were the ones to intervene. They even paid for her release.

Vimala now realized what she had not recognized before: the Royal Women were the reason they had managed to get as far as they had. The Gathering Women would not have survived without them. Each time a family member or property owner challenged, each time tensions flared, the Royal Women were the ones to step in. Without them, most refugees would have already been dragged home—back to the kitchens or brothels from whence they came. To the chains that were calling their names. Without them, the authorities would have mounted a formal assault, declared them illegal. After all, who did these women think they were to abandon their obligations? If every woman in the world followed in their footsteps, society would collapse. When you thought about it (and Vimala did), the Gathering Women made no sense. And yet here they were, walking away together from the obligations they were supposed to pay allegiance to.

The Royal Women were the ones making it all possible. The Queen was the wife of Suddhodana Maharaja—one of the greatest kings Sakya had ever known. She was a legend in her own time. If she declared the Gathering permissible, who would dare say otherwise? Vimala suddenly felt a rush of gratitude for the small women commanding their escape. They were protecting every woman who arrived, ensuring they had what they needed and were safe.

The price must have been significant. Vimala could only imagine the kinds of negotiations they had to have contended with at every turn—but she was certain that they never showed it. Royal Women were trained to wield authority; they knew how to carry a burden without faltering. Vimala believed that, like experienced courtesans, the Royal Women could slaughter an opponent with nothing more than the look in their eyes.

"Of course," Vimala answered with a warm smile. "We will bring her immediately."

Neelima bowed with her palms pressed together and hobbled back towards the golden tent, one little step at a time.

7

Patachara

Gotami, the once Queen of the Sakya Kingdom, had spent the previous evening negotiating the release of a young girl named Mutta, who wore flowers in her hair. The parents had pleaded for her return, using every argument they could dream up, but it was a lost cause. Legally speaking, Mutta was free to go.

Gotami felt for the distraught parents, but at the same time she was frustrated. The family had married their daughter off much too young—only moments after her first Bleeding. It was a tradition many families followed, but she could not see the point of it. She did not understand what harm would be caused by waiting just a few years instead. A girl in the first stage of puberty was more likely to die in childbirth than to survive it. If she did survive, she did not often survive it well. Everyone knew this, everyone saw the results time and again, but the tradition persisted. Girls who were just barely women were forced into marriage years before their bodies were old enough to manage it.

Mutta had been lucky. She had not yet become pregnant, so her young body was still intact, but she was terrified of the prospect. She knew it was only a matter of time before it happened to her too. The girl sobbed at Gotami's feet as she described one of her friends who had been leaking urine since the day she had given birth. Mutta could not even bear to sit close to her friend anymore, so bad was her friend's perpetual smell. She had begged Gotami not to force that future on her too.

To make matters worse, Mutta's husband was an old man with a hunchback—the only husband her parents could afford to pay. Whatever romantic hopes the young girl might have had about marriage were dashed the day she saw the man she was forced to wed. Gotami shook her head as she thought about all the ways a woman's life could disappoint. And how much worse women fared when poverty was at the source.

Thankfully, Mutta's husband had a thread of kindness in him. When she heard about the Gathering Women, Mutta begged for her freedom and he—unbelievably—granted it. And then she ran for her life, terrified he might change his mind.

In the end, it was her parents who pursued her, but they had no legal claim to her anymore. She belonged to her husband and her husband had set her free. They begged anyway, long into the night. Gotami simply had to wait for the arguments to run their course.

When the parents finally accepted their loss and began their journey home, Gotami asked Mutta to remain behind. Gotami could see the fire burning in the young girl's eyes—her enthusiasm and determination. She had run with the courage of a lioness, but Gotami knew that courage alone would not be enough. Mutta would have to be patient if she was going to manage the road ahead, and the young were never particularly good at that.

"The name you are called by means freedom, Mutta," Gotami instructed. "So be free from whatever holds you back. And know that, sometimes what we must free ourselves from are difficult conditions. At other times, though, the freedom we seek is inside."

She was not convinced Mutta understood what she was telling her, but Mutta nodded and bowed repeatedly as she wiped away tears of gratitude. Gotami hoped that in time, the words would take on the meaning she had intended.

The next day, Gotami received news of another woman who had wandered into their community. This one was not being claimed by anyone, but Gotami still wanted to meet with her. She wanted to be sure that every woman in the Gathering had what they needed and felt safe. This woman, so she was told, had appeared out of nowhere and looked battered and beaten. When she had made the decision to follow the Buddha, Gotami never imagined she would be carrying so many others on her back.

The new arrival stood by the entrance of the tent with two companions by her side. One of the tattooed guards had her spear out, blocking them from stepping in.

"They may enter," Gotami commanded as she settled onto a rolled up sleeping mat on the ground. Princess Yasodhara was busy organizing the evening meal. Gotami called out to her to join as soon as she was done.

"Please take a seat," Gotami offered as she pointed to the ground in front of her.

The women nodded, but first bowed low to the ground and reached out to touch the queen's naked feet. They then brought their hands back to their faces, infusing themselves with the sanctity of her royal presence. The lowest part of the queen's body was higher than the highest part of theirs.

Gotami watched the ceremony from a mental distance, having watched it unfold more times than she could possibly count. Whether she wanted it or not, every interaction, every meeting, every single day began with someone honoring her feet. When she lived in the palace, the ceremony always began with a quick wardrobe adjustment (clothing tucked, rearranged, maneuvered), and was completed with the sound of metals chiming. Women's jewels jangled and men's weapons clamored as devotees lowered themselves to touch her illustrious toes. But here in the forest, surrounded by women who had left everything behind, the rite had quieted. The women still took a moment to adjust their clothing, but there were few jewels left to jangle. Women lowered themselves without a sound to touch feet that were now stained with the earth's deposits.

Gotami wondered if the ritual would ever fade. They were honoring feet that were dirty and calloused. There was no mark of royalty left on her—not even royal plaited hair left on her head. But she knew better than to refuse an act that was so deeply ingrained. To the women in her care, she was still the Queen. Royalty was not a question of attire. It was an embodiment the community depended upon. An embodiment she had learned long ago how to wear.

"Why don't you tell us something about yourself?" Gotami asked, once the women had settled down.

A large black crow swooped into the tent with a loud caw and settled onto the bamboo scaffolding overhead. It looked down at Gotami, its small dark eyes blinking quickly. Gotami looked up and smiled.

And then Princess Yasodhara arrived and the three women immediately got up to prostrate all over again.

When the ritual of obeisance was finally over, Gotami made her request again. "Please tell us a bit about yourself." She was looking directly at the new woman who was wrapped in an old cloak.

The woman, however, was silent. She did not even raise her eyes.

Neelima arrived next with a tray of copper cups. Steaming ginger broth rose out to greet them. Neelima first offered cups to the Royal Women. She then offered a cup to each of the others. Vimala and Bhadda Kundalakesa accepted graciously. The woman in the cloak, however, did not move. Neelima placed the cup on the ground beside her and hobbled away.

Gotami sipped the broth as she contemplated the woman's silence. Princess Yasodhara was the one to speak next.

"We don't mean to pry, but we would like to help you."

The nameless woman kept her eyes on the ground. She seemed to have disappeared, despite sitting right there with them.

They waited.

Sat in silence, sipping the ginger broth. Each falling off into their own thoughts.

Gotami then tried again.

"Can you tell us your clan name?"

The woman shook her head.

A response, finally. But one that warned of trespass.

"Perhaps you might tell us where you're from?" Princess Yasodhara suggested.

Vimala was struck by the way the two women worked in tandem, like two sides of a rope pulley bringing up water from a well.

"I did belong somewhere once," the woman in the cloak suddenly replied without looking up. "But they're all gone. I don't belong anywhere now."

It was the first time the woman spoke. Her voice sounded parched, pain piercing through her throat like a dead branch. Vimala's mouth hung open with surprise. Bhadda Kundalakesa was biting her lower lip. Princess Yasodhara was staring at Gotami, and Gotami sat very still. She was straight and attentive, looking directly at the wild woman as though she was trying to interpret a new language. Trying to decipher the wild woman's own particular sound.

Eventually, Gotami leaned back on her seat with a look of resolve.

"You need a name," she declared. "And you need to belong somewhere. So, for now, we shall call you Patachara, the Cloak-Walker. And you will belong with us."

The woman, now called Patachara, looked up.

"We do not know why we are condemned to suffer the way we do," Gotami continued. "The sages have a million answers, but the answers never really satisfy. At the end of the day, all we know is that we must live the lives we are given. I don't know why you have been forced to suffer, Patachara, but you obviously have. And now you need to find a way to live with what is left."

8

Beads and Mirrors

"Were you always an ascetic?" Vimala asked Bhadda one morning as they began yet another day's march. They were walking together, as had become their habit, with the one they called Patachara trailing quietly behind.

"I was certainly not raised this way, if that's what you mean."

Vimala laughed. "Obviously!"

Bhadda looked at Vimala with unconcealed annoyance. "It does exist, you know," she said.

"What does?"

"Child ascetics."

Vimala's eyebrows shot up. *Child ascetics?* She had never heard of the practice before.

She was about to ask one of the many questions that was forming rapidly in her judgmental mind, but she stopped the moment she spotted the village up ahead. Village encounters were unpredictable.

Some villages provided joyful hospitality. The Gathering Women might be rounding a corner when celebration burst through the trees. The gossip grapevine would have done its work, alerting locals to their impending arrival. Meals would be steaming and ready to serve before the women had even rinsed the dust from their feet. Music would be blaring, trumpets and stringed instruments and sacred conch shells all at once. Elders would be bowing, children would be screeching, women would be working quickly with busy hands. When the Gathering passed through those villages, they knew to expect a long night. Vimala would drop her bag and grab a spot at the base of a tree, prepared to watch local entertainment while she was fed.

But at other times, the response was different. While most communities were eager to greet the Queen of Sakya and catch a glimpse of the spectacle the Gathering Women provided, for others it was a threat to be avoided. They were a band of women defying tradition, uprooting the rules of the land, demeaning the men who depended on them. In those villages, the response could be so hostile, it seethed with silence. The Gathering Women would walk through those villages with the doors shut against them.

Vimala eyed the village. It was eerily quiet. Not even a child peeking out from around a tree.

"Do you think we missed a turn?" Vimala asked.

"There was a fork in the road earlier on. Maybe we were supposed to go the other way?" Bhadda Kundalakesa replied.

The three of them turned around to look at the road just travelled, squinting their eyes against the sun to see if they could find where they had gone wrong. There was no one in either direction.

"It's just impossible to figure these paths out most of the time!" Vimala stomped at the earth with frustration. "How does anyone ever find their way through here?!"

Bhadda chuckled at Vimala's reaction.

"*We* had a child ascetic . . ."

Vimala and Bhadda stopped what they were thinking and turned to stare at the Wild One.

"What?" Vimala asked, feeling a bit disoriented.

"A child ascetic. We had one in the town where I lived."

Vimala's mouth hung slightly open. This was not how she anticipated conversation to materialize with the Cloak-Walker. Truth be told, she was not sure she had imagined any conversation at all.

Bhadda Kundalakesa, however, was quick to recover.

"Where was that?"

Patachara scratched her dirty hair and looked away.

A child ascetic, Vimala pondered again. The idea intrigued her now that it had returned to the surface. She imagined little ones tripping over long robes, scurrying up narrow stairs into temple halls. Carrying bowls of clarified butter and trying not to spill any. It was a rather sweet picture, even if she herself had never seen it.

But then her imagination led her elsewhere. To temple priests with grubby hands. Children unprotected. Rituals used and justified for a life of darkness that should never be. Vimala thought of her own mother who had protected her fiercely every day of her life. And the devastation that followed the moment her mother was gone. A child ascetic sounded like the most vulnerable little being in the world.

"Those poor children," she whispered like a prayer.

Bhadda looked over at Vimala with a curious expression. Then she looked at the road, at the two directions, and rubbed her bald head with both hands.

"Which way shall we try? Go back and look for a turn we might have missed? Or straight through the village?"

Vimala wished a sound would alert them to the answer, but there was none.

"I guess we go into the village," she replied. "If the Gathering didn't pass through that way, someone might at least tell us where we went wrong."

If, of course, they agreed to open their doors.

Bhadda Kundalakesa nodded with approval. Forward it was. They started walking again.

"No one knew the real story of how she'd gotten to the temple, but rumor was that she'd been abandoned by an unwed mother. She was left at the door in the middle of the night, swaddled in a cloth."

Patachara had spoken again, right out of the blue.

"Who?" Vimala asked, confused.

"The child ascetic in our town," she answered matter-of-factly.

Vimala shook her head. Patachara never spoke. And then suddenly she did, with that wild nest of hair on her head and nothing but a cloak on her naked back.

Vimala paced herself with patience. She had thirty-six thousand questions she wanted to ask Patachara. Questions about her life, her history, this mysterious town she had just referenced. About what had led her to the forest, naked and alone. Vimala was achingly curious and desperately impatient. But one look at the Wild One confirmed that she should not ask any of them. She had to follow Patachara's lead and accept the morsels she provided. So she asked about the child ascetic instead.

"Was the child . . . safe in the temple?"

"She was happy."

They had entered the village and were passing the first house. It had mud-baked walls and a thatch roof. A covered verandah stretched out alongside the home, where people would normally be congregating after a midday meal. But on that day, with the sun burning bright, the verandah was empty. No one was there.

"The head priest doted on her," Patachara continued. "He had no children of his own, so he adopted her. He took care of her and even taught her how to read. And he always had a few sweets tucked away. So many times, I found her wandering the grounds as she licked her fingers clean of the syrup. I'm sure she was sad sometimes, but I also know that she was loved."

That was not quite the picture Vimala had conjured in her mind a moment earlier.

"You're sure she was not . . . used by him?" she asked. She was trying to temper her cynicism, but it was not easily achieved.

"She was my friend," was Patachara's answer. "I'm sure of it."

Vimala looked at Patachara uncertainly, searching her face for more information than her words revealed. But Patachara had completed her sentence.

The following few houses were similarly vacant. No one resting on the verandahs. No one working the fields.

"There is a child ascetic in the Buddha's community," Bhadda Kundalakesa said, providing a contribution to the subject. "I'm sure we'll meet him when we arrive."

"In the Buddha's community?" Vimala repeated incredulously. "Why is he there?"

"He's the Buddha's son."

Vimala was now the one scratching her head. *The Buddha's son is a child ascetic? But why?* Presumably, he had not been abandoned by his mother. He had a palace and a family all his own. What was the purpose of bringing a child into the forest when he had everything he needed at home? Vimala could not imagine a reason for such a decision. Questions chased each other around in her mind.

But it was not the time to pursue any of them. Vimala took the information Bhadda provided and tucked it away for future consideration. They had an empty village to figure out.

They kept walking, passing one vacancy after another. Covered verandahs without anyone there. Rows of cultivated gardens. A stall with a few water-buffalos, another with goats. Random chickens clucking as they pecked at scattered grain. This village made no sense. It was cared for, but it was empty.

"Maybe we should turn back," Vimala finally reasoned. "What if the people here have been killed by a sickness?"

Bhadda Kundalakesa considered the possibility. She looked around, her sharp eyes seeming to pierce through the walls and into the homes, scavenging the rooms for an answer.

"I don't think so," she concluded. "This village doesn't seem contaminated."

"There are a few people down that way," Patachara noted.

She was pointing in a different direction, to the left of where they were standing. Vimala and Bhadda turned to look. Patachara was right.

Bhadda Kundalakesa changed course without another word and strode towards the villagers, her white robe billowing behind her. Vimala imagined how intimidating Bhadda Kundalakesa might seem to strangers as she charged forward like a bald-headed bull. A thought she privately enjoyed.

A group of tribeswomen was standing by a well. They stopped what they were doing as they watched Bhadda Kundalakesa make her strident arrival.

"Greetings," Bhadda Kundalakesa announced as she got close.

The women did not respond.

The women were, however, magnificent. They were dressed in outfits the likes of which Vimala had never seen. They wore skirts that were tied with a sash and a separate top that was stitched to fit exactly to size. And a long heavy scarf that was loosely laid over the head that matched the rest.

One of the women was dressed in red fabric, the second was in yellow, the third was in black. And all of them had intricate beading stitched along the edges of their clothes and down the middle of the front, creating vivid textures and patterns. Even the black dress, which Vimala found a shocking color at first, was somehow vibrant given all the beadwork incorporated. Vimala was tempted to reach out and feel the thick fabric, run her fingers along the edges and look more closely at the detail. She leaned forward and noticed tiny mirrors woven into the patterns, making the outfits almost blindingly bright.

But that was not all. The women were covered in jewelry that somehow blended into the rest, as though the jewelry was part of the clothing. Beaded necklaces strung together, piled over the beaded clothing so that you could not always tell what belonged where. And big round earrings the size of Vimala's palm. And nose-rings just as big—giant golden discs that pierced through one nostril and covered half the face. The women were extraordinary in their regalia. Vimala wondered if they were carrying their family fortunes on their backs.

A few children were playing in the dust behind them. Their clothing was simpler, but the girls wore hooped nose rings and thin beaded bangles.

"We are making our way to Vesali," Bhadda explained. "We seem to have lost our way."

The three women still did not respond. They just looked at their intruders, eyes wide, body language halted, heads cocked to the side.

Vimala pulled at her head scarf instinctively and tucked some hair behind her ear. What a sight the three of them must have been. Here were these magnificent housewives, dressed and decorated and entirely at ease, while Vimala wore nothing more than a grey rag of a dress. Bhadda's white robe was dusty and stained. Patachara was not even worth mentioning, so wild and tangled was her appearance. The tribeswomen were right to stare.

Bhadda Kundalakesa took another step forward. She used a different language, assuming they had not understood Magadhi. *How many languages did Bhadda speak?* Vimala suddenly wondered.

One of the women finally spoke up.

"We understood you the first time," the one in black said with a foreign accent. "We were just surprised."

Bhadda's shoulders, which had been raised and tense until then, finally dropped.

"Of course," Bhadda Kundalakesa replied, ever their spokesperson. "We are admittedly not a conventional sight. We must have given you a start."

"You're certainly *not* conventional!" the same tribeswoman replied with a big hearty laugh. She then reached out to Bhadda with her tattoo-covered hands. "Apologies for the silence, Mother," she said. "Come join us. We have lots of fresh water here. Bless us with your presence and accept our hospitality in return."

The children, at first distracted by the new arrivals, lost interest after that and resumed their banter. One of the boys was holding a cricket cupped in his hands that he refused to let the others see. "I caught him so he's mine!" he complained as he tried to pull himself away. "That's not fair!" another argued, and then the boys were chasing each other in the dry dust while the girls laughed giddily. One of the tribeswomen yelled at the children in a foreign tongue, then turned to the others with an obvious complaint Vimala could not understand.

The interaction between women and children was so ordinary and familiar, and yet . . . Vimala could not help noticing that the mother spoke to her children in a foreign language, while the children spoke to each other in Magadhi.

The tribeswomen drew up a bucket of fresh water from the well and poured it into a bronze vessel. Then they poured the water freely over the tired feet of their guests. More water was pulled up to rinse hands and faces. Another bucket lifted out of the well and the water was poured into small drinking cups for each to enjoy.

The women were soon in full conversational mode. Questions bubbled out from all directions. Where are you from? What is your clan name? Who are your parents and grandparents? Bhadda directed the traffic, moving the conversation away from personal histories where required, asking her own questions in return. "How many clans in this village?" she asked. "Who is the headman? What is he like?"

And then, eventually, Bhadda Kundalakesa asked the one question Vimala had been waiting for. "Where *is* everyone? This village seems completely empty. You are the first people we've seen."

Apparently, one of the more illustrious families in the village was celebrating their daughter's wedding. The bride left her parents' home that morning and the community was accompanying her to her new home. She was carried in a palanquin to the village on the other side of the river, the rest of the village dancing alongside her as she made the journey.

"I don't expect any of them will be back before tomorrow," said the woman in black. "You know how elaborate weddings can be in these parts."

"But then," Vimala inquired, "why are *you* still here? Shouldn't you be celebrating with the village too?"

"Oh, but we aren't from here. We come from Bharukacchaka. Our clan is settled a bit further away. We just came down for water, which the headman has permitted us to use when the well is not occupied."

"Bharukacchaka . . ." Bhadda mulled the word over. "That name sounds familiar . . . It's by the ocean, isn't it?" She then looked up at the women, as though seeing them properly for the first time. "Of course!" she said, as she slapped her forehead. "*Now* I recognize the jewelry."

The women smiled so widely you could see all of their remaining teeth.

"You've been to Bharukacchaka?" the woman in the black dress asked eagerly. "We rarely meet anyone who has been there!"

"Bhadda has been all over Bharata," Vimala announced with surprisingly personal pride. "She's been everywhere!"

After that, Bhadda Kundalakesa began to share their tale. She wove the threads of their stories into the larger tapestry that had become the Gathering Women, telling them about the journey they were making, about the Royals leading them and their collective hope that the Buddha might receive them when they arrived.

"But we seem to have lost our way. Our companions were right ahead of us and then they disappeared."

The one in black explained that they had missed a turn. There was a fork in the road and they should have taken the other path.

Vimala took this as a signal to get moving again. It was, after all, not wise to remain far from the others—particularly as the day was drawing to a close. She picked up her bag and started getting to her feet. But the tribeswoman in the red dress missed the signal and pressed the conversation further.

"I just don't understand your journey," she said, with an almost pleading tone. "You're saying that dozens of women have left home, just like that? They're all just walking away? How is that even possible?"

Bhadda Kundalakesa, who was likewise getting to her feet, settled back down.

"I suppose it is a rather startling thing," she agreed.

The woman in red scratched at her forehead, struggling to make sense of it all.

"But . . . how can you leave everyone behind?" she asked. "What about your responsibilities? And your families? I don't understand how any of this is possible."

Baddha Kundalakesa rubbed her bald head with both hands, a habit Vimala was becoming fond of.

"Not every woman in the Gathering has the kinds of responsibilities you're referring to," Bhadda began. "Of course, some of the women do. Some have families and loved ones, but many others do not. Some of the women are widows. Others are prostitutes." Vimala feared for a moment that Bhadda might point to her, but Bhadda had more tact than that. "Others have been given permission by their loved ones to walk away. We are all making this journey with different circumstances behind us."

"And the Royal Women . . . they accept everyone?" the one in red asked again with her lilting accent. She was sitting beside Vimala. Her body was leaning forward, her question seemingly as weighty as her long beaded head dress. The edge of it trailed over Vimala's lap.

Bhadda Kundalakesa nodded.

"The Royal Women accept everyone."

The woman in red looked bewildered. She stared at Bhadda Kundalakesa. Then she turned to the children who were still playing behind her. She seemed to be calculating something.

"Vaddha," she called out to the one with the cricket cupped in his hand. The boy looked up. She then said something in her own language and tapped her lap, obviously asking him to come sit with her. The boy looked at his cupped hands with no small measure of concern, but then looked again at his mother and begrudgingly let the cricket go.

"We also left our homes," the one in black explained as the boy called Vaddha settled onto his mother's lap. "And we created a new home not far from here. But we did not leave as individuals. We left as a clan when war broke out. There was no choice for us."

The one in yellow had a desperately sad look on her face as she stared into the horizon. The one in red was holding her child tight.

"The cost of leaving home cannot be measured," the one in black continued. "Some of the Old Ones did not survive the journey. Some arrived so exhausted, they never recovered. We broke with our history when we left, abandoned the land we are connected to. There are trees in Bharukacchaka that we had been worshipping for generations, temples we are supposed to care for, traditions we are responsible for passing on. But we had to leave it all behind. And now our children are growing up so far from their ancestral home that they don't even speak our language anymore. They have grown accustomed to the local language here and they speak it more naturally than our own."

Vimala was the one leaning forward now, listening with rapt attention. These women had lost everything; they had become strangers in unwelcome territory. They could only use the well when no one else needed it, which must have been a terrible burden on top of all the rest.

Vimala had lost everything too. Her story was her own personal catastrophe, something she had convinced herself that no one else could understand. And yet . . . how different was her catastrophe from theirs? Their lineage was broken, just as hers was. They were strangers in this village just as she had been a stranger for most of her life. And while she at first found it shocking that the children did not speak their mother tongue lightly anymore, she began to realize that this was similar to her own fate too. The courtesan tradition was its own language of refinement that one had to learn from birth. She did not speak that language lightly anymore either. She could recognize it, she could interpret and translate it, but she could not really speak it with ease. She had lost her language too.

"Forgive me, but I don't understand what you've done," the one in black concluded. "The ties that bind should never be broken. Without them, life is not bearable."

Vimala lowered her head. *How very true*, she thought to herself.

But Patachara kept her head up.

"Sometimes the ties break of their own accord," she replied with unusual clarity. "And then nothing is left to keep you bound."

It was time to go. The three companions had to find their way back to the Gathering before sundown. It would be dangerous in the dark otherwise.

"Thank you for your hospitality," Bhadda Kundalakesa said as she got to her feet. "It gave us respite. We are grateful."

"And you have shown us the way," Vimala added. "We were lost until we found you."

Vimala had grown attached to these women in the short time they had spent together. Especially the one in red, who felt familiar to her, like a sister from another life. She reached out and laid her hand on the red dress. She felt compelled by the intricacy of the beadwork. She marveled at the workmanship and detail.

The woman in the red dress smiled at her.

Everyone was now back on their feet. The one in yellow collected the drinking cups, busying herself with work as must have been her habit. The one in black was holding Bhadda's hands, invoking final blessings.

But the one in red now stepped away from the group and stood elsewhere, her gaze landing far into the distance.

The one in yellow took note.

"Come help me with the pulley, Vaddhamata," she said. "You know I can't do this by myself."

The woman in the red dress, the woman named Vaddhamata, did not move.

Now the one in black was paying attention.

"Vaddhamata," the one in black said, a note of caution in her voice. "I know what you're thinking. And it's time to go home."

The one called Vaddhamata ripped herself out of her reverie and turned toward her elder. "You *don't* know what I'm thinking," she replied defensively.

"I most certainly do. It's time to return to your clan, where your responsibilities lie."

Vimala watched the interaction with increasing curiosity. She had no idea what was happening between them, but it seemed to be something they had wrestled with before. The one called Vaddhamata remained where she was, feet planted. Apparently refusing to go home.

"We must be on our way," Bhadda decided. "We must find the Gathering before the sun sets."

Vimala picked up her bag and slung it across her shoulder. She looked at Vaddhamata one more time. Tried to interpret what Vaddhamata was saying inside herself, but Vaddhamata, the tribeswoman in the red dress, would not reveal more.

Her son, the boy called Vaddha, came forward and took his mother's hand into his own.

The three companions began their walk away.

9

The Long Road

The Gathering Women kept moving, each day a little more distance traveled. Villages greeted them, food was offered, more women joined the ranks along the way. Sometimes drama unfolded with another woman escaping and family members trying to stake their claims. The Royal Women intervened when things became too rough. Most of the time, though, the days passed quietly.

Vimala could feel the approach of Vesali.

Or to be more accurate, she felt herself approaching it. She began to recognize bits of landscape—a hill in the distance or a monument by the side of the road. The birdsongs became more familiar—not that the birds were particularly different, but somehow their songs sounded more like home. One evening, after setting up camp for the night, Vimala overheard someone say something that confirmed her fear.

"What did you say?" she asked the woman.

"We will be in Vesali tomorrow. Isn't that exciting?"

Vimala took a step back.

Tomorrow?

It was too soon.

Vimala looked for a spot of quiet, somewhere far from the buzzing community. She ducked beneath a few trees, away from the trail.

Vesali is tomorrow, she repeated.

She stepped over a folded branch. Moved aside another and walked further into the forest. Her bare feet were sore, but hardened now, capable of navigating the roughness. Further she went, fleeing into the darkness without even realizing what she was doing. *Vesali is tomorrow*, she repeated over the clamor of chattering insects and buzzing birds. What was she going to do then?

Her steps became more hurried, moving more quickly over the complicated terrain. She pushed greenery out of her way. The sounds of the forest grew with intensity, as the sounds of the Gathering Women faded. Panic became her momentum. She was moving without looking. She was not paying attention. As though she suddenly could not get away fast enough. Or far enough.

"This is getting to be a habit," she heard from behind her. "Where do you think you're going?"

Vimala halted. The voice that had called her back once before.

"I just needed a moment to myself," she replied without turning around.

"You have spent a lifetime alone, Vimala. There is no need for that anymore."

Vimala turned around to find Bhadda Kundalakesa staring right at her. Patachara stood behind Bhadda, twigs caught in her unkempt hair.

"What's going on with you?"

Vimala sighed heavily. She kicked a dry leaf by her foot.

"The journey's almost over," Bhadda added.

Vimala looked away.

Silence settled over them as they waited for the next piece of conversation to materialize. They had spent weeks navigating quiet together. Had gravitated towards each other without commentary or explanation. The quiet had become their refuge.

"Maybe that's the problem," Patachara whispered.

Vimala and Bhadda both looked up, surprised. Each time Patachara spoke, it felt like a cage door flung open. Vimala always felt the urge to try catching the words in her hands.

"What do you mean?" Bhadda Kundalakesa was the one to ask.

"The journey's almost over. Maybe *that's* the problem."

The Cloak-Walker was perceptive. Despite her consistent sadness, despite the flow of tears that accompanied her wherever she went, Patachara could see what was right in front of her—better than Vimala, whose eyes were almost always dry. The journey was ending and Vimala was not ready for the part that was supposed to come next. She had spent a lifetime wishing she could run away, but now that her wish had come true, she was not sure what she was supposed to do next. It felt like only yesterday that she was trying to survive the brute who bit into her thigh. And now she was here, so close to Vesali, she could taste it. She heard it in the birdsongs overhead. In the buzzing excitement among the Gathering Women. In the familiar markers alongside the road. What would she do when she got to Vesali? What would happen then?

"I guess that *is* the problem," she admitted.

If only she could disappear. Fall off the world and drown in the infinite blackness.

The sages said that there was only darkness on the other side, off the edge of the Cosmic Ocean. She had always wondered what that looked like, what it would feel like to dip into vast nothingness and disappear. It would be easier than staying here—of that she was certain. Everything would be easier than what she was doing now. Even surviving Kumari's had been easier. When she belonged to Kumari, there was nothing for her to do. Nothing to decide or direct. She just had to lie on her back and wait as the string of customers took their turns, taking what they paid for. She would stare at her rotten ceiling, at the mildew that grew green between the cracks, barely registering the men on top of her. That was something she knew how to do.

But she did not know how to do this. How to travel for miles with a gathering of hopeful women. How to face the gates of Vesali and all the memories it contained. How to go back to a place that had rejected her. That was something she did not know how to do. That required more energy than she knew how to find.

"Change is always difficult," Bhadda said. "But running from it won't stop change from happening."

Vimala looked up with incredulity.

How did Bhadda keep moving forward, without hesitation or fear? How did she always seem to have an answer—any answer—even if she was wrong? She still made decisions, moved forward, tackled the steps in front of her without so much as a stumble. Why was she able to do all that while Vimala could barely keep her head up?

"Don't you ever just want to quit?"

Bhadda Kundalakesa patted Vimala on the shoulder, like an elder who had seen it all before.

"No, I certainly don't want to quit," she said as she steered them all back towards the Gathering. "I have been travelling a long time looking for the right teacher. Now he's finally within reach. The last thing I want to do is quit.

"But what I don't understand is why you always *do* want to quit," Bhadda continued. "You're walking with us, but you're barely even here most of the time. You're like a ghost, the memory of you walking with us, but the rest somewhere else. When are you going to stop quitting and take yourself more seriously?"

Vimala was so unprepared to be challenged, her mind went temporarily blank. *Did Bhadda Kundalakesa just call her a ghost?* Vimala had thirty-six thousand words of retaliation inside of her, but she could not catch any of them. They were tangled up in her throat like a pile of bullock carts in a road accident. What did Bhadda know of her life? She clearly had no idea, no appreciation, no inkling of what it was like to risk everything and run from someone like Kumari. Vimala had done the impossible, broken the bonds that had kept her imprisoned for most of her life. Did Bhadda not see her at all?

"Vesali is tomorrow, Vimala," Bhadda Kundalakesa continued. "You've left Kumari's and your debts are paid. You're not a prostitute anymore. So why are you still running? What are you running from?"

"I'm not running!" Vimala cried out with hurt. "Who do you think you are?"

A stunned silence followed. Vimala had never raised her voice against Bhadda before.

Bhadda eyed her for a moment. Then she raised herself up until she was towering over her.

"Who do *I* think I am? I am Bhadda Kundalakesa, the most feared debater in all of Bharata. I have travelled this land in every direction, competed against the fiercest opponents, toppled the most brilliant tacticians ever known. *That* is who I am."

The two women stared at each other fiercely, titans facing off in battle, neither one prepared to back down.

"I did not insult you, Vimala," Bhadda went on. "I spoke the truth, and it's about time you heard it from someone. You saved yourself when you ran from that brothel, and that was an accomplishment, but if you think you're done making efforts, you're wrong. You broke free from that life, but now you have to build a new one. You have to stop running, Vimala. None of us gets to live forever, but you're living as though you have lifetimes to waste."

Vimala dropped her eyes in defeat. She knew Bhadda's words were true, even if she didn't want them to be. Bhadda Kundalakesa was the most feared debater in Bharata. Whatever that meant, Vimala knew enough not to argue any more.

A rustling noise caught their attention.

The three women looked up to find a man stepping out of the forest shadows. They were so caught up in their argument, they had not noticed him earlier.

"Well, well," the man purred. "What do we have here?"

The argument that, a moment earlier, seemed like the most important argument of Vimala's life was swiftly forgotten.

The man took a moment to evaluate his prey as he twirled a knife between his fingers. Vimala watched him as he watched them. His hair was filthy and his clothing old and torn. She assumed he was a thief, or perhaps an escaped prisoner, a thug of some kind lurking in the forest. Vimala then noticed that his satchel was bulging. A gold necklace with a ruby pendant was dangling out. That piece of jewelry was clearly not his.

Vimala could smell the stink of alcohol on him, even from where she stood. How many men like him had she been forced to face over the years? She remembered the last customer who bit into her thigh.

Drink always made them worse, more difficult to maneuver. A strike that might cripple a sober man had little effect on someone drenched in spirits. Vimala took a step back, her arm out protectively in front of her companions. She kept her eyes trained on the knife that kept moving between his dirty hands.

"What are you ladies doing out here all by yourselves?" he said as he crept forward, oozing violence. "No husbands around to protect you?"

He spit out a glob of betel juice at his feet. Then he wiped his nose along his sleeve with a disgusting sound, like a grunting animal.

Vimala expected Bhadda to step forward, maybe argue or threaten him with the Royal Women who were not far away, or simply abuse him with her stinging vocabulary, but when she turned to look at her, she found Bhadda Kundalakesa completely still. Vimala looked at Patachara, who was on the other side of her, and realized that she was not likely going to be of any help either. Her cloak was hanging slightly open, exposing her naked breasts, and she was scratching at the nest of hair on her head. What easy prey they must have seemed.

Vimala assessed her surroundings, tried to evaluate his body weight compared to hers, then slowly took a step forward as she waved the other two back. Her entire body was trembling, but she tried not to show it.

The man laughed when he realized Vimala had moved in.

"So, we're beginning with you, are we, princess?" the man said as he kept twirling his knife. "If you keep still, I promise it'll be over quick. Then we'll have a turn with the others, although . . ." he looked up at Bhadda and Patachara, "they're less appetizing, I must admit."

He took another step toward Vimala, so that he was now almost within reach, his knife pointed straight at her. The smell of alcohol was so strong it made her want to retch. She flung her disgust aside and planted her feet firmly on the ground, waiting for him to close the gap.

He took one more step. He was right in front of her, the blade almost touching her chest. And then, before she could think twice, Vimala threw a kick into his groin with all her might. He doubled over with a cry, dropped the knife, and cupped his injury with both hands. Then he let out a string of curses that would have put a sailor to shame.

Vimala was so stunned by her own instinctive response that she just stood there. She should have bolted, or at least struck again, but was frozen.

He started pulling himself back up. She had waited too long, missed her opportunity for escape, and now she was cursing herself for her stupidity. She looked around frantically for some answer or way out, when she saw Patachara moving behind the man with a great big rock in her hands. Before he saw her coming, Patachara smashed the rock right over the man's dirty head.

He fell with a heavy thud.

The three women stood where they were. No one dared breathe. Vimala felt the blood draining from her body. She stumbled backwards, but Patachara caught her. Her whole body was trembling feverishly.

Bhadda approached the man and stared at him for a moment. Then she lowered herself onto her knees and checked for signs of life.

"He's breathing," she concluded quietly. "But he has a deep gash here on the side of his head." She tore off a piece of her white robe and used it to staunch the blood.

"Are you mad, Bhadda?! Why are you helping him?" Vimala demanded.

Bhadda Kundalakesa did not reply. She bandaged his head carefully, then got up and dusted herself off.

"We should never cause unnecessary harm," was all she said.

The Gathering Women were in full festive mode, cooking and organizing and chirping happily. Without consulting each other, the three companions walked over to the river's edge, to sit apart.

Vimala was replaying the scene in her mind. She kept seeing his face, the way he looked at her, hearing the sound of his body as he hit the ground. She could not believe she had been so blindsided. He had caught them all off guard.

"Where did you learn to kick like that?"

Vimala was so far away she did not hear the question.

"Vimala, that kick of yours. Where did you learn to do that?" Bhadda Kundalakesa asked again.

"I don't know . . ."

She felt more flustered than she had in a long time. Probably because she had not expected the attack. The Gathering had lulled her into a false sense of security. She had gotten used to feeling safe, surrounded by women. That man had torn the safety right out of her hands.

Bhadda reached out for Vimala's hands and repeated the question. Vimala turned toward Bhadda, as though only just then registering that she was there.

"Where did you learn to kick like that?" Bhadda repeated softly.

"Oh . . . I am not sure I ever learned it exactly," she finally replied, coming back to herself. "I certainly never practiced. I guess it just comes with the territory. I can't even count the number of men I've had to fight off over the years . . ."

Sadness was seeping out of her.

"But I did get a few tips from Surasa once," she added, now remembering. "She was a seasoned prostitute by the time I'd arrived at Kumari's. She taught me that you should always aim for the middle parts: the nose, the throat, the groin. That's how you hurt a man if you need to get away fast. But the groin is the best option. It's the easiest to reach when you're in close. The only thing is that if you're going to go for it, you have to commit. You can't be even a bit tentative. You have to hit as hard as you can the first time. That's what Surasa always said."

It was strange to hear herself recite this lesson now, with Vesali just a few hours away. Her mother would have been horrified by the violence she had learned to wield to get herself by.

"We should have run the moment he doubled over, but it all happened so fast. Patachara, if you hadn't come in with the second strike, the Great Goddess only knows what he would have done to us."

"You saved us first, Vimala," Patachara said with a loving smile.

Vimala appreciated her more than she knew how to say.

"You know, I wasn't raised for any of this," Vimala said. "I was raised to be a courtesan. Not a prostitute in a dirty brothel. This wasn't supposed to be my life."

Vimala's life was supposed to be beautiful and loving and safe. For the first time in as long as she could remember, Vimala wanted to speak her past out loud.

10

Flying Horses

Vimala could not believe Vesali was so close. In beautiful Vesali, she grew up with her mother always beside her, teaching her the craft she was meant to inherit. Watching courtesans decorate themselves with expert precision, plait each other's hair, paint each other's faces. They had had a garden and servants, and a small water tank filled with lotus flowers. And at the edge of the garden, in a fenced-off enclosure, they had one perfect, beautiful horse. Vesali was not a place she ever imagined she would have to run from. She thought she would live in Vesali forever.

Early morning was her favorite time. Her mother, along with the other courtesans of the house and their many servants, would work late into the night. Vimala therefore had the house to herself in the mornings. She would wake up and go straight through the garden toward the horse enclosure at the edge of the property. She would then open the gate at the end of the long wooden fence, drop her sandals into the swaying grass, and summon the horse she had loved all her life.

Assavata was tall and black, and embodied a kind of dark liquid grace. She would trot towards Vimala with such ease, you would think she was floating. And when she lifted her head to look at you, it was with such dignity, you were almost compelled to bow. Vimala could spend hours caressing Assavata and speaking secrets in her ear. Or braiding her thick mane into sections, taking her time as the sun rose above them both. Assavata would shift her weight from one side to the other, her hoofs pawing softly against the earth, but Assavata would otherwise remain perfectly still as she listened to Vimala's young voice and the stories she had to tell.

Best of all, though, was when they rode. Vimala would never insult her with a saddle or choke her with a bit. Instead, she would climb onto Assavata's bare back with her robe tucked up into her sash. She would knit her fingers into the horse's mane, squeeze her thighs tight, lean forward and . . .

"*Run.*"

Assavata would surge like the wind, just as her name—Windhorse—promised she could. Vimala stretched her imagination as Assavata stretched her legs, the two of them tearing through the countryside with unbridled freedom. Vimala could feel her world expanding with every step the horse took. She felt certain Assavata should have been built with her own pair of wings.

"You might be right about that," Patachara said. "When I was a little girl, my grandfather told me the story of a great horse that was born with wings."

"I never heard of a horse with wings."

"Oh yes. The horse was one of the seven treasures churned out of the ocean during the great battle between the gods and demons. It's a long story, filled with betrayal and intrigue that I loved hearing about as a child, but at the end of the story, they churned the milky ocean until it released its celestial treasures. They used Mount Mandara as a churning stick and the great snake Vasuki wrapped himself around it like a rope. They churned the ocean until it frothed like butter. The magical treasures rose to the surface one at a time, and one of them was a seven-headed horse with wings. I can't remember his name, but he was white and had great big wings that he flapped like an eagle. When he neighed, my grandfather said that the ten thousand universes shook."

Vimala had never heard Patachara speak so much at once.

"My grandfather told me that the horse was too magical to be kept on earth, so the gods brought the horse into the heavens and Surya, the Sun God, adopted him as his chariot driver. Every horse thereafter has its wings clipped before it's born, but if you look closely, sometimes you can see where the wings were supposed to be."

That made so much sense to Vimala. Horses were *obviously* supposed to have wings. She wished she could go back in time to tell Assavata all about it. Her Windhorse would have appreciated it. Or perhaps her Windhorse already knew.

"The horse's name was Ucchaihshravas," Bhadda said. "Some say he belonged to Surya, but others say that Indra was the one who took him. I have even heard that he was kidnapped by one of the demon kings, but I never believed that, for sure."

Vimala suddenly recalled the argument they were having before the man intruded. She felt a wave of regret wash over her for having raised her voice. Bhadda Kundalakesa was only trying to tell her the truth. She wanted to apologize, but she did not know how.

"I wasn't permitted to spend all my time with Assavata," Vimala continued instead.

Although everyone understood their bond, Vimala required training if she was going to manage as a courtesan and Assavata was not part of that. On the contrary, her horse represented an extravagant expense. It was not, after all, a beast of burden. Horses could not pull a heavy cart or plough a field nearly as well as oxen, and no one was prepared to use them for food. The only practical reason for keeping a single horse in Vesali was to showcase it. A single horse was a symbol of prosperity, left out in the open for everyone to see. Vimala's mother had every interest in displaying their wealth, and so she was happy to indulge Vimala on this front, but at the end of the day her mother watched over the coffers like a hawk. If Assavata ever proved too expensive, Vimala knew what the outcome would be.

Vimala could therefore not spend her entire day with Assavata. Eventually, she was forced to trudge back to the house where hours of tedious instruction awaited.

The day would begin with her music teacher who demanded breathing exercises and posture corrections, singing lessons, and practice with her stringed instrument. "Stand up straight," he would bellow, perpetually frustrated by her mediocrity. "Don't drop your shoulders. You're not a *gopi* chasing cows in a field."

"I'm trying," she would complain.

And then came the slap upside the head.

"You are not expected to try. You are expected to succeed. You think your patrons will be pleased with someone who is content just to *try?*"

He would fume. Throw his hands into the air and wail at the gods. Vimala had centuries of tradition to carry on her shoulders. "When will you understand the role you have been entrusted with?" he would demand. "You are a courtesan, the daughter of a great tradition. You must be perfect to honor the gods. Pull back your shoulders and breathe into the base of your spine. You must use your whole body to sing."

But no matter how much he would yell at her, it was obvious that Vimala would never be as good as she needed to be. Every lesson ended with her teacher storming dramatically out the door.

In the afternoon, Vimala would meet with her dance teacher, Natyaguru. Thankfully, her skills were more promising here, but after a morning of unrelenting condemnation, motivation was difficult to muster. She would return to her room after the midday meal to prepare herself, but the moment she walked through the door, she would collapse on her bed instead. It stood in the center of the room, its jute ropes coiled to perfection, with a soft mattress laid on top.

"Your teacher is waiting!"

The call of her servant always grated against her ears.

Vimala would squeeze her eyes shut and burrow her face deeper into the pillows, but they were soon torn away. "How can you be so slow?" the servant demanded. "And look how you treat the family manuscripts! I will tell your mother about this!"

Vimala always had a collection of manuscripts strewn about in her room, despite the fact that she was repeatedly warned to leave them in the house library where they belonged. It was a source of perpetual argument.

She would pull herself out of bed with a long sigh, collect the stray pages she had left scattered about, pile them into a corner, and walk despondently towards the door.

"Your jewelry!"

Vimala would touch her face, her ears, her neck, and only then would she register how late she was about to be. Soon she was tossing her pillows around in a storm of panic, throwing aside bed covers, ransacking her room with fury as she searched for the accessories that always managed to elude her when she needed them most. Eventually, a necklace would appear from under the bed, thick dangling earrings would manifest by the window. Bangles would be discovered in every hidden corner, along with the ever-evasive string of pearls that she would hook to her ear and clasp to her nose-ring with impatient fingers. And at the last minute, always the anklets—big leather straps covered with chimes that she would strap and tighten as she hopped around in maddening circles.

"Your dance teacher spoils you," the servant would scold as they flew through the hallways together. "If only the teacher used a bamboo stick, you would learn to get dressed on time."

Natyaguru would be waiting in the courtyard with his faithful drummer. Vimala would come charging in like Nandi the bull and then screech to a stop right in front of him.

"You're late," he would say.

She would mumble her apologies, head bowed.

And then he would smile.

"So much like your mother," he would reply as he shook his head. "Let's begin."

She would take her position, heels touching, toes pointed outwards, tucking her flying strands of hair behind her ears. . . .

"You are forgetting the most important part."

For a brief instant, she would wonder what might have slipped her mind. And then she would flush with embarrassment (for the hundred and eighth time) and run toward the small makeshift shrine he would set up before every lesson.

A bronze image of the dancing god Shiva would be waiting for her on a decorated folding table. Shiva would have his four arms outstretched, each one in a different position. His long locks whirling around him as he stomped on a demon's back. Carrying the sun, the moon, and the stars like a crown. Shiva was the cosmos incarnate.

Vimala got on her knees and dropped her forehead to the ground. "Om Shiva," she would whisper. "I bow to you, the destroyer, the dancer, the beginning and end of the universe." She would then touch the deity's feet with her hands and bring them to her face.

She would get back up to find her teacher staring at her with his arms crossed.

"You are not done yet . . ." he would taunt, amused despite himself.

She would look up, puzzled. And then smack her little forehead.

Quickly she would drop back to the ground and touch the floor with her fingertips. "My apologies, Earth Mother, for the stomping I am about to do."

Only then would the drumming begin.

Her teacher would clap to the rhythm and call out instructions as Vimala was taught how to perform the oldest rite of all: the dance of stories. She would use her hands to create props out of thin air, use her eyes to express surprise, despair, or a flash of anger. She would pound the ground with her bare, painted feet to create the movement that brought the gods to life. Vimala would dance and sway and pound and twirl. She would shake the jewels that were fastened on every limb.

Sometimes, her teacher would push her to the point of collapse, forcing her to repeat and repeat again as the sweat poured down her back.

At other times, he would stop everything and focus exclusively on her facial expressions. "When you become Krishna and are seducing Radha, you must seem playful and mischievous," he instructed. "But when you are Radha and you are being seduced, you must look shocked, but also secretly delighted." Vimala had to become everyone all at once, move through the stories flawlessly from one character to the next, so that the audience felt like they were seeing an entire caravan of performers, even though she alone would be on the stage. In the story of Lord Shiva descending to earth in a pillar of fire, she had to engulf the stage with her own body of flame.

Vimala worked hard for her beloved teacher. He encouraged her to find the divine inside herself, to become a conduit of divinity for her audience. "Dance is a sacred act," he would remind her every day. "You are bestowing your audience with divine presence. Feel it flowing through you. Then reveal it with movement." For Natyaguru, dance was not just about seducing her patrons. It was a devotional experience. When class ended, she did not need to be reminded to touch his feet.

Just before the day's end, just before the patrons arrived and the house became a public space, Vimala would be summoned to her mother's chambers for the day's review. This was always a precious time for the two of them—a sliver of quiet intimacy, far from prying eyes. Vimala would sit on a low wicker stool and massage her mother's feet. And then she would watch as her mother prepared herself for the night.

Rows of jewelry would be laid out on a chest. A selection of outfits would be spread out on the bed. Vimala's mother might walk over to the mirror and, with hands on her hips, would examine herself in detail. She would turn sideways to inspect her profile, or she would lean in to check her skin. And she would hum all the while—a few verses from a favorite poem, or perhaps a song she had prepared for a patron she expected that night. Vimala would watch her mother with fascination. She could not wait to grow up so she could be just like her.

As her mother moved through the elaborate stages of ornamentation, she sometimes provided a bit of her own instruction—the kind that male teachers were incapable of providing.

Her mother would explain the art of seduction in all of its colorful possibilities, show her the secrets of every body part. She would teach her about the different points in the body that elicited pleasure (the obvious areas and the ones that surprised) and explain the different tools that could be used to enhance the experience. She would explain . . .

"Wait," Bhadda interrupted. "Did you say *tools?*"

Vimala turned to look at her. She had disappeared into her past and forgotten that the others were there.

"What?"

"You said something about *tools.* What are you talking about?"

Vimala almost blushed.

"Maybe not so much tools as . . . enhancements? Does that make it clearer for you?"

Now it was Bhadda's turn to blush. She clearly had no idea what Vimala was talking about.

"How can I put this delicately . . . ?" Vimala wondered aloud.

"You don't need to be delicate with me."

Of course.

"Well . . . sometimes men enjoy a bit more than the usual routine. You can enhance the experience by adding a few things."

"Such as . . . ?"

"Well, there are simple things that I am sure most women discover during their time in the bedroom, like . . . using your fingernails?"

Both women looked baffled.

"When you scratch down a man's back, for example, it can heighten his experience," she tried explaining. "Or he can scratch down yours."

"That sounds painful," Patachara said.

"It is, but pain is part of the bedroom experience. Pleasure and pain almost become one during sex. Have you never noticed that?"

The women stared at her.

"Some people enjoy pain *as* pleasure."

Nothing.

"Well, it's not only about pain of course," she said, trying to alleviate the tension. "Some enhancements are much more pleasure-oriented."

"Such as?" Bhadda again.

"Well . . ." She wondered for a moment if she should really go through with her explanation. She looked at her companions with some uncertainty, but they remained right where they were. Waiting.

"We had a few objects that clients could use on us. Smooth wooden pieces that had been carved to fit inside a woman's body. We had a whole collection. Some were very beautiful. Men often liked to use those pieces instead of their own bodies, so that they could watch us, watch our bodies as they entered us from a different position."

Neither of them responded. Both of their mouths hung slightly ajar.

Vimala now felt sweat materializing on her brow. Her heart began to palpitate. She had gone too far (and yet she had barely told them anything at all!). She never should have said anything. She should have stopped at the nails, but she did not want them to think that everything was pain-inducing. Their craft was ultimately about pleasure, even if some clients experienced pleasure through pain. Familiar worries were scrambling to the surface. She crossed her arms against her chest protectively. She should never have said so much.

Patachara turned away.

And Vimala felt her heart sink.

What had she done? She watched as Patachara busied herself with the stones by the riverside. Picking them up and moving them around like a madwoman distracted by a world no one else could see. Vimala did not even dare look at Bhadda Kundalakesa. She could just imagine the condemnation she was certain would be written right across her stern face.

"You mean something like this?" Patachara had returned with an oblong stone in one of her hands. "Is this kind of shape you meant? As one of your tools?"

It was Vimala's turn to be shocked. She thought Patachara had turned *from* her . . .

"I guess . . . although that seems a little large to me . . ."

The three of them stared at the rock. Imaginations going to places they probably should not have been.

"Well, you said pleasure and pain went together, right?" said Bhadda.

Another moment of silence. Of staring.

And imagining.

And then the three of them broke out into a great fit of laughter. They clutched their bellies and they laughed. They were embarrassed. They were shocked.

And for just a brief moment in time, they were oh so free.

"A courtesan's life isn't only about the bedroom," Vimala ventured once the laughter had passed. "Of course, the bedroom is essential, but we are trained for so much more than that." She had loved the laughter, but she could not leave her story there. She came from a long line of distinguished women and she wanted to honor them. Neither laughter nor shame were appropriate endings. "What we do requires skill."

Vimala's mother taught her how to read people and manage different character types. Her mother carefully dissected the politics of their household, making sure Vimala understood the history of the relationships they were bound by and the lingering resentments that lay hidden beneath polished smiles. She explained the weight of Vimala's eventual inheritance and all the ways it made her vulnerable, warned her of the traps that were lurking, the other daughters who would try to steal her place. Her mother provided her with every bit of information she could think of, every tool and trick and ploy, in the hopes that her daughter would move into her future safely. A courtesan's life is like a spider's web, her mother always said: to the spider, it was home. But to everyone else, it was a trap, and Vimala could never afford to forget that.

The sun had long since set. The Gathering had quieted. Vimala let herself fall back on the grass.

"Although I have seen many things throughout my years," Bhadda said after a while, "and I have learned about different kinds of lives, I really knew nothing about the life of a courtesan. You make it sound . . . almost attractive."

Vimala was relieved. Her lineage was worthy of honor, even if she herself no longer was.

"Our education is unlike any other," she replied with a note of pride. "I suppose that in some ways, it must be similar to the education Royal Women receive. At least, that's what my mother always thought. Like them, we learn the ancient crafts of our culture, the songs, the dances, the stories. And we even learn to read and write, so that we can discuss the texts our patrons are most interested in and share their burdens."

"That you learned to read and write impresses me most of all," Bhadda admitted.

Vimala smiled.

"We had a whole library of manuscripts in our household," she replied with pride. "I obviously don't know what royal life is like, but their training is probably not that different from ours."

The stars were beginning to fill the sky. Soon the entire sea of celestial waters would be filled with twinkling lights, like a rolling ocean speckled with waves.

"So why did you leave?" Bhadda Kundalakesa asked. "It sounds like you were well on your way to inheriting your small kingdom. What went wrong?"

"Everything."

11

The Flying Sage

One morning, Vimala woke to find her sheets stained with blood. She panicked at first, but then realized that it was what she had been waiting for. She jumped out of bed and raced towards her mother's chambers. It was the first time in as long as she could remember that she did not greet Assavata first.

Her mother had only gotten to sleep a few hours earlier, so she was initially confused by the intrusion, but once the news registered, she leapt out of bed with delight. "You're finally a woman!" she cried as she hugged her daughter. "How do you feel?"

Before Vimala could answer, her mother grabbed her by the hand and pulled her towards the bed. "Climb in with me, the way you used to when you were little," she said. "We have so much to discuss!" But Vimala stayed where she was with a look of distress on her face. She was bleeding. She did not want to soil her mother's delicate bedding. "How silly of me," her mother said as she slapped her forehead. "Look how excited you've made your mother. I'm not thinking straight." She picked up a thick cloth that she used to mop up the rain when it came in through the window. "Here, this is clean. It hasn't rained in days. Tie it around your waist and climb in. You never bleed very much at the beginning so it won't be a problem, and I want to hear *everything*!"

They talked for hours, snuggled in each other's arms. The Bleeding announced all kinds of changes in Vimala's life and they needed to dissect each and every one. Her mother told her to expect cramps, possibly headaches, mood swings, and oily skin. Most of all, though, she should prepare herself for the swelling of desire. "As courtesans, we are trained to harness other people's desires, but that doesn't mean that we don't have desires of our own." Her mother had never spoken to her about her own desires, but the Bleeding was a first step into womanhood. "You will have to be very careful with desire and learn to master it. It will otherwise become your destruction."

Vimala was still too young to understand, but she was sure there would be lots of time to ask questions. She was only just beginning her journey. There was supposed to be a lifetime of conversation ahead.

More pressing than the bodily changes, however, was the issue of her ritual deflowering. A courtesan's life might have begun the day she was born, but her real life opened the night of her deflowering. This was a ritual that had to be crafted by the young courtesan's guardian and it required weeks of planning. The clients had to be strategically enticed, announcements delivered in just the right way, and all of it had to happen with the required discretion and decorum. A dropped hint here, a subtle suggestion there, and soon the offers would be pouring in. Vimala's mother had to dangle her daughter with meticulous care, so that desire would froth and purses would empty.

"You mean that your virginity was going to be *auctioned* off?" Patachara interjected.

Vimala was surprised by the question.

"Of course."

Patachara looked down at her hands, as though she had gotten lost, despite still being right where she was.

"Patachara, I was a *courtesan*. What did you think was going to happen?"

She shrugged.

"I think we got carried away by some of your descriptions," Bhadda answered instead. "You painted such a glorious picture, we forgot where you were ultimately heading."

"I suppose I can understand that," Vimala admitted, although she could not hide her disappointment. "Courtesans are complicated. We are educated and refined and very beautiful, but at the end of the day, the purpose is not subtle. We *are* selling ourselves."

"To the highest bidder?" Patachara added.

"To the highest bidder," Vimala acquiesced.

Patachara's head dropped. As though the very reason for Vimala's elaborate education had only now started sinking in.

"What if the highest bidder was . . . not what you hoped for?" she asked.

"That's the least of our worries. Sometimes the highest bidder is cruel or even violent. Many courtesans have lost their lives that way. That is part of our tradition too."

Patachara shook her head, the weight of the information seemingly too difficult to bear.

And then a surge of age-old defensiveness rose up like bile. Vimala was speaking before she could stop herself.

"How can you react that way when most women are auctioned off to future husbands?" she demanded. "What do you think the bridal gifts are for?"

"But those gifts are an expression of the wife's value. It's what she brings to the marriage and what she can take away." Patachara replied innocently.

Vimala wanted to pounce. She was on the verge of saying more. Of arguing that a bride is bought and paid for and then still works the rest of her life to prove her worth. And in the end, she might wind up beaten or dead too. How different were any of their lives when you thought about it? Why had so many wives joined the Gathering if marriage was such a prize?

But one look at Patachara's pained face was enough to stop her. These were not her words to throw.

"We should get some sleep," Vimala said.

"You can keep talking," Patachara replied.

She wanted to hear more.

Vimala's mother had successfully created a bidding war between two interested candidates—one a local prince who had had the honor of deflowering most of the young courtesans over the years (Vimala was to be added to his long list of conquests), and the other a wealthy landowner who was trying to establish himself as someone of renown. He was hoping that by claiming Vimala's virginity, his status in the community might be taken more seriously.

The two men circled the household like vultures. First one would appear with gifts of perfume, then the other with a new piece of jewelry. Then the first would return with something else. Back and forth the two of them went, competing against each other, trying to get at the prize without appearing too desperate, fingers drumming against every surface, waiting for the decision that was out of their hands.

Each time one of the men called, Vimala made a carefully constructed appearance. Her clothing became her costume, her behavior a role she was taught to play. She would enter the room just a little bit late, wearing the clothes chosen for her on that particular day. Her jewels would jingle, her robe would shimmer, and her eyes would feign humility. She would serve some food, pour a drink, whisper a delicate note of flattery. And then, just before flitting away, she would "accidentally" reveal a small bit of skin—her veil would fall to the side or the hem of her robe would hike up over her ankle. Nothing dramatic, always inadvertent, but just enough to keep the client captivated.

Vimala's mother, in the meanwhile, managed the negotiations with expert precision, holding court on an almost daily basis as she deftly maneuvered between the patrons and their demands. She clapped her hands at the staff, reminding them of how important it was to keep the household in pristine condition. The walls were scrubbed and repainted, the floors repeatedly swept. The kitchen had to fill the home with smells that kept the palate whet. There was so much to do every day, it was no wonder that Vimala's mother began to tire. There were days when she did not emerge from her room before the sun began to set. At other times, she seemed pale and out of breath. Vimala normally would have paid attention to her mother's fatigued demeanor, but she was distracted. There were new clothes and pretty jewels to play with, and so many cosmetics she was finally allowed to try. Turmeric paste to brighten her skin, black kohl to trace around her eyes. And bright red lac for her fingertips and toes. The door of Vimala's world had been blown wide open; she barely considered how drawn her mother's face had become. She was preoccupied by the gifts piling up at her door. It was exciting and it was new.

And it was daunting . . . although she would never openly admit to that.

Vimala privately worried about the rite and how much it would hurt. Her mother had explained the details, had instructed her to place a clean cloth underneath her so that she would not stain the sheets. She told her to expect a pinch, but warned that it could be sharper than that. Either way, Vimala was instructed to be brave. Patrons did not pay hefty sums to watch courtesans drown in a puddle of tears.

Vimala had nodded with feigned maturity as her mother explained the stages of deflowering, but the more she imagined the moment, the more worried Vimala became. Her Bleeding sometimes caused her to double over. Sharp stabs struck through her belly and reached all the way into her lower back. How much worse would the deflowering be? How much more could she take? She promised herself that she would bite into her fist when he mounted her, to stifle whatever scream might otherwise escape.

But the fears tortured her. And when they did, the walls of their home felt like they were pressing in. She would burst out the door and race towards Assavata. It was only in Assavata's trusted company that Vimala would finally feel safe.

But most days were not like that. Vimala learned how to push her worries aside and fill her mind with fantasies of unparalleled success instead. Once she was deflowered, she would be a full-fledged courtesan. She could take her place beside her mother, learn to rule their small domain as her second-in-command. She imagined the glory she would be greeted with after that first night. The celebration and applause. She wondered who would win the bid and how much he would pay. Maybe she would break the household record? Maybe they would pay even more than they had once paid for Ambapali? Maybe she would become famous like Ambapali and have a mansion all to herself? Her fantasies took her in all kinds of directions, swirling inside her young heart and mind. She was so preoccupied by it all, she simply did not notice how sluggish her mother was becoming.

She did not take the time to ask.

Vimala had stopped talking. She was still lying on her back in the grass, looking up at the stars, but the words no longer found a voice.

"Maybe it's time to get some rest. Tomorrow is going to be a big day," Bhadda suggested gently.

Vimala missed her mother so much. Everything would have been different if the Skin Disease had not taken her. She would have been safe; she would have had a place to call her own. She would have had a proper deflowering, the honor of a craft, a clan, a tradition. Instead, she had lost it all before it had even begun.

"I just don't understand how you can have everything one minute, and nothing the next," Vimala said, almost to herself. "I was ready. I was just moments from finally becoming a courtesan like all the women in my family before. I had everything I could hope for. And then the earth opened her mouth and swallowed everything up without warning. I still can't wrap my mind around it, even after all these years."

She kept her eyes on the sky above, on its immensity, and wondered what any of it was even for. A shooting star flew across the glittering darkness. She watched its trajectory until it faded out of view.

"I understand that," Patachara whispered.

Vimala turned to look at her, but Patachara did not say more.

"I came across a story long ago that I still think about sometimes," Vimala said.

Cicadas were welcoming the night with their songs.

"Actually, more than sometimes. It's a story that I go back to all the time. Some days, it feels like the story is haunting me, following me around, pushing itself into my head. Like the story has a spell attached or an enchantment of some kind and it just won't leave me alone. Like it's knocking on my door and I don't know how to let the story in."

"What is it?" Bhadda asked.

"It's the story of a sage named Markandeya. Have you heard of him? Bhadda, maybe you have, with all of your travels?"

A tiny flame of hope sparked inside her as she asked her question, but when neither of her companions replied, the flame died out.

"It's just as well," she sighed. "Maybe Markandeya is a puzzle that I am supposed to decipher on my own."

"Would you tell us the story anyway?" Bhadda asked again.

"The truth is that I don't know much about Markandeya. I can't tell you where he came from or what his life was like. I only know this one story about him that I discovered in our library long ago. It was just a fragment that I found on the back of a shelf, so I am sure some of the story is missing, but according to this fragment, Markandeya was a sage who had learned how to fly.

"Of course, many sages know how to fly, but according to this story, Markandeya was particularly good at it. He could fly anywhere. Sometimes when I was little, I would sit under my window, my knees tucked under my chin, hoping to catch a glimpse of him. But he was too evasive for me to find.

"One day, Markandeya flew out so far, he lost track of where he was. He lost every reference point. He must have been terrified, but he kept going because there was nothing else for him to do. I imagine him tumbling about in the darkness like that, not knowing which way is up. Just twirling in the void. Drowning in emptiness. But then, just as he was about to despair, a hole in the darkness opened up. He raced towards it and flung himself at the light without a second thought."

"What was it?" Bhadda asked, listening on the edge of her seat.

"It was the last thing he expected. It was a doorway into another universe."

She could never think about this part without her heart palpitating. To fling yourself with desperation, to stretch yourself against your own shackles so far that they burst, only to find yourself landing dangerously far away . . . it terrified her every time she thought about it. He was just trying to save himself, but instead he had torn through the fabric of the familiar. And there is no coming back from something like that.

"The thing is," Vimala continued, "Markandeya did not land on dry ground. The moment he crossed that threshold, he dropped like a lump into the Cosmic Ocean."

"The Cosmic Ocean?" Bhadda exclaimed. "How can that be?"

"The Cosmic Ocean holds up every one of the ten thousand universes. Every planet, star, and galaxy is like a small island floating on it. When Markandeya was flying through the night, he thought he was seeing the biggest expanse of reality that there was. He thought he was already travelling over the Cosmic Ocean, but he had it completely wrong. The whole time he was flying, he had been safely tucked inside Lord Vishnu's body. He had barely covered any distance at all."

Vimala gazed at the stars that were floating above. So far away.

"He discovered that we are nothing more than tiny specks floating inside a god's body. He hadn't even reached the Great Immensity yet. He wasn't even close."

Bhadda turned her head to look at Vimala. Wonder filling her from the inside.

"But then . . . There's something I don't understand."

"What?"

"Well, if he was locked inside Lord Vishnu's body that whole time, how did he fall out?"

Vimala smiled.

"He fell out of Lord Vishnu's mouth when he yawned."

And then she could feel the other two smiling beside her.

"Vishnu opened his mouth to yawn and that created a great burst of light. Markandeya raced for the light and fell right out. And that's how he landed in the Cosmic Ocean. Which you would think would be soothing, but as soon as he caught his breath and looked around himself . . . well, the sight of the Cosmic Ocean completely overwhelmed him."

"What do you mean?" Patachara asked. Now she was the one on the edge of her seat. Or perhaps they all were.

"I mean he panicked. He looked out at an immensity that was too big for him to understand and he fell apart. The once wise and accomplished yogi lost complete control of himself and flailed about in the water like a madman.

"That's when Lord Vishnu realized what had happened. He was floating in the Cosmic Ocean, reclining on Ananta, the Serpent of Endlessness, when Markandeya fell right out of him. Vishnu looked down at the water and saw the little flailing sage. So, he scooped him up and popped him right back into his mouth. And that was that."

Vimala felt a familiar emptiness rising inside her.

"The piece that really haunts me about this story, though, is that Vishnu realized that Markandeya had to return to the safety of the inside. That human beings were not built to understand great immensities. So, he returned Markandeya to a more limited reality than the truth."

"Why does that bother you?" Bhadda asked, with a note of almost maternal concern.

"Because . . . ," Vimala replied, "it means that none of us sees things the way they really are. Because it means that I am missing so much."

12

River Mud

The three fell asleep to the sound of the bubbling river, covered by the glittering blanket of stars above.

"Are we ready?" Bhadda asked as she dusted herself off early the next morning.

Vimala kept her eyes closed. She was deep inside a flight dream and did not want to shake herself awake. She could feel the lightness of her body as she soared. She did not have them often, but whenever she did, her flight dreams were always the same: she never flew the way Markandeya did. Instead, her dreams had her making long jumps across vast expanses of space. She would soar for a while, land on the earth, bend her knees and then jump up again into the bright blue sky above without making any effort at all. Then she would land, survey the area, bend her knees, and jump once more.

She was trying to find her way back to the dream, to hold onto it for just a bit longer, but the dream was fading, slipping from her grasp.

"Come on, Vimala," Bhadda bugged her impatiently.

The last trail of the dream vanished.

Vimala opened her eyes. Bhadda Kundalakesa was standing over her, the sun like a bright halo over her prickly bald head. She had that familiar look on her face. She was itching to move on.

"It's too early," Vimala mumbled.

"The day has started," was Bhadda's answer. "Everyone's getting ready. It's time to get up."

Vimala rolled onto her side and covered her head with her arms like a petulant child.

"Go without me."

She would remain right where she was by the river and sleep.

"Suit yourself. I am going to see about a morning meal. I won't waste my time trying to convince you not to waste yours."

Bhadda Kundalakesa marched off. She had woken up with the sun and was ready for the next chapter. Vimala shut her eyes in the hopes that the world would go away.

"Bhadda is right, you know," Patachara said.

Vimala's eyes shot open, surprised to hear Patachara's sudden opinion.

"Right about what?"

"You act like a child sometimes."

Vimala removed her arms from her face and looked up.

"I don't remember her saying that."

"She did in so many words . . ."

"What are you talking about?" Vimala asked as she lifted herself onto her elbows.

"She said it yesterday. It's like you want to waste your own time," Patachara said. "Every day, we get closer to Vesali. It's the city you were raised in. The city you have been avoiding for most of your life. We're almost there. We will reach Vesali tonight, and yet here you are covering your eyes and rolling back to sleep. This is the moment you've been waiting for since your world fell apart. The city is finally within your reach. What are you doing sitting here with your eyes closed?"

Patachara the Wild Woman was looking directly at her without a hint of madness. Her hair was a mess of tangled knots, her cloak the only piece of clothing on her back, and she was even dirtier than the day they found her. But her eyes were bright and clear.

"My eyes are not closed," was all she could think of saying in reply.

She fingered her hair and felt the nest of tangles on her own head.

"I need a bath," she decided.

Without further commentary, without a shred of modesty, Vimala dropped her clothes and walked straight into the river. She slipped in like a dragon lizard, and when the water reached her waist, she dove in like a fish. When she broke through the surface, she lifted her face to the sun, smoothed back her hair and smiled.

"Why don't you join me?" she called out, ignoring the earlier conversation.

Patachara recoiled and pulled her knees up into her chest.

Vimala shrugged.

Bathing in the river was a delight Vimala would not take for granted. At Kumari's, she had been forced to bathe with a bucket behind the brothel, hiding her polluting presence from public view. Prostitutes were not welcome to bathe in the river alongside respectable women, so Vimala was forced to bathe in secret where no one could see her, alone after a long night of clients, before the sun came up. Her back up against the wall.

She had always hated bathing that way. Instead of being a pleasure, it was reduced to a necessity. It was not the kind of bathing she had been raised to enjoy.

Vimala moved the water with her hand, pushing it back and forth playfully. A school of fish arrived and her face lit up like a ray of light. She twirled with pleasure as she moved through them. Vimala danced like the courtesan she was raised to be, tantalizing the fish with her seductive nature, beckoning them to her and then swishing them away.

Eventually, Vimala lifted herself out of the water and settled onto the bank. The air was cool, but the sun felt warm on her shoulders. She leaned back and closed her eyes, water dripping down her back and pooling around her naked body.

"My mother always said that the sun has healing properties," she ventured. "I find it hard to believe during the dry season when the sun is blistering, but on a morning like this, it feels true, don't you think?"

Patachara did not answer.

Vimala shrugged.

The pebbles by her feet were quite beautiful. They were soft and waterworn. Vimala picked up a dark grey stone with a streak of white shot across the middle.

"This looks like a bolt of lightning." She held it up. "And this one looks like . . . Oh my! Look at *this*!" Vimala exclaimed. She tossed the stone aside and sank her fingers into the mud. "I haven't come across this stuff in years!"

"What is it?" Patachara asked.

"It's beauty-clay. Every week, my mother would have the servants bring up whole jars of it from the river. I can't believe I didn't notice it before."

"What do you do with it?"

Vimala smiled as she grabbed a big chunk of the wet slop and plopped it onto her own head.

"You wash with it."

She massaged the clay into her hair. She dug it into her scalp and then coated her long strands, one section at a time, until her whole head was covered. The clay was soon dripping onto her bare shoulders and running down her back.

"You could use a wash too," Vimala said.

And then without asking for permission, without even a second thought, Vimala grabbed another handful and plopped it onto Patachara's head. She thought it would be funny. Or at least that it would encourage the Wild One to clean herself up.

"Don't!!!" Patachara screeched as she scrambled backwards. "*Why did you do that?!*"

Vimala retreated instinctively, her eyes wide with surprise.

"I'm so sorry," she stammered.

But Patachara's horror sliced up the space between them. She seemed to have smashed herself up against the cage of her insides.

"I am so sorry," Vimala repeated desperately. "I didn't mean to upset you." She felt such a wave of regret. What had she done? "We can wash it out in the river," Vimala suggested. "It really isn't hard to remove."

Patachara's body scrambled backwards even further.

"Patachara, we can fix this," Vimala said with all of her heart. She put out her hand, reaching for the friend who seemed to have jumped ship without warning. "Just a bit of water and the clay will be gone, I promise."

Nothing.

"I am so very sorry, my friend," Vimala whispered. "I wasn't thinking . . ."

She could not believe her own stupidity. How could she hurt the one person who had been hurt so much already? She could see the suffering that followed Patachara like a hungry ghost, even if she knew nothing about it. Vimala kicked the ground with her foot in self-recrimination. If only she could take it back.

"It's just . . ." Patachara mumbled.

Vimala looked up.

"I don't like rivers."

Vimala breathed out with relief. Patachara had not disappeared. She was still here. Vimala closed her eyes and thanked the gods for the reprieve. Then she opened them and looked at her friend, who carried a boulder of pain on her back. Vimala did not understand Patachara's suffering or what rivers had to do with it, but she would not ask for more than the Cloak-Walker was prepared to give.

"You don't have to like rivers," she answered. She crawled toward her frightened friend and put her arm around her.

"You don't have to like rivers at all."

The two women sat quietly together for a time after that. The clay was drying out in Vimala's hair, causing the strands to turn brittle and hard. Vimala wondered what effect it would have on her hair, since she normally rinsed it out quickly after applying it. But she dared not move. She could feel the Cloak-Walker's tension slowly seeping out of her, one small breath at a time.

"Why do you think they do that?" Patachara suddenly asked.

"Why does who do what?"

"Why do birds sing so much in the mornings? What do you think they're saying?"

Vimala looked over at her companion. She smiled gently, loving her more than she could explain. Then she looked up at the trees overhead. There were magpies and finches, and a family of tiny green warblers in a nest. A woodpecker was hammering against a tree trunk further away, and she was certain she had seen a crow perched somewhere on a branch. The forest was full of birds of every variety, all of them chattering with early morning enthusiasm.

"Well, they're talking . . . that's for sure," Vimala answered. "But my singing teacher once told me that their conversation is not nearly as inspired as we tend to imagine."

Patachara waited.

"According to him, birds don't actually sing, even if that's what it sounds like. There are a few birds who might sing the way we understand the term, singing a song for pleasure, but for the most part birds are not singing that way."

"So, what did he say they were they saying?"

"According to my teacher, their songs are mating calls. The male birds put on a show in the hope of attracting a female. Once he gets the girl, the singing stops."

"Oh."

Vimala assumed she was disappointed.

"So then male birds are just like male men?" Patachara asked.

"Male *men*?"

"Yes. Male birds spend all their energy trying to attract females and when they get what they want, they quit, just like male men."

Patachara was smiling with mischief. It was good to have her back.

Bhadda returned to the riverside and was surprised to find her companions as they were: Vimala naked with dried out clay in her hair and Patachara huddled beside her.

"I seem to have missed something," she said, as she took her seat across from them. "Are you planning on getting dressed, Vimala?" she asked. "Or will you be travelling to Vesali that way?"

Vimala felt the rush of instant retaliation, thirty-six retorts on the tip of her tongue . . . but she withheld them. She had done enough damage for one day.

Instead, she got to her feet and slipped back into the water to rinse herself off.

It was then that Patachara began to speak.

Walking with her companions and listening to them had been stirring something inside the Cloak-Walker. "My past seems to be calling me," she said. "Asking me to remember pieces from long ago." While Bhadda Kundalakesa and Vimala argued, Patachara had been sifting through the past, molding her story like clay.

Despite appearances to the contrary, Patachara had had a wonderful childhood. She was raised by loving parents in a beautiful home in the great city of Savatthi. Her father was one of the richest men in the city and they had everything you could ever imagine wanting. Their wealth was so abundant, they even had different kinds of rice to choose from. They grew three different types of rice on their property alone, each one a slightly different flavor. But sometimes they splurged on red rice, which she adored. Her father had it brought in from the Himalayas and it had a wondrous nutty flavor. Her favorite meal was a bowl of plain red rice with buffalo yogurt. If her parents had let her, she would have eaten it every day.

They lived in a beautiful two-storied house with more servants than any of their neighbors. And those servants took care of everything—they washed her clothes and flattened them out in the sun. They cleaned her room, aired out her mattress, placed fresh flowers in a vase. And they even arranged her toys, every day in a new configuration. Some days she would wake up to find her favorite doll sitting at a small table, as though awaiting the morning meal, while on other days her toy elephant would be carting a bundle of honeyed sweets on his back. The servants cooked and cleaned and watched over her like an army of doting caretakers, and late at night, just before she went to bed, one of them would bring her a cup of warm goat milk to help send her to sleep.

Her servants were not the only ones spoiling her with affection. When the goat milk failed to send her into the dreamworld, her mother's bed was only a few steps away. She would sneak into her mother's room, trying not to make a noise, and would very carefully climb in, praying the bedframe would not creak. She would then snuggle up against her mother's warm back and sigh contentedly.

Of course, most families in Savatthi slept together. The idea of sleeping apart would never even cross most people's minds. But when you were as wealthy as they were, with each member of the household having their very own room, an attempt was made to sleep apart. It was silly of them—families were meant to stay together. But they tried. They were wealthy enough to at least put on a show of it.

"One morning, as I sat in the garden raking the earth with my toy plough, one of the servants offered to pluck me a mango from the tree," Patachara reminisced.

Mango was her favorite fruit. She watched, mesmerized, as the servant wrapped his arms around the trunk and scooted up like a monkey. "It looked so effortless. When he got down, I begged him to show me how to do climb the tree myself, but he refused. He knew how much trouble he would get into if my parents found out. He offered me the mango, but I no longer wanted it. I threw it away and stomped my feet, spoiled as spoiled could be. If I could not climb the tree, I would not eat mango."

When the servants proved adamant, little Patachara ran to her parents and begged for permission to try climbing from them. She loved her mangos, but she no longer wanted them delivered. She wanted to get them herself. She wanted to climb, to feel the sky on her skin, to grab a fruit with her own little hands. She begged and begged and begged. But a girl of her station was simply not allowed.

She would not accept their refusal. "Please let me, Father," she asked with her sweetest little voice. "No one will know. I will only climb the trees in our garden. Who will ever find out?" But her parents refused. It was an impossible request. What if she scratched herself? What if she fell? What if the neighbors came by just as she was hanging from a branch? They could not imagine saying yes, but Patachara could not accept their saying no.

The young stable boy was the one to save the day. He had watched the whole story unfold. He could see how eager she had become, but he also understood her parents' concerns. So, he built a ladder and painted it blue and he tied ribbons along the side so that she might feel like she was flying. He presented it to the family as a proposed solution. She would not climb *onto* a tree (and risk ruining her delicate clothing or scratching her delicate knees), but she could climb into one safely enough. Her parents finally approved.

Patachara bounced around the garden with giddy delight, clapping her hands and shouting as loud as she could. The ladder looked like her very own stairway to heaven. Just like the ones the gods used when they visited humans on earth. She could imagine Lord Brahma using it to visit her when his celestial swans were too tired to carry him down, or Lord Vishnu if he felt the need to repair the ten thousand worlds. Lord Shiva, however, would never use it. That much she knew for certain. Shiva would never use something so dainty. He would fire-breathe his way down if he ever felt like visiting.

The first time she used the ladder was a big household affair. Her parents and all the servants came out to watch. The poor stable boy was a nervous wreck. He was sweating profusely from every pore. If he made even the slightest mistake, he knew he was done for. He prayed the ladder would hold. He prayed she would not slip. He prayed the gods would not send a sudden gust of wind. He prayed for protection against every possible scenario as he walked ceremoniously into the garden with the ladder in his arms.

He brought the ladder to the great mango tree and laid it against the trunk. Patachara was ready to pounce onto the first step the second it was planted, but the stable boy would not hear of it. He needed to be sure it was properly set. He checked that the legs were safely rooted and examined every rung to make sure that it was as solid as he needed it to be. He studied the different angles and considered weight distribution, while she paced with impatient exasperation behind him on her little legs.

When he finally declared the ladder safe, she threw herself on with wild abandon. She forgot to tuck in her robe and she forgot to worry about the wind lifting it up. She forgot to worry about anything at all. She was climbing her bright blue stairway to heaven all by herself, while the stable boy held her steady (and tried not to look up). When she reached the first fruit-bearing branch, she screeched with delight. She wrapped her little fingers around a mango and everyone cheered. She could not believe she was plucking a fruit by herself. For once, the fruit was not given to her. It was not chosen for her. It was a fruit she had chosen from a tree that she had climbed. She felt absolutely triumphant.

"It was the best moment of my little life."

A memory she found herself returning to these days, although she was not quite sure why.

Vimala was back on land, dressed and washed. She was wringing out the water from her hair as she listened. She tried imagining Patachara as a carefree little girl surrounded by servants, climbing a bright blue ladder with ribbons. The contrast seemed impossible to reconcile.

"The stable boy sounds like a kind person," was all she could think of saying. "It sounds like he made you a wonderful ladder."

"It *was* wonderful," Patachara replied. "I had so many expensive things, but I loved nothing more than that stairway to heaven."

The stable boy became her trusted confidant after that. He was supposed to remain in the stables, but Patachara called on him so often, the head servant eventually rotated responsibilities and placed him in the main house instead.

"Uh oh . . ." Vimala mumbled. "I think I know where *this* story is going."

"Is it that obvious?"

Vimala smiled. Bhadda Kundalakesa nodded like a wise old bird.

"I guess you're right," she replied matter-of-factly. "The story went right where you are both imagining."

Patachara and the stable boy fell in love. They were not supposed to, but they did. Eventually, they ran away together to marry in secret, far from her parents and their hierarchical concerns. "I spent years away from my beloved parents, terrified of their recrimination. So many wasted years far from the family I loved."

When she finally did try to return home a few years later, it was too late. She approached the city of Savatthi, trudging slowly along the path, lifetimes of suffering weighing down her dirty feet. She saw smoke rising in the distance.

"What is that?" she asked a familiar face, passing by.

The man looked her up and down. She was so different from the innocent girl she had once been that she was almost unrecognizable. The man stared at her, scratched his head, and then suddenly pulled back with a yelp of surprise. The girl who once belonged to the Great House of Savatthi had become a haggard old woman almost overnight.

"It is your parents' funeral pyre," he said.

Her whole family was gone.

13

Vesali

Vimala had forgotten how pretty Vesali was.

It was quite unlike the other cities of Northern Bharata. Or so she had heard. Kapilavatthu, a city she did know well, had never built itself into a fortress, but Vimala knew that most cities in the region had. She had heard descriptions from her clients over the years. Most of these cities were surrounded with thick ugly walls that towered over the inhabitants. The walls were peppered with heavy bolts and surrounded by vile-smelling moats. Cities built to keep the world out, to barricade themselves in. Masculine architecture at its most fearful and defensive.

But Vesali looked like it had been drawn into existence by a woman. The walls were only a few stories high, so that you did not feel as though they were pressing down as you approached. The stones did not stick out unevenly the way most city walls did, like a jumble of protruding elbows that you tried to avoid. Instead, these walls were sanded down to create a smooth, almost glistening surface.

Vesali was not, however, a vulnerable city. It had a surrounding moat like all the others; the walls were pierced with small openings for archers to aim and shoot; there was a rampart above for strutting surveillance and towers that provided excellent views. Vesali had everything a city of its stature required. The difference was that it also took the time to beautify along the way. The moat, for example, was not a muddy eyesore filled with rotting fish. It was as wide as a strong river and filled with fresh water instead. The openings for the archers, as small as they were, were all exactly the same, separated at regular intervals and framed with beautifully carved spirals. The drawbridge was not just a collection of random wooden boards nailed together. It was gracefully crafted with iron handrails that were as elegant as they were strong. Vesali was a masterpiece. A city like a many-sided gem.

Vesali was, moreover, unusual for its style of governance. Vimala had not been old enough to appreciate this when she had lived there, but she had learned since that Vesali governed itself differently. Her people, the Licchavis, had abandoned the notion of a sovereign king years ago and instead rotated governance among their noble families. No one ruled forever in Vesali. Everyone, rather, ruled for just a bit of time. There were skirmishes and political infighting, but on the whole the Licchavis had ruled well.

Vimala had grown up believing that all cities functioned this way, but she was relieved of that illusion as soon as she left. Vesali was in fact the exception. The rest of Bharata was the rule. Kapilavatthu, for example, lived and died by the king's commands. She could never quite get used to that fact, but given Suddhodana Maharaja's benevolence, she did not mind as much as she might have. Kapilavatthu was a good city. Few other Royal Cities could claim as much.

Gotami was leading the women toward the drawbridge.

Vimala stopped walking and watched. When Gotami stepped onto that drawbridge, Vimala would be connected to the city that had shut her out. The city that had had ejected her like unwanted trash.

Gotami placed her Royal Hand onto the railing. Vimala reached for the pendant around her neck. Gotami then stepped forward, her Royal Foot taking the first step. She walked across the drawbridge and presented herself to the guards standing sentry at the gate.

The guards had their spears planted firmly beside them. Gotami's bodyguards stood stoically behind her. Vimala held her breath.

And then, all of a sudden, the Vesali guards moved their spears aside in a choreographed gesture as a lady stepped forward from behind them. This lady was covered in sparkling jewels and swaying fabrics. Long hair plaited like a rope down her back. There was something familiar about the way the woman moved, but Vimala could not see her clearly from where she stood. She watched as the lady lowered herself to touch Gotami's feet. She then lifted herself back up and pressed her palms together with a bowed head.

The Gathering Women were invited into the city. Vimala followed behind the others, but when she reached the top of the drawbridge herself, she stopped. The women shuffled forward, one after the next, babbling excitedly as they walked past. She, however, remained right where she was. Her feet had turned to lead.

After so many years of running.

All that time, feeling shame and rejection. She was just a child when she left. Had just begun the process of becoming a woman. She had lost everything before she even knew how to appreciate any of it. There one moment, gone the next, and then she was running for her life. Charging through that very gate on Assavata's back.

Bhadda Kundalakesa laid her hand on Vimala's shoulder.

"Will you be all right?" she asked.

Vimala looked at her friend and nodded. Bhadda went ahead.

Vimala waited for the last of them to go through. Then she set down her bag. She raised her hands over her head, palms pressed together, and bowed to her native city.

Tears slid down her cheeks.

Vimala lowered herself onto her knees and bowed again.

She had not allowed herself to cry in years, but now the tears were flowing like a rapid river. She dropped to the ground and prostrated her entire body onto the bridge, her forehead pressed against the wood. With arms raised in reverence, her eyes closed, she let herself cry and cry and cry. The tears fell between the slats and dropped into the moat below. Vimala cried and cried.

After all that time.

She whispered prayers of gratitude. She begged the guardian deities to receive her softly, to forgive her, to help her find her way. She did not know how long she stayed that way, face down on the bridge. She did not know if others were staring or whispering or wondering who she was. Vimala stayed as long as she needed to, until all the tears were spent and the prayers had run their course.

When she was ready, she got up, dusted herself off and crossed over to the other side.

The women were up ahead.

She walked through the archway and into the city, racing to catch up. She did not take the time to look around, to remember more than she already had. As much as she needed to be alone a moment ago, now she yearned for the others. She wanted to slip into the sea of female bodies that had become her protection.

The women seemed to be moving towards the city center. She assumed they were being welcomed by one of the noble families. She kept going, rushing through the maze that had once been her home. She knew that if she turned left, she would find the trail that would lead back to her mother's home, that if she veered right, she would reach the vegetable market. And that just around that corner, she would find Vesali's most famous jeweler. She knew so many things about Vesali, but the point now was to reach the Gathering. There would be time later for the rest. She raced to catch up.

And then she realized where the Gathering was headed and she screeched to a stop.

The Queen of Sakya was leading the women into Ambapali's residence! Why were they going *there*? Ambapali was the High Courtesan of Vesali. Why would she be inviting the Queen of Sakya in? It made no sense. The queen should be welcomed by high officials. Women of stature. Men of nobility.

Was Ambapali the lady who had greeted Gotami at the gate? Was that why she seemed so familiar? The questions were reeling and colliding all at once. Vimala could not think straight. But then she remembered when Neelima had stopped by the brothel for a cup of water. She acted as though it was the most natural thing in the world to sit with a prostitute. Bhadda Kundalakesa had urged her to join the Gathering Women, knowing full well that she was a prostitute and that she even had debts. Princess Yasodhara had fought Kumari to set her free. At every turn, the Gathering had made room for her. "Prostitutes and queens together," was what Bhadda had said. Prostitutes and queens.

Vimala watched the women walk through Ambapali's front gate. Many years earlier—a lifetime ago, really—Vimala had been rejected at that very spot.

She remembered it like it was yesterday.

It had been pouring. That halfway point during monsoon when the rain has become an unrelenting assault. When the fields are drowning and the terraced hills are on the verge of collapse. When the relief you feel upon the rain's arrival becomes a distant memory and you begin to worry that it will take more than it will give. It was pouring like that when Vimala's mother died. The clouds were thick and black and fierce. Rain was smashing against the shuttered windows. Vimala cowered in the dark, afraid of what would happen once the others realized that death had come.

Funerals were not permitted when someone died of the Skin Disease. The flames of the fire god were too sacred to touch a polluted body like that. The traditional rites were cancelled and Vimala's mother was dumped in a charnel ground instead. There was no procession to carry her to the river. No cremation pyre for Vimala to light. Not even a flower garland tossed in her direction. Vimala's mother was left where Agni the Fire God would never find her. He would never lick her skin to set her free.

It did not take long after that. The other courtesans accused Vimala of contamination and turned her out of the house. She had no symptoms of the Skin Disease, but they slammed the door right in her face.

Vimala still remembered the feeling. Of the rain pouring over her little head, as she stared vacantly at the closed door that created a boundary between what was and what would never be again. Eventually, she turned around and trudged through the mud toward Assavata's enclosure. She opened the gate and approached her only remaining friend. She hoisted herself onto Assavata's back, wrapped her arms around the horse's neck, and sobbed like the little girl she still was.

She did not know how long she cried. It seemed like forever to her then. It seemed like it was forever ago now. Eventually though, she asked Assavata to take her away. They slogged through the empty streets together. Everyone in Vesali was huddled indoors, shielding themselves and each other from a storm that would not relent. Indra, the God of Thunder, must have been angry that day. There was no explanation other than that.

The streets had fast become a rushing river and it was difficult to move forward. Debris was swirling in the dark water. A withered flower garland drifted by, the orange petals already curling into death. "Keep going, Windhorse," she whispered. She was guiding her horse toward Ambapali's residence. She could think of nowhere else to go.

They were both exhausted by the time they reached the gate. Vimala lowered herself down, her hand still clutching Assavata's mane. She steadied herself amid the swelling waves. Then she banged on the door.

"Ambapali, let me in!" She banged and banged with her little fists. "Somebody please let me in!"

But no one answered.

Perhaps they could not hear over the clamoring waters. Perhaps the guards were hiding indoors too and did not even know she was there. She banged again.

"Somebody please!" she cried. "Help me."

But no one came. Her hands became bruised and sore. She slid to the ground, collapsed with despair.

Assavata stepped forward, nudging Vimala with her nose, but Vimala's head was folded into her arms. She had lost her mother. She had lost her title and her home. She had even lost her clan. Now she would never be a courtesan. Ambapali would not even let her in.

Assavata tried to push her back to her feet. She shifted back and forth, neighing restlessly in the face of Vimala's dejection. "Get up" was what she was trying to say.

Assavata stomped and neighed again, this time more loudly. She clamped onto Vimala's clothes with her teeth and pulled, but Vimala would not get up. Assavata got angrier. More flustered. Impatience turning to panic. She stomped again, this time so hard, Vimala felt the ground beneath her shake. Assavata then stepped back and reared onto her two hind legs and let out a howl that challenged Indra himself. She was banging at the earth the way Vimala had been banging at the door.

And then, just as Assavata was about to break down the gate, someone unlatched a small window in the door and slid it open. A guard's face peered through.

"Who's there?" he asked, through the curtain of water falling over him.

Vimala scrambled quickly to her feet. She lifted herself onto her toes and stuck her face inside the frame.

"My name is Vimala. Please, sir, I am here for refuge. Please ask the High Courtesan if I might be let in."

"How do you know Her Mistress?" he barked.

"She knows my mother, a courtesan from the house down the road." She pointed in the direction of her home.

"You are the daughter of a courtesan from *that* house?"

Vimala nodded eagerly.

"You're not bringing your dirty Skin Disease in here!" He slammed the window shut. "Get out of here, street rat!" he bellowed from across the gate. "You're not wanted here!"

Vimala did not have the Skin Disease.

Not that day, not ever. She was not contagious or sick and she never had symptoms. But she had been too close to it all—too close to the illness as she cowered in her mother's room, too close to inheritance as she stood next in line. The Skin Disease served as a perfect pretext to send her away. By the time she reached Ambapali's residence, the damage was done.

Vimala was now standing on that street again, staring at the door that had once closed against her. She watched the women of the Gathering filing in, chattering with animated curiosity, most of them probably never having been invited to a courtesan's estate before. The closer they got to the entrance, the more they peeked over each other's shoulders. Trying to catch a glimpse of the forbidden treasure house on the other side. When they reached the threshold, she watched as each one was welcomed with a fresh flower garland placed around their neck. No one was interrogated or refused. No one had the door slammed in their face.

Vimala fiddled with her head scarf.

Would she be allowed in this time? Or would she be recognized as the daughter of the Skin Disease? She tapped her foot, crossed her arms, unsure of what she should do. The line was petering out.

It was now or never. She took in a deep breath, pulled back her shoulders and approached. She looked at the guard squarely in the eyes. Daring him to respond. But he said nothing. He barely even looked at her. The young courtesan beside him bowed politely and placed a flower garland around her neck.

"Great Goddess, I had no idea . . . !" she heard one of the women say as Vimala followed the line inside. "I have never seen anything . . ." exclaimed another. The women had barely crossed the threshold and they were already entranced. Ambapali's courtyard was a work of art, just as it was supposed to be.

The floor of the courtyard was paved with seashells and the walls were painted every possible shade of blue, so that it looked like the ocean had been pulled in on a wave. Creepers sprouted between the paved stones and climbed the walls with their lush greenery, while bright pink rhododendron flowers flopped into the courtyard from the street outside. Delicately carved furniture lined the walls, each piece abundant with colorful pillows. And at the center of it all, a holy fig tree, with branches that spread out so far and wide, it looked like it was trying to hug the sky. Its heart-shaped leaves fluttered in the wind, along with hundreds of tiny windchimes that dangled and decorated it. The birds were chirping, the bees were buzzing, the sun was shining bright. "It feels like we've landed in a celestial heaven," Vimala heard one of the women say. It felt that way indeed. And they had barely seen anything at all. Vimala put her shaking hand to her amulet and thanked the Great Goddess for her return.

Courtesans sashayed between the women of the Gathering, sparkling with sensuous hospitality. Carpets were flicked into position and spread along the floor. Silk pillows were delivered for tired limbs. Moist towels scented with rose petals for dirty hands and faces. And a meal began circulating that promised to put them all to sleep instantly. Saffron rice topped with bright green coriander leaves. Fried eggplant with spiced yogurt and pomegranate seeds. Black lentils stewed in rich cream. The courtesans moved through the cacophony of tired women like gentle spirits, delivering respite with a delicate touch.

Vimala took to a corner and watched as her two worlds intertwined. The young girl called Mutta who wore flowers in her hair was taking it all in with big bright eyes. The woman with blue-black skin was trailing her hand over the walls, marvelling at their luxurious color. Bhadda Kundalakesa was sitting stoically with a few others, careful not to overindulge in the food. Patachara looked almost feral with her wild tangles of hair and dirty cloak, while the Queen of the Sakya Kingdom and the mighty Princess Yasodhara sat at the center of it all, graced by the chiming fig tree, accepting hospitality with practiced elegance. Of everyone in that courtyard, they seemed the most at ease.

Vimala smiled to herself.

She was watching Royal Women receive hospitality in a courtesan's courtyard. The Queen of Sakya and Princess Yasodhara were smiling lightly as courtesans showered them with offerings.

Vimala shook her head again and again at the wonder of it all.

14

Hollowed-Out Mess

A few days passed. Hospitality required as much.

The Gathering women busied themselves with tours of Ambapali's residence, marveling at luxuries most had never imagined possible, or stared with unconcealed amazement at the beauties who were their wards. Some dedicated themselves to ardent conversation, legs crossed on cushions as they negotiated their hopes and fears.

Vimala, however, sat by herself.

She could not believe that she had arrived. That she was sitting in Ambapali's courtyard, leaning against the wall, her feet tucked beneath her like the child she used to be. She remembered the hours she had spent twirling on those very same seashells that blanketed the floor. The windchimes she had tried to reach on tiptoe when no one was looking that hung on the branches of that majestic tree. Her mother had brought her to Ambapali's each time a guild meeting was called. She was too young to understand most of the happenings then, but her mother wanted to familiarize her with the community, have her see what it was all about.

Vimala could still see the old courtesan mothers who dominated with willful tempers. They squeezed her cheeks with decorated hands and commented on her shape as though she was a fruit to be plucked. Or the competing proprietors who argued price points, threatening suicide if the city's taxes were raised just one more time. She remembered a friendly kitchen maid who gave her sweets when no one was looking, a gardener who whistled while he worked. And most of all, she remembered the newly inducted courtesans, just a few years older than her, freshly deflowered and already convinced that they knew everything. Ambapali's residence was Vimala's favorite place in the whole world as a child. She could still taste the disappointment each time her mother said that it was time to go.

And now here she was, a lifetime later. The seashells sparkled just as they always had, the walls were just as liquid blue. Ambapali remained the uncontested leader of the courtesan guild. Everything was as it had always been, all of it just as she remembered.

But one look at the rag robe she was wearing and Vimala knew that everything was different too. Vimala's mother had always fussed about her appearance when they were summoned to Ambapali's for a meeting. Vimala's hair would be decorated and her face wiped clean. She would never have appeared in a rag robe with her hair a tangled mess. Her mother would have died a thousand deaths. Vimala looked down at herself, at the poverty she exuded. After weeks of walking, of worn-out feet and tired limbs, after escaping Kumari's, risking imprisonment, cowering in shame as others negotiated her person's worth, Vimala finally recognized the truth she had avoided until then: Vimala was not a courtesan anymore. Ambapali's was not her home.

"Are you well, dear?" Ambapali asked Vimala each time she passed. "Can I get you something more to eat?"

Vimala tried not to stare, but she could not resist. She had expected Ambapali to be the brilliant young courtesan she had once known. The one who could command an army with a flick of her delicate wrist. The one with a tiny waist and hips that swelled like ocean waves.

But Ambapali had aged. She had crows' feet etched around her eyes, lines running down her cheeks, thinning hair, even yellowed teeth. Her waist had thickened; her hips no longer swelled.

"You are a perfect hostess," Vimala would reply as she got to her feet. "You have provided more than enough."

Sometimes Ambapali's gaze drifted over Vimala's face just a bit longer than was appropriate. As though she might have recognized something in her, some detail or wisp of familiarity, and Vimala's breath would catch in her throat. She would wait, looking with anticipation, wondering if this would be the time when Ambapali would finally see her, finally know that she had come. But then the moment would pass. Ambapali would shake her head, as though tossing a disconcerting thought aside, and bow to Vimala before she shuffled away.

"Won't you ever say something to her?"

Bhadda Kundalakesa was standing beside her, watching Vimala with a knowing gaze.

"Probably not."

"But you came all this way to find her."

Vimala watched Ambapali as she made her way through the courtyard, acknowledging each guest with the appropriate greeting. Bowing, smiling, being the perfect courtesan.

"Maybe finding her was enough."

Vimala sat back down and retreated into silence. She was finally back in Vesali, in the little treasure house that she had always admired. She was in Ambapali's protection, *finally*, after all these years. The very place she had tried so hard to take refuge in when everyone else had turned her away. She had done it.

But Ambapali's estate was not her refuge anymore. It was home to an old woman she barely knew.

"I won't continue with the Gathering," Vimala told her companions the following day. She was clutching at her string amulet around her neck.

"There's talk that they might be leaving today, but I need to take care of something first. I can catch up with you later."

"We're coming with you," Patachara answered, not skipping a beat. "We figured you would not be done with Vesali just yet."

"But don't you want to stay with the Gathering?" Vimala asked. The Buddha was just around the corner. Only a few minutes outside the gate. How could they delay when they were so close?

Patachara did not reply. Instead, she threaded her arm into Vimala's and Bhadda threaded her own on the other side.

They left Ambapali's later that day and headed for the house Vimala never thought she would see again. They walked down the busy city street, navigating animal dung and bullock carts, street vendors and armed guards. They were quite a sight, particularly given how sparkly the inhabitants of the jeweled city tended to be. Bhadda was bald, in a white tattered robe. Patachara was wild looking and barely dressed.

Vimala wore little more than a thin greying rag. What a sight they were to see.

At the end of the road, the three companions turned the anticipated corner. Vimala's fists had closed into tight balls of anguish. She prayed for the courage to face whatever it was that was left. She hoped the house was still standing, hoped it was as beautiful as she remembered, hoped to find Assavata's grassy enclosure filled with young horses neighing with delight.

Most of all, though, she hoped for anonymity. The kind she had gotten used to over the years. She did not want to see anyone who might recognize her. She now knew that she had not come back for that.

They turned the corner, arms still interlocked, Vimala's heart beating wildly. Vimala had her eyes closed, but when she felt the others stop, she knew they had arrived. She counted under her breath: one, two, three. And then she looked up.

It was devastating.

The home Vimala had been dreaming about since the day she was evicted was a dilapidated, hollowed-out mess.

"How could this have happened?" Vimala asked once she recovered from the initial shock. "There used to be a garden right over here, and a field of apricot trees along the side of the house over there. And the front door was a work of art—heavy rosewood that I could barely manage closing by myself. I can't believe anyone would steal a front door!"

Vimala approached the remains of her home in a daze. It looked like an amputated veteran, barely able to hold itself up. When she reached the cracked doorstep, she put her hand on the frame, as though looking for something in the dark. Feeling her way through the absence. "Our door had magnificent carvings of couples lying together," she said.

"The wood was probably too valuable to waste," Bhadda Kundalakesa answered, pragmatic as ever. "Either it's been repurposed, or someone else is enjoying those carvings now."

"We could try looking for it," Patachara suggested. "Maybe it's become someone else's front door?"

Vimala had no answer to that. She did not think she could stomach the idea of finding it hanging in someone else's home. Their door had been famous. Children used to sneak their way towards the house when mothers weren't watching, just to catch a glimpse of the positions they were forbidden from thinking about.

"Must have been good for business," Bhadda Kundalakesa said.

It certainly was.

Vimala ducked under the ripped doorframe and stepped inside. The world it had once been danced in her imagination. Pieces of glitter seemed to be peeking out from between broken shards. She could see her mother up ahead in her mind's eye, whirling her seductive body, shaking bangles on her slim wrists. Beckoning her to come in. She could hear Natyaguru clapping a rhythm in the courtyard. She heard the sounds of servants scurrying about, getting the house ready, changing sheets, filling the rooms with sweet smells, lighting butter lamps in the dark. Vimala closed her eyes and breathed in the memories that were swirling all around her, seducing her with nostalgic charm. Begging her to hold on.

"I don't think the building is safe," Bhadda interrupted.

Vimala's mother vanished in an instant. Natyaguru's rhythm was silenced. The once brilliantly painted plaster from the walls lay in large dusty chunks on the floor. When she looked up, she found that some of the wooden beams were missing. The house was hanging together by a thread.

"We will be safer outside," Bhadda said as she steered them away. Vimala watched as her entire story melted into loss all over again. Nothing was left to hold onto anymore.

They walked away from the house and toward the field that had once been home to her beloved horse. The grass had grown wildly high. What was left of the enclosure lay in heaps like unwanted wreckage. Vimala walked into the heart of the land and lay down on the ground. As though she was trying to embrace the earth that had once been her own.

Patachara got down beside her. Bhadda hesitated, but then lay down on the other side. No explanations were required.

"I lost my family too," Patachara said.

Vimala turned to look at the Cloak-Walker lying on the grass beside her.

"I was so young when I ran away," Patachara said. "We both were, my husband and I. We had no idea how difficult the road ahead would be."

Patachara was finally prepared to tell another piece of her story. Seeing the remains of Vimala's story allowed her to look at her own.

Patachara and her husband escaped in the middle of the night and made their way to a new life in a town further away. "We did well at first. My husband found work with a local carpenter; we made a home out of the shed next to the shop. It was nothing like the home I was raised in, obviously, but we thought we had enough." They created new identities, never letting themselves get close to their neighbors for fear that they would be found out. "It was a lonelier life than either of us was prepared for. I never imagined how much I would miss the comfort of my community until I found myself alone."

People were kind, but always more curious than the couple could afford, so they learned to keep to themselves. When Patachara finally became pregnant, she decided it was time to go home. "I begged my husband to bring us back to Savatthi. I missed my parents terribly. I was sure they would forgive us and take us in, but he was terrified. He hemmed and hawed, and delayed in every possible way, until I was giving birth right there at home on the shed floor and the idea of returning to Savatthi was abadoned.

"But when I became pregnant a second time, I was determined. I wouldn't let him delay again." When she felt the time approaching, she packed her things and walked right out the door. Her husband had no choice but to follow. "But then everything went wrong."

Patachara closed her eyes.

Vimala, lying in the grass beside her, reached for her friend's hand. "You lost your baby, didn't you?"

"I lost them both," she answered. "I lost everyone."

With a belly bursting like a ripe melon, she left the village with her son and aimed for the river that led to Savatthi. Her husband was right behind her, begging her to turn back, but refusing to let her get too far ahead.

By the time they reached the river's edge, the weather had turned and a storm was churning up the sky. The clouds had blackened and soon rain was whipping away at them from every direction. "We had to stop where we were. My husband ran off to get some wood for a shelter and I waited by the foot of a tree, praying it would not break over our heads. I sheltered my baby and bore the storm on my back."

Her husband was gone a long time. First an hour, then two. By the middle of the night, Patachara was terrified, but her Birthing had begun and there was nothing for her to do but stay where she was. "I waited and I breathed, and then I was howling into the stormy night as the Birthing split me apart." Holding onto one child with one arm, grabbing at the tree's limbs for support with the other, "I prayed and prayed to the Birthing Goddess, begging her to keep us safe."

By the next morning, she had a newborn in her arms. She lay exhausted on the wet earth. The storm had subsided. The clouds were sailing away.

"But still my husband had not returned."

When she felt strong enough, she got to her feet and tucked her newborn under her arm. She begged her eldest to walk on his own little feet beside her. A trail of blood poured out from between her legs and followed her as they went off in search of a husband she was certain was dead. "And then I found him, lying in a heap by an anthill with a snakebite on his arm, the wound swollen and blue. A branch lay broken beside him. I knew he was planning on bringing that branch to us to build the shelter he had promised."

She had no choice but to continue towards Savatthi without him. She left her husband behind and trudged through the muddy earth with her children until they reached the river's shore. But what had once been a small riverbed had now swollen to twice its size. The river was rushing through the landscape with sickening speed. Savatthi lay just on the other side, but there were no rafts or boats or bridges.

Vimala was still holding Patachara's hand, but Patachara's chest was tightening. She needed air. She dropped Vimala's hand like a dead weight, sat up with a quick movement. She folded her knees into her chest and wrapped her arms around them. The other two sat up beside her. They waited for her to finish the story she had been carrying in silence since the day they met.

"I asked the eldest to wait for me. I told him that I would cross with his baby brother and then come back for him. He was such a dutiful boy! I had no doubt that he would listen. He nodded his beautiful head and agreed to the instructions. He smiled with his big beautiful black eyes, and even tried to reassure me that everything would be all right. 'Don't worry, mama,' he said." She kissed him on the forehead. Then she waded in, the newborn clasped to her breast.

"We made it without mishap and I breathed out a sigh of relief. I thought everything would work out now. I had figured out a way. I put my baby down on a flat rock and turned around to go back for the

other one." She was half-way across the river when she caught site of
an eagle flying dangerously low. She realized just a moment too late
what was about to happen and she let out a blood-curdling scream.
She watched in horror as the eagle swooped down and grabbed her
baby in its talons.

Vimala gasped despite herself.

How could a mother survive having her baby ripped away like that?
Vimala wanted to grab Patachara in her arms and hold her tight. But
Patachara sat stock still. Hardened behind the words she was finally
speaking out loud.

"It all happened so quickly," the Cloak-Walker continued. "I was
screaming and waving my arms, trying to call the eagle back with my
pleas. And then I caught sight of my other son stepping into the river. I
turned and screamed at him to get back, but he couldn't hear me over
the sound of rushing water. He must have thought that I was calling
him towards me instead. He looked up and smiled and then plowed
forward, right into the waves . . ."

Before she could reach him, he was swept away.

Silence settled over the three friends with a heavy weight. Bhadda
and Vimala barely breathed. They stared at Patachara with eyes wide.

"It's why I don't like rivers," Patachara concluded.

She lost both her children. She lost her husband too. All in one day.

15

The Great Woman Tree

They walked back to Ambapali's estate in silence. The sun was setting. The bats hanging in the trees were unfurling their wings. Vimala watched as they stretched themselves out and lifted their dark bodies into the sky.

"Do you think the others will have left?" Vimala asked as they neared the front gate.

No one answered.

They reached Ambapali's residence. Vimala tensed instinctively, but the guards let them through.

The women were still there. They were sitting in circles or standing in small groups here and there. Some were arguing fiercely, while others were steeped in quiet conversation. In one corner, some of the women were waiting in line to have their heads shaved. Vimala could see Mutta, the young girl who had once worn flowers in her hair, sitting still as the blue-black woman cut off her long locks.

"What's going on here?" Vimala asked.

Bhadda Kundalakesa was the one to answer.

"I think it's time I told you how this journey began."

They crossed the courtyard without needing to consult each other, making their way to their favorite part of Ambapali's estate: not one of the elaborate dining rooms or any of the sumptuous lounges, but outside, where they were most at ease, in the famous Mango Grove behind the house.

According to legend, Ambapali was found at the foot of a mango tree and that was how she got her name (*amba* being the word for mango). She was so beautiful, even as a small child, that men immediately fought to lay claim to her. The governing body of the city therefore decided to step in. No one wanted to see the city torn apart over a little girl, so they decided that Ambapali would not belong to any one person exclusively. She would belong to everyone instead. She would be raised as the future High Courtesan of Vesali.

"I'm sure it was hard for her," Vimala had explained to them the first time she took them to the Mango Grove. "She became the chief courtesan before she even had her deflowering. And she did it without a mother's protection. Surrounded by hungry men. There were attempts to dethrone her, betrayals to navigate and schemes to survive, but she never faltered. My mother said that Ambapali could tame an emperor with one hand while arranging flowers with another. Ambapali has been the uncontested leader of the Vesali courtesans for decades. Few have managed half as much."

Vimala herself had barely lasted a few minutes. She lost everything the moment her mother died. Despite everything her mother tried to teach her, every skill she tried to instill, Vimala was out the door in the pouring rain before she even realized the game had begun.

"Ambapali sounds like a warrior, the way you describe her," Bhadda said with genuine admiration.

"Ambapali could take down Arjuna if she wanted to," was Vimala's natural reply.

Vimala had surprised herself with her own words. She had spent years nursing resentment and accusation against Ambapali. Years blaming her for not opening the door that night. If only Ambapali had agreed to see her, everything would have been different. Her beloved horse would not have died on the side of the road. A piece of her would not have died either, as strange men deflowered her without permission. If only Ambapali had opened the door, she would have been safe. But Ambapali never opened the door and Vimala had been forced to follow a trail of servitude and humiliation instead. For years, all Vimala could think was, *if only Ambapali had opened the door.*

She thought she hated Ambapali, that she would launch accusations into her perfect face the moment she saw her again, or fall at her feet sobbing, begging for the protection she had so long been denied.

But now that she had arrived, now that she had looked upon Ambapali's real face, seen the lines of time drawn into it, her feelings had changed. Ambapali was not the reason her whole world had fallen apart. She was just the last thread that pulled the rest undone. The certainty Vimala had been raised with, that everything would be taken care of, that her future would play out exactly as planned . . . that was the real mistake. There was no certainty to depend on. No future, no assurances, no substance upon which to rest anyone's head. Vimala's life felt no different from the house that had once been her own. It may have been sturdy and beautiful once, but now only dust and rusty hinges were left. Everything was impermanent, fading, coming to an end. Of what use was anger when it falls apart so easily in one's hands?

Each time Vimala went through these thoughts, she was left empty. The past had withered. The future was not hers to determine. Only the present remained. What could she do with that?

"What was the story you wanted to tell us?" she asked Bhadda as they reached the grove together. The smell of sweet mangos filled the evening air. Bhadda had stopped walking and was reaching out for a mango that seemed on the verge of letting go.

"It's about the Queen's hair," she said. Bhadda tested its resistance and decided to leave the mango where it was.

"But the queen *has* no hair," Vimala answered impatiently. "The queen's a widow."

Bhadda picked up her stride, her hands locked behind her back.

"That's not why she has no hair," she said as she looked ahead. "Not all widows follow the tradition of head shaving."

Before Vimala could launch another retort, Patachara lay her hand on Vimala's arm. Vimala held her tongue.

Weeks earlier, when the Queen of Sakya, Mahapajapati Gotami, walked out of her palace in Kapilavatthu, she still had a full head of hair. Bhadda Kundalakesa was standing at the palace gate when the queen emerged with Princess Yasodhara beside her. She watched as the queen led their pilgrimage towards Banyan Grove. The queen did not make small talk with anyone; she did not accept offerings or invite devotional reverence. She walked straight towards the Buddha on her bare royal feet, with her long braids swaying behind her back, wearing nothing more than a simple white cotton robe. She was walking to Banyan Grove to ask the Buddha for permission to join the order. The Gathering Women followed. Bhadda Kundalakesa was there.

At the very edge of the grove stood the Great Woman Tree. It was a boundary unto itself, a demarcation that separated one world from another. The Queen of Sakya stopped before the Great Woman Tree and turned to face her newly formed community. "This part of the story I must do alone," she said.

No one argued, not even Princess Yasodhara. No one said a word. The Queen of Sakya bowed to the Great Woman Tree and then walked on, further into the grove where the Buddha promised to be. Even her tattooed bodyguards were told to stay behind.

Time passed. The sun rose high into the morning sky. The air grew wet with humid heat. The women waited clustered around the Great Woman Tree, sitting in silence, sitting with questions and worries and time.

The Great Woman Tree was a beloved tree that had been worshipped for as long as anyone could remember. It was almost as wide as it was tall, with branches that reached up like fingers to the sky. The sages of stories long ago said that a woman lived inside the tree, that she could bless anyone with anything if she decided she would. If you looked carefully, you could see her shape inside the trunk, her hips, her torso, and breasts, and her long flowing hair that reached into her branches and spread out like Shiva's locks when he danced.

Every once in a while, someone would dismiss the tradition. They would say that no tree could really be a woman, that the stories weren't true. But those views never lasted. The sages knew of what they spoke. She was the Great Woman Tree, a goddess incarnate. She was protected by the king's command. No one was permitted to cut any of her branches or collect any of her leaves. The Great Woman Tree could make herself as wide as she wanted to be, with pieces of herself falling back into the earth whenever she felt like dropping them, while other pieces of forest added themselves on. No one was permitted to disturb her growth.

Gotami soon returned from the grove.

The women rose to their feet beneath the tree that looked like them. On soil that coated her intertwining roots. The women were sheltered by her thick branches overhead. They were knit into the tree's world without even realizing it. The black crow that had been following Gotami through Banyan Grove set himself down on one of the moss-covered branches and swiveled his head. Bhadda Kundalakesa thought she saw him bow.

Gotami looked at the women. At their hopeful, worried, complicated faces.

Before taking her seat, she turned to face the tree and bowed with her palms pressed together. Whatever would come of this adventure she had started, she knew she would have to pace herself to survive it. She would have to become like the tree that had weathered countless seasons, sheltered myriad creatures inside itself, become home to a world of living greenery. The tree was a piece of the forest, an embodiment of its complexity, solitary and yet wholly communal all at once. Gotami looked up into the tree's branches, smiled at her magnificently voluptuous shape, whispered a prayer of thanks for her rooted wisdom. Then she sat down at the tree's base, straightened her back, and placed her braids behind her.

"I know you are all waiting for the story," she began. "But I ask you to first settle inside yourselves."

The women murmured. Lines of concern appeared on foreheads. For many, the crow alone was not a good omen. Gotami waited for quiet to arrive.

"I asked the teacher for permission to join the order," she began when she felt it was time. "I asked him for the right to sit beside the monks as a community of female renunciants. Unfortunately, his answer was not what we had hoped. He suggested that we not ask the question."

The murmurs returned.

"I asked him three times. And three times he replied with the same words: it is not a good idea to ask the question."

"What does that mean?" one of the women blurted out.

"It means he said no," Bhadda Kundalakesa answered. "He was just too polite to say it directly."

And that was all it took.

Some of the women began to cry. Others covered their faces with their calloused hands. A few threw their arms into the air, invoking the inevitability of women's suffering. These women may have had idealism in their feet, enough to get them walking out the door, but they scared easily. They had broken every rule to follow Gotami into the wilderness. They feared retribution at every step. It would take time for their confidence to grow.

Women belonged to the home. That was what everyone always said. They were meant to dedicate their lives to the men who supported them. Cook and clean for them like servants until death did them part. Reproduce children as often as their bodies would permit. It was their role in the cosmos, their place to hold without question or argument.

To leave the home was to disrupt the way things had always been. To threaten cosmic harmony. To destroy the social bonds that kept everyone else afloat. These women broke all of those promises and challenged every expectation the moment they walked out the door. It took every ounce of courage they had. They did not have much left. Some risked the wrath of violent husbands. Others risked property owners, taskmasters, temple priests. If the Teacher said no, what would happen to them then?

But retribution was not the only concern. For some it was, but for others, it was the risk of a broken heart. And a broken vow after that. Many of the women followed Gotami not to get away from one thing, but to aspire to something else. To achieve something greater than culinary competence. To count their scores by more than the number of male children they reproduced. For these women, the vow they had whispered as they walked out the door was unbreakable. Returning to the dishes was impossible. If the Teacher said no, there was nowhere else for them to go. They would have to continue as renunciants, homeless and wandering in ways they had not anticipated. They would do it, but that was not how it should be done.

Gotami looked at the women around her. She felt their panic, understood their fears. They were attempting the impossible and already the road was blocked. They were a community of female renunciants who had renounced before they even knew if they were allowed.

What madness.

But then again, she thought to herself, *what else is renunciation if not that? If the first renunciants had to wait for permission, they would never have left.*

"Before you all throw yourselves into the fire," Gotami declared, "listen carefully to the words I used: the Teacher said that it was not a good idea that we ask for ordination."

The women stopped their worries and stared at her. The answer was out there, but just out of reach.

"He did not *actually* say no."

"But isn't that the same thing?" one asked.

"No, it is not the same thing at all."

If he did not say no, according to Gotami, then there remained a chance that his answer might eventually become yes.

"I am not sure what his reasons were for denying us today. But whatever they were, one thing is clear: the decision was not final. He left the door open, which means the conversation is destined to continue."

"So, we go on?" one woman asked.

"We do."

They were not going back. They would follow the Teacher to the next town and they would ask again. And if need be, they would ask again after that. There was still a path beneath their feet and their role was to keep following it.

But before they took another step, Gotami needed to do one last thing. Renunciation of this calibre required a symbol. A gesture that went further than walking out the door. A sign that tells everyone—outside and in—that the act had been taken. A confirmation of commitment. She needed a way to communicate what she had done.

She knew precisely what it had to be. The Teacher had not granted her permission to adopt it, but he had not forbidden it either. He had left her in the grey zone of the in-between. A place where there was no teacher, where she was the one to make the call. Gotami took out her knife from her shoulder bag and removed the jewelled sheath. She whispered another prayer, asking the gods to guide her hand. She then gathered her silver plaits and—without the slightest hesitation, without even announcing that it was about to be done—she sliced her plaits off right at the base.

The moment the hair was severed from Gotami's head, thunder cracked against the silence. Shards of lightning pierced the open, clear blue sky. The earth growled; the forest swayed; the whole cosmos felt like it was rattling with energy. The women seated in front of Gotami clutched the earth, gripped the soil with their fingers, trying to hold on. The leaves above trembled. The roots below slithered. The crow that had been following Gotami lifted off its branch and circled overhead.

The shaking grew stronger. As though something inside the forest was about to break. The Great Woman Tree behind Gotami was groaning. Her branches seemed to be spreading themselves out wider like a terrifying fan. Was the world collapsing? Or rebirthing? Impossible to tell—death and rebirth are so intimately tied. Bhadda Kundalakesa watched the forest bare its fangs.

But then, right there before her eyes, the woman's shape inside the tree moved.

Rippled.

And then the Great Woman Tree was ripping herself apart, thundering with noise, clawing at the seam that kept the world stitched together.

The woman whose shape was inside the tree stepped out.

And all the noise vanished and all the rumbling ceased.

The woman who had been a tree was really a woman. And the woman was really a tree, just as the sages had always said. A forest spirit embedded inside an ancient trunk. A *yakshi*. A beautiful creature who wore moss for covering and flowers in her long shiny hair.

Gotami had her eyes closed, but Bhadda could see the presence standing behind her—the presence that had pulled herself out of the tree.

They waited. They breathed.

The *yakshi* then stepped through Gotami's body like a cloud slipping through a landscape and turned to face the woman who was once a queen.

Gotami opened her eyes.

The *yakshi*—part tree trunk, part moss, covered in foliage and shining bright—bowed with reverence.

She then picked up the silver hair from the ground in both her hands, cupping it like sacred treasure, and raised it over her head.

And then, before anyone knew it, the spirit of the Great Woman Tree was gone.

16

Bhadda Kundalakesa

Bhadda Kundalakesa was there.

She was seated on the ground when the earth began to shake. Had felt the roots quiver beneath her palms. Had seen the lightning slice through the clear blue sky.

She thought she had seen it all. She had been on the road for a lifetime and had seen more than most. She had seen the vastness of the ocean and the crowning heights of the Himalayas. She had debated and argued and studied with teachers across the land, had seen them do things that had confused and amazed her.

But the past few weeks were of a different measure. She had seen things that defied even her imagination. A queen who walks barefoot. Another who steps out of a tree. She saw women choose excommunication, who were excommunicating themselves, rather than follow the road most taken. Never had women surprised her so much.

And the cosmos was watching. She was sure of it. The ten thousand universes were responding to these women as they stepped out of their lives and into something new. The crow that had followed Gotami, the crow that followed them still, was not a bad omen, no matter what anyone said. Most people were scared of crows. They were black and ugly and they feasted on death. But Bhadda Kundalakesa knew better. That crow was their protector. A wrathful guardian watching over them as they attempted the impossible. Never had Bhadda Kundalakesa seen so much.

"It's getting dark," Bhadda said.

The three friends had not seen the time pass as they lingered in Ambapali's Mango Grove. They were mulling over the story of the

Great Woman Tree inside themselves. Feeling it stir something in each of them, each in their own way. Without even knowing that time was passing, they sat still and listened to the sounds of the grove around them, pondering the changes happening within. Vimala was saying goodbye to Vesali, even if she did not voice it aloud. Patachara was speaking the loss she had until then kept sealed at the base of her throat. And Bhadda Kundalakesa was marveling. Preparing herself for a widening freedom she could feel tingling all along her spine.

They walked back in silence. The courtyard had emptied. Everyone had gone to bed.

Bhadda Kundalakesa did not want to retire.

I can sleep when I'm dead, she thought to herself. Right now, she was wholly and completely alive. Her belly was rumbling with energy. She had thoughts to think. An inner universe to engage. She bid her friends goodnight and watched them walk towards their rooms in silence. She would remain in the courtyard under the wide-open sky.

She looked around at the quiet space she had to herself. The only sound in the empty courtyard came from the windchimes swaying in the breeze. The holy tree was even more beautiful at this hour, its heart-shaped leaves silver against the moonlight. Bhadda walked over and reached for one of the chimes. It had a golden thread and was strung with seashells. She let the shells drape over her fingers, reminding her of the jewels she had once draped around her neck. *That was a lifetime ago*, she mused. *And yet it feels like it was only yesterday.* How strangely time flowed as one aged.

She reached for another—this one made of hollow wood, each tube a different length. When she ran her hand along those, they swung a melody. Other chimes were made of crystal. And there were small bronze metal bells, so familiar to her. The kind of bells that hang in front of temple shrines everywhere.

The roots of the tree threaded in and out of the earth into forever configurations. Bhadda knew that snakes were likely hiding therein, particularly at that time of year. Any experienced ascetic knew as much. But now she wondered if snakes might be creatures to sit beside and not against. For once, she decided not to avoid them.

"If you permit," she said aloud to the tree (and its sheltering serpents too), "I would like to join you."

She bowed slowly, like the old woman she had become. The breeze tickled the back of her legs and fiddled with the edge of her robe. She noticed the feeling, the softness of the worn cloth against her skin. She took a moment to look at the tree, then lowered herself to the ground, despite the creaks in her joints and the accusations from her lower back. She settled carefully between a tangle of its roots. "I am here for a moment of quiet," she said to whoever was listening. "I promise not to harm."

Harm.

It was the second time in recent days that the word had fallen from her mouth.

She remembered when the word first entered her emotional vocabulary. It was years after harm had already taken root. She had been running for her life. Her dress was torn, her jewels had been ripped from her neck, her hair that she had carefully combed and oiled earlier that morning was a screaming mess. She did not see the teacher because she was looking behind her while she raced forward and then she careened right into him. She looked up with eyes frightened and shocked.

The teacher caught her by the shoulders. He waited for her to catch her breath. She was missing a sandal. When she had calmed down, he let her go. She stayed where she was and looked at the man who had held her fear in his hands.

He touched her cheek like a kindly grandfather. He called her 'daughter' and told her that everything would be all right. That whatever it was that she was running from, she did not need to run from anymore. That she was safe and that the past could be left behind her. That it was time to let go.

Bhadda Kundalakesa could have argued with him. It certainly would have been in character. She could have told him, *mind your own business, Old Man*. The past does not disappear just because we decide that it has. He had no idea who she was or what she had done. She could have argued thirty-six million things, but Bhadda Kundalakesa looked at the old man standing barefoot and bald before her, and she found herself without arguments to voice. She wiped her face with her bejeweled hand and nodded obediently instead.

The past is gone, she repeated to herself.

She had shoved it right off a cliff.

She let the old man guide her to wherever he was going next.

He led her to the community. The Niganthas were living in the forest together. He introduced her to the others, gave her food and a place to rest. When he felt it was the right time, he also gave her teachings. He did it softly, asking for nothing in return. Telling her about "harm," describing it as the primary reason for the cycle of rebirth. He said that she had to root harm out of her life if she ever hoped to find peace. Every type of harm, every kind of pain, even the most minute.

Pretty clothes lead to pride, he had said. And pride leads to harm. So, she abandoned her colorful clothes and glittery jewelry and adopted white cotton garb like the rest of them. She stopped eating meat, gave up milk provided by cows and goats. Even gave up eating honey. These foods were taken, not given, he had said. And theft leads to harm. She learned to be careful where she walked. Did not want to step on an animal inadvertently. Even insects had to be protected if they could be. She had to eliminate harm wherever it could be found.

Eventually she even gave up her hair, because hair leads to vanity and vanity leads to harm. She did not cut it off with one quick slice, the way Gotami had when she had stood before the Great Woman Tree. Instead, the teacher suggested she remove her hair another way, by facing harm, learning to feel it so that she would become repulsed by it, so that she never caused harm again. Bhadda Kundalakesa may have been skeptical, but she agreed. She wanted to be free. So, she sat down and plucked her hair out of her head. One solitary strand at a time. She bled. Her scalp became swollen and raw. But she kept at it until every individual hair had been removed. It had taken hours and it was agony, but she saw it through to the end.

I don't want to see his face anymore, she begged of herself. But she saw his face every time she closed her eyes. Each hair ripped out of her scalp was accompanied by a prayer to be free of him. To be released from the mess she had been swirling in all her life.

She had killed her husband.

She needed to be free of that.

"You seem lost in thought."

Bhadda looked up to find Vimala standing over her.

"Do you mind if I join you?"

Bhadda considered saying no. She wanted the courtyard to herself.

"I thought you'd gone to bed."

Vimala smiled. "I feel strangely awake tonight."

Bhadda Kundalakesa nodded as she patted the tree roots beside her. Vimala dropped her shoulder bag and crashed down without even considering who she might be squashing in the process. Bhadda clucked her tongue in disapproval. No Nigantha would ever take a seat like that.

"What are you thinking about?"

Bhadda trailed her fingers along the twisty roots. *How does one summarize a life*, she wondered.

"I guess I'm remembering."

"I think everyone is doing some of that these days."

Bhadda closed her eyes and returned to the images she had been watching in her mind. She saw the kindness of a teacher from ages past. The one who had seen through her young, frightened face.

"So, what are you remembering?"

Bhadda opened her eyes and looked at Vimala, wondering again how to respond. She was not used to sharing her story with others. Truth be told, she was not used to keeping company at all. Most of her life had been spent as a wandering ascetic, walking barefoot and solitary from one town to the next.

"I am thinking about the mistakes of my youth," she answered. "The ones that eventually led me here."

Vimala could not hide her surprise. Bhadda never spoke of herself.

"Would you tell me about it?" she asked, tiptoeing towards her with her words.

Bhadda looked up at the tree. She was annoyed. And yet . . . *Everyone is remembering these days.* Perhaps that was why they were all there. Maybe it was time she voiced some of her story too.

Bhadda nodded. Vimala leaned back, her knees tucked into her chest, like a child preparing for a bedtime story.

"It's not a pretty tale," Bhadda warned.

Vimala was the one to nod this time.

"None of our stories is."

"I was raised stupidly," Bhadda began. Not the smoothest entry point, but it was the truth. "My parents loved me terribly, but they said yes to everything."

She looked over at Vimala, as though checking to see how her story-telling fared.

"And I mean yes to *everything*," Bhadda added for emphasis. "Stupid."

Bhadda's parents raised her without reason, spoiled her at every conceivable turn. Whatever she wanted, they immediately delivered, no hesitation or questions asked. But whatever she *needed*—education, temperance, wisdom—these they did not know how to give. Parenting was an act of devoted materialism in their household. Her parents hoped that if they gave enough, it might prove to *be* enough. But no child can be raised that way and turn out well.

They gave her everything she asked for, so that in the end, all she learned was how to ask for more. By the time she reached the age of maturity, she had become impossible. A walking hurricane with no sense of discipline, no sense of right and wrong. Loving her with devoted materialism had proved not to be enough at all.

And then one morning, Bhadda Kundalakesa heard the sound of a criminal parade coming down the street. A thief had just been sentenced to death. He was making the traditional walk to the town square and the authorities were calling the town subjects to come bear witness to justice served. "Come one, come all!" they cried to whoever might hear. Bhadda Kundalakesa raced to the window.

Any reasonable person would have expressed relief that the thief had finally been caught. Or they might have felt sorrow for the suffering the man represented. Or better yet, she should simply not have been watching the scene at all. After all, who watches a parade of criminals that way? Noble ladies knew better than to watch something like that. But Bhadda Kundalakesa *was* watching and what she felt as she watched the thief walk down the road surprised her. Instead of relief or sorrow, or anything else that might have been appropriate, what Bhadda Kundalakesa felt was flushing desire.

And what Bhadda Kundalakesa desired, she had to get.

Her parents were beside themselves. They begged her not to ask for that. Anything but that. Of all things, how could she ask for *that*? But she was adamant. She used every trick in the book. She was practiced in the art of getting. She cried and pleaded and batted her lovely eyelashes. She tossed her long curly locks and pouted just at the right intervals. It was only a question of time before they relented. And when they did, her father raced down to the street, caught up with the executioner, and paid for the thief's release.

"They *actually* did as I asked, despite the obvious madness of my request."

Who asks for such a husband? She asked herself for the three hundred and thirty millionth time. Who grabs the first criminal they see and binds themselves for life? Bhadda shook her head again, amazed by her own stupidity. By the stupidity of everything she was surrounded by. He was beautiful—there was no doubt about that. But beauty as the sole criterion?

"Stupid," she muttered to herself again.

"At first, he was delightful," Bhadda continued. "I really thought I had made the right choice, that I had seen through him, seen his potential, where everyone else had failed. I thought it would make me special in his eyes. And at first, it seemed like it did. He showered me with attention and swept me off my feet." Bhadda turned away from Vimala as she felt her cheeks redden. "But soon, he got restless."

"Did he abandon you?" Vimala asked quietly.

"If only . . ."

Her husband was a criminal through and through. Even though he technically inherited everything the moment they wed, it became increasingly obvious that inheritance was not enough for him. He wanted everything for himself and he did not want her in the way. He did not want her at all, it turned out . . . How could she have even imagined that he would?

The pain of that truth still stung, even all those years later. The fact that she was not loved, that she was not even wanted, even after she had saved his life . . . it was still so hard to see.

"He wanted my jewels. He never wanted me. It was obvious, but I didn't want to admit it. One day he asked to see my jewelry collection. He had seen individual pieces when I wore them, but suddenly he wanted to see everything all at once. A small inner voice warned me to beware, but I refused to listen. I was too eager to please, so I brought the chest to him and opened it with my key . . .

"You should have seen his eyes! He poured his hands into the chest and scooped out the jewels in one big greedy heap. I remember watching my pearl necklace with an emerald pendant dripping from his fingers like it was trying to escape."

"Oh Bhadda," Vimala whispered. "I'm so sorry."

Nothing hurts quite like being used.

"He was different after that. He looked at me like I was prey. He tried to hide it, but his eyes betrayed his ambition. I could see it, but I kept my eyes closed at the same time. I didn't want to see what I was seeing every day.

"And then one afternoon, I found him in my dressing room. He had not heard me come in. He was standing with his back to the door, staring at the contents of my jewel chest again. He had my key in his hands, had taken it from the safe place where I normally kept it hid. The cover was lying open against the hinges, the mirror looking right back at me. I could see his face in its reflection, but he did not see mine . . ."

Bhadda paused.

"What was he doing, Bhadda? What did you see?"

"I saw . . ." she paused again, struggling with the memory of it all. "I saw the look on his face as he looked into that treasure chest. I saw desire and hunger and want. He was looking at the jewels the way . . ."

Bhadda's voice caught.

"The way you hoped he would look at you?"

Bhadda turned away again. Embarrassed by the truth of a time so long ago.

"And then I saw him do something else," she continued. "He closed the chest, locked it with the key, and got down on his knees. Right there in my dressing room. He got on his knees and he began to pray."

Bhadda covered her face with her ageing hands. The memories belonged to a faraway time, and yet speaking the words brought them so close she could taste them again. She could hear his prayer as clearly as she had that day. She could hear the sound of his voice.

"I stood by the door of my own dressing room and listened as my husband begged the Mountain Goddess for help. He told her that this would be the last time. One last kill, one last plunder. In exchange for his safe escape, he would dedicate one of my jewels to her shrine. The one he was holding in his hands, that he had raised over his head in supplication. My pearl necklace with an emerald pendant hanging at the center."

Her husband's prayer pierced her like an arrow. She wanted to collapse right there and then, but she held herself together and backed out of the room silently instead.

Her husband wanted to kill her, she recited to herself. He wanted the jewels and he wanted her dead. And after everything she had done for him, after saving him from the executioner and giving him all of herself! After lying with him in their bed. He was prepared to kill her, to take her jewels, to run from the life she had offered on a silver platter. He was going to destroy it all. He wanted her dead.

Vimala was sitting perfectly still. Listening intently to a story she could never have imagined was Bhadda's heritage.

"I don't know how I did it, but I didn't say a word. For days, I pretended like there was nothing wrong. I was as loving and dutiful as ever, performing my wifely tasks, smiling on command, acting my part as innocently as I could make myself seem. But inside, I was a roiling mess. I was terrified and heartbroken and furious all at once. What had begun as a moment of incredulity had morphed into thirty-six million other things. My husband was going to kill me after all I had done for him. It was a truth I did not know how to understand.

"And then one morning, my husband woke me up gently, and with his most tender-loving voice, he suggested we make a pilgrimage to the Mountain Goddess to thank her for his reprieve. I knew that the moment had come.

"I don't know how he didn't see the truth on my face, but he was probably so focused on his own worries, he never bothered to consider mine. When I agreed to join him on the pilgrimage, he jumped with enthusiasm. He kissed my forehead and then got up to leave. But just before he was out the door, he turned around and, as though it was a last-minute thought, said, 'Wear your nicest jewels, my darling. Wear all of them if you can. We must be at our best.'"

He really *was* preparing to kill her, she realized again. He wanted her jewels and he did not want her, and he would spill her blood to get them. She had married a monster.

Bhadda Kundalakesa watched the door close. Her body was trembling, but she refused to give in. She calmed herself down, got out of bed, and got dressed. She put on her most beautiful silk outfit. She added as many jewels as she could fit. Rings on every finger, bangles up to her elbows, a ruby nose ring and layers of pendants around her neck. She topped it off with her pearl necklace, the one she had seen him holding in his hands with the emerald pendant. Everything just as she knew it should be.

Then she stepped out to greet her criminal husband.

And he smiled.

And stupidly, just for a moment, she melted.

They took her father's palanquin as far as the road permitted and then walked the rest of the way. They hiked uphill. Her jewels jangled. Her sandals chimed, but husband and wife did not speak a word to each other, the silence muffling them both like a heavy blanket.

The trail got steeper and she felt increasingly uncomfortable in her clothes. The silk did not breathe the way cotton would have. The jewels were sticking to her skin. But she kept going, wiping her forehead with her headscarf over and over again.

They met an old man by the side of the road selling coconuts. It meant that they were getting close. Coconuts were used as offerings for the Mountain Goddess. Someone once told her that the coconut was a replacement for a severed head. Every Mountain Goddess required a sacrifice. Mountain deities feasted on blood.

"Husband, dear," she said in her most pleasing voice, "can we buy a coconut?"

"Of course," he replied with a charming smile.

Bhadda Kundalakesa held the fruit tight against her chest as they climbed the last bit of trail. When they reached the top, the temple was waiting for them. She had not visited it since she was a child and had forgotten how lovely it was. She stopped in front of the entrance and bowed.

The temple was surrounded by natural springs—one of the many reasons the site had been identified as home to the gods. A series of bronze spouts poured the spring water out into individual streams. Bhadda walked along the path of streams with her hand held out, feeling the sacred water gush out of each spout, one at a time. She counted them.

One hundred and eight.

Her husband stood back and watched her circumambulate the sacred waters, but eventually he grew impatient.

"Let's go look at the view," he suggested.

She bristled at the sound of his voice. Her back was still turned. She was facing the waterspouts. She could feel the moment getting closer.

She turned to look at him. She looked straight into his eyes.

"First I must make the offering."

She returned to the temple entrance. Stood alone in front of the deity. The Mountain Goddess was dancing naked on a lotus flower. Almost mocking her with her uninhibited power. Bhadda Kundalakesa closed her eyes. "Please, Shaktidevi," she whispered with the coconut raised over her head, "stay with me."

The coconut was the symbol of human sacrifice. The replacement for her own human head.

She smashed the coconut as hard as she could on the stone floor at her feet. The coconut cracked in two, its juices gushing. The sacrifice was a success.

Her husband was waiting for her on the precipice. Apparently to show her the view. She approached, time moving slowly. Her heart beating so loud, she was certain he could hear it. Husband and wife were completely alone, isolated on a mountaintop. Instinctively, she knew he was on the verge of killing her with his bare hands. Instinctively, she knew she was on the verge of killing him too.

"We are here to thank the Goddess for your reprieve," she said as she approached. "Please, husband, allow me to circumambulate you. It is my responsibility as your devoted wife."

He was surprised, but he consented. It was her role to worship him by paying him the appropriate sign of respect. She lowered herself to the ground to touch his feet with her head, her jewels glistening in the fiery sun. She then got up and began the slow walk around him, with her head still bowed and her hands folded in reverence.

When she was squarely behind him, she whispered one last prayer to the Goddess . . . and then Bhadda Kundalakesa shoved her husband right off the cliff. She tore off her pearl necklace—the one with the emerald pendant—and sent it trailing after him. It was his if he wanted it.

And then she ran.

Vimala stared at Bhadda for a long time. Never had she imagined that this was the story Bhadda was carrying. Fierce, stalwart, powerful Bhadda Kundalakesa.

"When we first met on the road a few weeks ago," Bhadda said, "I asked you what you were ashamed of, what was holding you back. I asked you if you were a criminal and you took offense. Do you remember?"

Vimala nodded.

"You never imagined that the person you were speaking to *was* a criminal, did you?"

"But you *aren't* a criminal, Bhadda. You were protecting yourself . . ."

"Don't try to conceal my life from me. You know as well as I do that when a woman kills her husband, no matter what the circumstances, the law condemns her."

Vimala knew this to be true. She wanted the truth to be otherwise, but she could not look Bhadda in the face and lie. It would have made no difference even if she did.

"I am a criminal, Vimala. I have been wandering and homeless ever since."

17

Muttering and Mad

The city was quiet, with most of the residents still asleep. But the Gathering Women were moving. They had woken up early and were finally on their way. They were stepping out of Ambapali's courtyard, walking to the forest beyond the city gates where the Buddha was residing. He would be surrounded by his male monastics. Vimala wondered if he knew that the women were on their way.

Many of them now had shaved heads. When the Gathering had started, only a few had cut their hair—presumably following Gotami after she had cut her own. Most of the women then still looked the way they had before. They wore the clothing they had left home with and their hair was still plaited down their backs. They had walked in the bright colors of domestic compliance, looking like they had stepped out of the house just for a moment and promised to be back soon. But as Vimala looked around now, she found most women had shaved their heads. She remembered Mutta having her hair shorn in the courtyard the night before by the woman with blue-black skin. Vimala tugged at her own hair self-consciously.

The women of the Gathering were all so different, despite their growing similarities. Some of the women were there as practiced renunciants—Bhadda Kundalakesa more than anyone else. She had not shaved her head that morning for the first time. She had started the routine many years earlier. She had joined the Gathering Women in the hopes of finding a new meaning to the baldness of her head. Other women had stumbled upon the Gathering almost accidentally. Ready to toss their realities to the side the moment the opportunity presented itself. Vimala was obviously one of those. She had used the Gathering as a means of escape rather than a path toward anything else. And Patachara had stumbled right into their hands, disoriented by loss, drowning in suffering. She followed because they suggested she should. There was certainly no plan in her case. She just moved forward with them because she did not know where else to go.

But then there were others. One old woman named Chanda had called out to them as they passed her sitting by the side of the road. "Please, Sisters, tell me where you are going," she had pleaded with arms outstretched. She was dirty and destitute and covered with flies. Most of the women ignored her, but Patachara stopped and asked what was wrong. "I have lost everything, Sister. My family was taken by sickness. I have nothing left. I am a childless widow, hungry and alone."

Patachara could have ignored her. She could have just erased her from view. But unlike almost everyone else, Patachara refused to pretend not to see. She squatted on the ground and listened to what the old woman had to say. "I am reduced to begging now," the old woman explained. "But even that does not work most of the time. No one wants to see me. No one wants so much bad luck crossing their path." In rural settings, widows were as dangerous as black cats.

"Come with us, Sister," Patachara eventually offered. "We have food and community. You will not be invisible here." She helped the woman to her feet, took her earth-encrusted hands into her own and welcomed her in. Chanda joined the Gathering not because she was looking for teachings. She never pretended to have such high aspirations. She just wanted some company in old age. And some food if there was any to spare.

Sama joined the Gathering after watching her beloved burn to death. She arrived still smelling of smoke and with her hair singed all along the edges. Sama was Queen Samavati's confidante. She was also her friend *and* her lover (when no one was looking). She took care of the queen, doted on her, loved her more than anyone else ever had. But King Udena's court festered with jealousy. He had multiple wives (as kings often did) and he played them against each other, creating competition where collaboration should have been.

One of his wives eventually took matters into her own hands. She set Queen Samavati's house on fire while the queen was still inside, because she wanted the king all to herself. Sama was forced by the flames to stay outside and watch. She could hear the queen screaming but there was nothing she could do. The building crashed down onto itself and took the beautiful Samavati with it. Sama was never the same after that. She was found wandering in the woods with her heart broken when women from the Gathering found her. They opened their arms and welcomed her in.

The Gathering was becoming an extraordinary situation. Never before had so many women from so many different backgrounds come together in that way. In another lifetime, most of these women would never have even met. They would never have been given (or received) the time of day from each other. Princesses did not walk with beggars. Nigantha renunciants did not travel with prostitutes. Wild women did not sit with queens. And yet here they all were, walking together, each with her own story and her own reasons. It was a gathering for the ages, a story that would be told for generations in every possible way.

What most of these women had in common, Vimala was beginning to realize, was that they all seemed to come from a story of pain. Hearing Bhadda Kundalakesa's story the night before had awakened her to this fact all over again. It was, of course, not surprising, but it was worth taking a moment to recognize. After all, what would be the point of all of them leaving home otherwise? What would have been the point of her own escape? If the brothel had been heaven on earth, then surely she would have stayed? If she could have found a place for herself, if she could have forgotten the disorientation that constantly tugged at her heart from beneath the grimy surface of her life, perhaps Kumari's could have been enough? Perhaps then, she would have felt some sense of belonging, some sense of home. She would not have looked elsewhere if she had belonged where she was.

Vimala glanced at Patachara, who was walking quietly beside her. Her suffering was not even a question. She had lost both her children before she could even say goodbye. Lost her husband and her parents too, all in the same day. How does someone come back from that? How does someone move forward when they've lost so much? Vimala shook her head. This was a Gathering of women who understood broken promises. Who knew that no matter how hard one might try, no matter how many assurances one might make or believe in, the world would eventually disappoint them. Even worse, it would break their hearts. For most of them, it already had.

There was one woman, though, who defied all of these generalities. She had appeared partway through the journey to Vesali and had been walking with them ever since. Try as she might, Vimala simply could not make any sense of her.

"Good morning," the woman chirped with every sunrise.

Vimala would look up to find her grinning exuberantly.

"Beautiful day, isn't it?"

And then she would bounce off before Vimala had a chance to reply.

Vimala had been accosted by her that very morning. "Who *is* that woman?" she had asked Bhadda Kundalakesa as she rubbed the sleep from her eyes.

"Infuriating, isn't she?"

Vimala spotted her in the crowd as they walked. She was chatting enthusiastically with Neelima, a bit further ahead.

"Do you know anything about her?" Vimala asked.

"Only a bit. Her name is Bhadda Kapilani," she answered. "She comes from Savatthi."

Vimala cocked her head to the side.

"Her name's Bhadda? But that's *your* name . . ."

"Obviously."

"Another reason not to like her. She stole your name."

Bhadda was about to reprimand Vimala for her pettiness, but her smile betrayed her. *Indeed*, she thought to herself. Bhadda was *her* name.

"So, what's her story?" Vimala asked as she adjusted her shoulder bag back into position. It had a way of slipping down her arm, no matter how high she placed it against her collarbone. She wondered if she was crooked.

"Apparently, she left home with her husband. They became renunciants together. He went searching for the Buddha in one direction, and she went the other hoping to find female company, but they took the decision to renounce together. As a couple."

Vimala was used to hearing unusual backstories by then, but this story caught her off guard.

"I don't believe it."

"What do you mean? What's not to believe?"

"What's not to . . ." she stammered. "Everything!"

"Vimala, you will have to do better than that."

Vimala scratched her head as she looked at the Gathering, at the women they were surrounded by. "I don't believe it because husbands don't go off into the sunset with their wives. Husbands leave their wives behind. Your story makes no sense."

"What makes you say that?"

"Are you serious? Look around you?" Vimala demanded with sudden ferocity. "How many women are here with their husband's blessing? Really, how many? How many happy families have you seen here waving goodbye? Women don't get to leave home that way. Women have to run and hide. Look at Crazy Sama over there, still smelling of charred flesh. She watched her lover burn to death! Women don't get permission to live as they want. They have to wiggle and squirm and fight just to get past the front door. And you're telling me that *that* woman left together *with* her husband? Your story makes no sense."

Bhadda stared at her friend. Wondered what had gotten into her so suddenly.

"Not all men are so bad . . ."

"Bhadda, your husband tried to kill you, for goodness' sake. You can't seriously be arguing with me on this."

Bhadda stopped walking and rubbed her face with both her hands. Then she rubbed her bald head. For a moment, she wondered if she had made a mistake telling Vimala her story.

"What's this about, Vimala?"

Vimala closed her internal door. Slammed it shut and looked away.

"Who hurt you?" Bhadda asked quietly.

The door flew back open.

"Bhadda, I was a common whore for most of my life. Almost *everyone* I met hurt me. I have been abused in so many ways, so many times, by men who paid Kumari for the pleasure of it. By others who didn't even try to pay. Are you really asking me that question?"

For the first time in recent memory, Bhadda Kundalakesa stood down.

"No, of course not, Vimala."

Vimala watched her giant of a friend shrink at her own monstrous feet.

What am I doing here? Vimala wondered again.

She was feeling haunted by memories that pressed against her more with each passing day. Feelings and thoughts swirled around in her mind. Memories long repressed were now crashing into her, forcing themselves in. Memories of the many men who had taken their turn as she lay on her dirty mattress, staring at the mildew in the ceiling. Their smells, the way they moved, the demands they made without asking permission. She remembered the one who called out to his mother; another who covered her face with a pillow while he thrust. She remembered the last one who bit into her thigh.

She watched the parade of memories march on. Tried calculating the number of clients. The number of years. The fact of time passing without her being there at all. Sometimes clients were gentle. Every once in a while, they wanted to know her name. But for the most part, she was there to provide a service. It lasted a few minutes and it was done. She was irrelevant. As irrelevant as anyone could ever be.

Sometimes, though, it was different. She had to concede that much. Sometimes the clients were kind. It wasn't all bad. But it wasn't much good either. It was a life wasted. She was supposed to have been a courtesan. It was so difficult to let that fact go.

She remembered one young client who had come to the brothel in anticipation of his wedding night. He wanted to learn how things were done. The first time he visited, he was abrupt and awkward. He barely lasted a few minutes. He was in and it was over. He stumbled out of the room looking devastated and overwhelmed. But then he returned the following evening. Most men were desperate to assert their dominance, but this one stood at her door with a pleading look. "It went too fast yesterday," he said by way of explanation. She propped herself up on her elbow and stared at him.

"Pay first," was her reply.

He tried to move more slowly the second time around, but he could not resist. It was over before he could even register the fact, betrayed by the enthusiasm he was trying so hard to restrain. He bit into the pillow with frustration. "Can I try again?" he asked once he recovered from the shock, and for the first time in as long as she could remember, Vimala laughed. She looked at the pile of coins beside her.

"I know. Pay first."

His sweetness cut into her. More than almost any other. She never knew his name, but she carried the memory of him, like a puppy she wrapped her arms around. He stopped visiting after the wedding. His attention was redirected. He had moved on. She, however, had remained right where she was. As irrelevant as she had always been. A dust-heap in the corner of a hollowed-out mess, just as broken as the home she had left behind.

The forest thickened.

The path they were following eventually became so narrow, they had to file through one at a time. Bhadda Kundalekesa stepped in behind her. A fidgety woman in battered silk robes was walking ahead. Vimala did not recognize her immediately, but when the woman wheeled around at the sound of a snapped twig, Vimala knew who she was. She had walked with them from Kapilavatthu, flitting in and out of view, but had disappeared when they had reached Ambapali's. Her name was Kisa Gotami. She carried a dead baby in her arms.

Vimala remembered the first time she had noticed her. It was at the start of the journey. Kisa Gotami was muttering to herself, clutching what seemed like a package close to her heart. She bumped into Neelima and almost sent her flying. And then Neelima was the one helping *her*. Neelima, who seemed to be one hundred years old, brittle, and ancient, and small. She was concerned about *her* instead of the other way around. Neelima held out her hand and Kisa Gotami took it.

At first, Kisa Gotami was an anomaly. An unsettling mystery. Her tattered silk threads trailed behind her, gathering up leaves and dirt and mud. She spoke to no one, frightened almost everyone, her madness a sign of danger. But Kisa Gotami's story eventually threaded its way through the Gathering. No longer an object of horror, she became a precious heirloom that everyone learned how to hold dear. At first, she belonged to Neelima, but then she belonged to them all.

Kisa Gotami had once been a lively, precocious young woman. She had had friends and family and a belly full of laughter. She was poor, and unbearably skinny, so much so that her ribs poked through her clothes like embedded arrows and her legs looked like dried out bamboo sticks. But a man of nobility wanted her anyway. He decided to make her his bride. Kisa Gotami circled the sacrificial fire, confirmed the marital contract, and was taken to a new land far from everything she had ever known. She was given shimmery silks and glittery jewels. She no longer worked the fields. Someone else washed the laundry.

Her friends forgot about her and her family let her go. She turned her attention to her husband and tried to find happiness as his wife. But when the first slap came flying, she knew she had misunderstood. "Who do you think you are?" he had bellowed. The lavish promises he had made, the attention he had showered her with . . . it had all been a farce. He was a *rakshasa* in human form. A devil who knew no kindness, who beat her until he removed her kindness too. She tried to please him, tried to do everything she was taught wives should do, but it was all in vain.

"The food is too cold."

She adjusted.

"The food is too hot."

The next day it was too spicy and she was trying to kill him. After that, it was too bland and she was putting him to sleep.

"It's because you're so ugly," was what he always said.

He took what he needed from her and ignored her for the rest.

But when she became pregnant, something changed. He still stared at her with disdain, but he would not raise a hand against her. Every once in a while, he even seemed to dote on her. Once, he brought her a bundle of fresh bananas. Apparently, he had negotiated the price himself at the market (instead of sending servants). It was the only food she craved, the only food that did not make her sick.

She was elated. The bananas proved that he was sorry. He was not the brute of yesterday, but a husband who was trying to do what was right. She clung to those bananas like they were her salvation, convincing herself that the past was gone for good.

When the birth pangs announced themselves, she was terrified, but also excited. It was the moment she had been waiting for. The doorway to a happier life. Her husband called for the midwife, raced around the house with flustered impatience, yelled at everyone for not doing enough. She interpreted this as an expression of his love. She smiled benevolently as she listened to his anger on the other side of the door.

She delivered a boy and her delight multiplied. She had done it! Produced a male heir, provided her husband with a lineage, made a place for herself in the ancestral skies. Nothing could go wrong now. He would be happy with her forever. He came into the room and looked at the little bundle with pleasure. He even gave her a peck on the cheek.

But a few days later, she woke to find that her perfect son was dead. At first, she thought he was asleep and she tried to soothe him awake. "*Lu lu lu,*" she cooed. "Time to wake up, my sweet one." She kissed his face, nudged his little body gently with her hand.

But the infant did not move.

She nudged harder.

Still nothing.

And then she cried out, the sound of an animal caught in a vicious trap. She screamed and screamed, shaking him with desperation, trying to force him back to life. But it was of no use. Her son was deathly still. Her son would not respond.

The door flew open. Her husband took one look at the scene before him and walked out.

"The baby is dead. Get rid of it," she heard him say from the other side.

Her screaming instantly stopped. *What did he just say? Get rid of it?*

The world stopped spinning as Kisa Gotami stared at the door that he had shut behind him. *He is going to take my baby.* Toss him into the river like unwanted refuse or bury him in mud. She looked down at her son who had never even been blessed with a name and brought him to her leaking breasts.

And then a maddening rage whirled up inside her.

"He will not touch my baby," she seethed. "This is *my* baby."

She got up, threw on some clothes, wrapped her dead baby in a cloth, and slipped out of the house unseen. She would never go back to that house. Not ever. Their story was done.

She was the one walking directly in front of Vimala in the forest. She still clung to her dead baby, her insanity deepening with time, the smell of the child corpse getting worse. But no one tried to pry the corpse away from her. Something inside Kisa Gotami had snapped. Vimala wondered if anyone would ever be able to help her set things right. Either way, Kisa Gotami had been granted a place among the Gathering Women.

Muttering, mad, and yet somehow found.

18

Motherhood Lost and Found

The Gathering Women had gotten quieter as they neared their destination. The familiar chatter faded. The only sound left was of bare feet on dry grass. Nothing but crackles and snaps and fluttering heartbeats. Vimala tried to welcome the quiet, but she struggled. She felt fidgety. She kept readjusting her shoulder bag, moving the strap up and down the edge of her clavicle, looking for that sweet spot that would hold it in place, but never quite finding it. She scratched her hair, rubbed her arms, swatted flies. A black crow soared overhead and screeched.

"What was that?" she heard a startled voice behind her.

"A bad omen . . ." answered another.

The Gathering Women were uneasy. What had begun as an inspired revolution seemed to have morphed into frightened insecurity. They had all been so eager and sure of themselves at first. Women had poured into the Gathering from near and far, challenging their families, their owners, their own expectations of what life was supposed to be. They did not have to be shackled to a life of domestic drudgery. They did not have to accept the terms of their servitude. The Gathering offered a way out and so many had run for their lives. They would do something different, toss their bangles to the wind, be something more than they ever imagined they could be before. They wanted out from wherever they came, but they were approaching a community that had already denied them entry. They were mad. Reckless even. They were riding a wave of hope, where thinking does not follow. They had the Queen of the Sakya Kingdom leading the charge, the one who went by the name Gotami. Maybe they had a right to hope with her at the helm?

But the closer they got to their destination, the more skittish they all became.

They were attempting the impossible. The Buddha had already said no.

Every time they debated the issue, Bhadda Kundalakesa trembled with fierce emotion.

"Why couldn't he have just said yes?" she demanded as she flung her frustrations into the wind. Bhadda Kundalakesa knew it was possible for women to become monastics. She was one herself. The Nigantha teacher had offered monasticism to her like a gift without strings. She did not have to fight for it. She did not have to beg. She needed salvation and her teacher had opened the doors. Women could become nuns. Men could accept it. She knew this to be true because she was living proof.

"Then why did you leave the Niganthas?" Vimala asked.

"Because their teachings were not enough for me."

She had loved the Niganthas. Had felt devotion and gratitude and respect. The head nun of the community, Candana, had become like a mother to her. She was the teacher's first female disciple and she led the women with clarity and dedication. "But no matter how much I practiced, I could not find what I was looking for. I watched Candana sit with tranquility and could not help but wonder at what she had found."

Bhadda Kundalakesa eventually made the decision to leave. She touched her teacher's feet, embraced Candana with gratitude, and walked away. "They saved me from myself, from the violence I was drowning in when I killed my husband. It is because of them that I did not sink. But I couldn't stay. I needed something else."

Bhadda wandered for a long time. Years and years. Listening to teachers, hearing what they had to say. The first teacher she encountered sat her down enthusiastically and explained his many truths. She nodded politely as he rained his wisdom over her head. But then she asked a question and the tone changed. He flustered, compensated, wrapped his answer up in a flurry of empty words. Her question had apparently caused offense.

She moved on to the next teacher. She listened and then asked again. One teacher after another, one teaching after another, all of them falling apart in her dextrous hands. None of the teachings were as solid as they pretended to be. Her questions, as sharp as arrows, reached the mark every single time. Eventually, she gained a reputation. No one wanted to argue with her. She had become too skilled at finding the cracks.

One day, she came across a large crowd. People listening to someone speaking further ahead. She approached slowly, catching a few words here and there. When she got to the front, she found herself listening to a follower of the Buddha. And the monk was brilliant. He had answers to every question. He never flustered no matter what she asked. It was the first time in years that she felt as though she had finally found what she was looking for. When he was done speaking, she asked for refuge.

"You must take refuge with my teacher," he had replied. "He is the Buddha. You must go see him."

She was on her way when she heard about the Gathering. She followed the rumors all the way to the palace gates. She found the Queen of the Sakya Kingdom standing before a sea of women, all of them prepared to make the same request.

"I never thought the Buddha would say no," she would say each time they discussed it. Bhadda Kundalakesa shook her head with frustration.

The Gathering Women stopped.

After days of repetition, after journeying through the forest, trudging along beaten paths, after discussions, debates, questions . . . their destination was suddenly right there in front of them.

There he was. The Buddha.

The one they had come all that way to see.

He was once the Prince of the Sakya Kingdom. The one who had tossed his royal jewels aside, who had abandoned his earthly obligations, who had renounced his treasures with barely a glance as though it was nothing more than a ball of spit, the one who had once been the husband of Princess Yasodhara, the father of Prince Rahula . . .

Him.

The one who had become the Buddha was sitting right there in front of her. Right there in front of all of them. He was sitting on the grass under a tree bursting with bright orange flowers like a flame.

The Buddha.

The world in all its glory felt as though it was suspended in stillness.

Rows of steady monks sat quietly facing him. A colony of breathing statues with their backs turned. The only sounds were of birds chirping and leaves rustling, but the monks themselves were still. Not a hand flicking or a body readjusting in its seat. Vimala had never felt such deepening quiet before. She lowered herself down into a crouch, unable to keep herself up so high.

Vimala could not sense the other women around her. She felt as though she was vanishing inside herself, her world narrowing, her mind becoming a thin tunnel. Everything was disappearing, every thought, hope, and fear. Every worry and distraction. Nothing was left but this sight of the men resting inside themselves, following the Teacher whose resting state made him look like he was on fire. She could not process what she was seeing, could not understand what any of it could possibly mean or why it was affecting her so much. All she knew was that she could not remain upright, that she had to lower herself down or she would fall.

The Buddha seemed to flicker under the tree with orange flowers, like a flame dancing. He seemed to be there, and yet he also did not seem to be there at all. *What was she seeing?*

And then, without warning or explanation, the flame was gone.

He was sitting on the grass. An ordinary man. Almost unremarkable.

She pulled her eyes away from him and let them glide over the others instead. The monks sat in their organized rows, like a body of repetitive sameness. But then she looked more carefully and began to notice small differences. Some of the monks had freshly shaved heads, but others had a bit of new growth. Others still were not shaved at all, but had long matted locks that flowed down their backs.

Even their robes were varied, she noticed now, with some wearing yellow, others wearing brown, many in random shades of orange. The more she looked, the more variety she saw. A few of the monks in the back row were falling over into sleep, while the ones up front were sitting with backs straight and shoulders pulled back. She even spotted a child in there. He kept fidgeting, readjusting his seat, pulling at his robes and rearranging them over his knees.

Peak Hall, the Buddha's monastic residence, rose out of the forest behind them. It was a magnificent white jewel of architecture. The lower level gave way to an open courtyard, with rows of columns that held up the second storey above. Vimala recognized the meticulous Vesali workmanship, the latticed carvings framing the upper storey windows, the soft curvature of the walls, the delicate marble stones that paved the courtyard floor.

Vimala let herself sink into the earth. She had been crouching, but she felt knots she didn't even know she had coming undone. She did not feel like holding herself in position any longer. She settled into the soft grass, dropped her shoulder bag, leaned against a tree behind her. She closed her eyes and let her head fall back and breathed in the early morning air. She wondered, for the hundred and eighth time, what she was doing there. Was she going to join these women and shave her head? Maybe it was inevitable? After all, where else did she have to go?

But was she really prepared for such a life?

She shook her head, as though trying to rid herself of the question. It was irrelevant, in any case, because the Buddha had already said no. She did not have to worry about it. They had followed him to Vesali to ask again, hoping that this time his answer would be different, but do Buddhas even change their minds? If he was as perfect as they said he was, he would just say no again. The Gathering Women would have no choice but to accept the verdict and move on. She could live peacefully among them, wherever they went, with Gotami as their teacher. Vimala could do that. Join a band of free women, far out of reach of the world of men. Vimala was convinced that this was how the story would go.

Vimala eventually opened her eyes and looked around. The women had moved up ahead. They had placed themselves behind the monks and were bowing quietly, offering reverence. Some of the women were kneeling with their foreheads to the ground, while others were fully prostrate on the earth, their entire bodies laid out with humility and salutation. Bhadda Kundalakesa was beside Gotami and Yasodhara, the three of them standing with their palms pressed together, tears running down their faces. Patachara was rocking on her heels with her arms wrapped around herself, as though trying to keep her loose ends from coming apart.

Someone struck a metal bell and the monastic stillness instantly dissolved. The monks rose out of their seats in a flurry of activity, the silent uniformity of a moment earlier now quickly forgotten. A few picked up brooms and got to work. Others made their way to the river that gurgled to the side of the building. One group fell into play and began tossing sticks around like village boys.

The Buddha, however, did not move. He was exactly where he had been earlier. He had not fidgeted or readjusted or even swatted a fly. Vimala thought she saw a flicker of light moving through him again, but she was not sure.

The child monk was still there too. His back was to Vimala, so she could not see his face, but she was pretty certain he was not meditating. From where she was, he looked like he was concentrating on the dust at his feet, but then he pounced forward with cupped hands, as though trying to catch something.

Vimala laughed.

The child monk was living in his own world, carried off by his own imagination, catching dragonflies or chasing a cricket. Or maybe following an invisible friend who was trying to get away. Whatever it was, the boy was oblivious to his surroundings. She remembered how often she had done the same, disappearing inside herself for hours as she combed Assavata's mane. How many times would her mother have to call her name before she finally heard? How many lessons had she been late for because she was elsewhere in her fantasies, far, far away? She would barrel through the front door, her sandals forgotten in the field, her clothes splattered with mud. "You smell like a stableboy!" her mother would complain. "I don't know why we keep that horse around. It just distracts you from your studies," she would argue as she pushed Vimala into her room to get changed. Vimala would mumble half-hearted apologies as she cleaned herself up.

An older monk approached the child, urging him to get moving. He was wasting his time. There were things to do, the monk said as he clapped his hands for the child to hurry. Vimala watched as the little one pounced a few more times in the hopes of catching whatever it was that was evading him, but he eventually resigned himself to let it go. He scrambled to his feet and rubbed his face with what were probably very dirty hands. "I'm coming," he answered. He looked down at his robe—a long piece of cloth that was wrapped around his torso—and decided it required adjustment. He unwrapped one side and tried to toss it over his other shoulder with a dramatic wave of his hand, but the cloth barely made it across. It just fell limply by his feet. He sighed, picked it up, and tugged it back into place with both hands. Clearly not the effect he was hoping for.

And then from somewhere nearby, Vimala heard a cry.

Vimala turned and saw Yasodhara on her knees, her face filled with unconcealed anguish.

And then the child monk was running. Tearing across the clearing towards Yasodhara with wild desperation. He ran and ran and then he was in her arms, sobbing like the child that he was, crying out with the pain that only the young are free to express, clutching at her neck, his face buried in her chest, holding on for dear life.

The Gathering Women stepped back. Bhadda Kundalakesa and Patachara were beside Vimala again, each one with hands on their own hearts as they watched a scene of intimate love.

"Who is that?" Vimala asked.

"Prince Rahula," Bhadda answered.

Vimala was confused a moment. *Who was Prince Rahula?*

And then she recalled a conversation half-finished from ages ago, when they had found the tribeswomen from Bharukacchaka. This was the child ascetic Bhadda had mentioned during their walk. This was Princess Yasodhara's son.

Everyone in Kapilavatthu knew Princess Yasodhara's story. The night she gave birth, the Crown Prince of Kapilavatthu—her husband—had run away. Galloped off into the sunset in search of answers he could not find at home.

Vimala could well imagine the humiliation Yasodhara felt the next morning when she learned the news. And the sadness too. Many people blamed her; others sympathized. But none of it mattered. Yasodhara was abandoned with a newborn while her husband set off on a great adventure.

Rumors circulated, each one describing another facet of the princess' experience. Some said she spent her days walking through the gardens listlessly, speaking to no one. Others, that she was hurling dishes against her bedroom door. For a while, they said that she refused to hold her son. Princess Yasodhara was like a ship lost at sea, battled by storms, barely keeping herself afloat. Like so many women before her, like so many afterwards, the familiar stages of grief unfurled, until her ship finally found its way. She learned to pick up her son, learned to hold him, let her heart open until she felt the cords of maternity bind them together tight. Eventually, she learned to accept

her new title too—the Widow Whose Husband Was Still Alive—
and donned a widow's garb. She closed her Royal Wardrobe, gave up
her silks and jewels, and grew accustomed to a life dressed in white.
She learned to walk past her husband's bedroom without yearning,
to eat her meals without staring at his empty seat. Princess Yasodhara
learned her new life well, became a loving mother, and let her living
husband go.

But then he returned without warning or permission. The sages
promised that he wouldn't. That an ascetic could not return for at
least twelve years, to ensure the cords of attachment were properly
severed. If an ascetic returned early, he risked undoing all the severing
he had worked so hard to achieve. He had to be certain he no longer
felt any attachment, that he no longer thought of his family as his
own. And yet, only eight years later, there he was, standing at the palace gates, the conquering hero. *She* was not ready for him, *her* cords
were not severed yet, but her state of mind was not the point.

Everyone raced to the courtyard to express their devotion, to hear
his teachings, to catch a moment of *darshan* with this extraordinary
man. But Yasodhara refused. She stood by the window and watched
the scene from a distance. If he wanted to see her, she decided, he
would have to come find her. She would not go to see him herself.

It was a scandal. Everyone whispered about her defiance. About her
arrogance, as she turned around and walked away. But Vimala understood this part of the story all too well. He had devastated her. It
did not matter that he was a Buddha. He was also a husband and a
father (or at least he used to be), and he had failed as both. He may
have conquered suffering as a Buddha, but as a man, he had broken
her heart.

The Buddha did precisely as Yasodhara had expected. He went
to see her, visited her in her chambers like the husband he used to
be. And then he hurt her all over again. He asked for their son. He
wanted to take him back to the forest with him. "It's his inheritance,"
he explained, as though it was the most reasonable idea in the world.

Vimala shook her head as she thought about all these shapes of
loss. Yasodhara had stood at the helm of the Gathering, guiding the
women and supporting them, attending to them and ensuring everyone was safe. She had obviously scaled mountains of suffering and
she had somehow managed to reach the other side. Vimala watched
Yasodhara rocking her beloved son in her arms and realized again that

it was just as Bhadda had said on that first day when they met: the details might be different, but their stories were all the same.

The Gathering Women had formed a circle around Yasodhara and her son. A ring of silent support. The ache of the moment was familiar to everyone there. Yasodhara rocked her son in her arms and Rahula kept his eyes squeezed shut, as though he feared that if he opened them, he would wake from a dream. The Queen of Sakya stood over them both. The queen was Rahula's grandmother. She had lost her grandson too.

Vimala watched the scene quietly. But then a thought struck her so hard, she almost fell.

Gotami was the Buddha's mother.

It was so obvious, but she had not seen it until just that moment. Everyone in the Gathering knew. Queen Maya had birthed him, but Gotami was the one to have raised him as her own. The Buddha was Gotami's son.

And yet, until that moment, Vimala had not given this fact any consideration. Vimala looked over to where the Buddha had been sitting. Gotami had seen him right there in front of her, only moments earlier. Neither of them had run into each other's arms. Neither had even made a move of recognition. Gotami bowed to her son from afar with tears streaming from her eyes.

Vimala had initially assumed that Gotami's tears were tears of relief. Perhaps of devotion too. *But he was her son . . .* Maybe the tears were about lost love too? The possibility rolled over her with the crushing weight of an elephant. She felt the air pushed right out of her lungs.

Who was who in this story? she suddenly demanded. What were all these layers she felt herself embroiled in that she had not recognized before? Gotami had walked all this way to ask the Teacher for permission to join the community. But what if there was more to her request?

And what about Yasodhara, her second-in-command? The Buddha was her husband. Rahula was her son. *What were they all doing here? Why had they come?* For the first time since the journey began, Vimala doubted the seriousness with which renunciation was being claimed. Vimala looked over at Yasodhara and Rahula, still wrapped in each other's arms, and felt devastatingly insecure. How could she not have asked herself these questions earlier? How could she have been so blind? How many other mothers of sons was she surrounded by? How many other secret stories were there to tell?

Yasodhara was kissing Rahula's face, smothering her child with adoration. It was suddenly all so very obvious. She could not believe she had not wondered at any of it before.

And yet . . . if she was right . . .

Could she blame them? How many others were here with similarly layered aspirations? Why was *she* even here? Why was any of them?

The one thing Vimala knew for certain was that if she had had a family to reclaim, she would have moved heaven and earth to find them too. She would have created a Gathering herself and walked the length of Bharata just to catch a glimpse. She watched Yasodhara folding her son into herself and knew she would have been no different. Vimala laid her palm against her belly. If she had been allowed to keep any one of her pregnancies, Vimala would have done that and so much more.

She remembered the first time it had happened. It was not long after Kumari had purchased her. She woke one afternoon feeling flushed and feverish. A moment later, she was retching out her insides on the floor. Surasa was the first to look in.

"What's going on?" she asked as she watched Vimala spit out the remains of her vomit.

"I must have eaten something bad."

Surasa watched her skeptically but said nothing. When Vimala repeated the scene the following day, Surasa was the one to explain.

"You're pregnant."

Words Vimala was not prepared to hear.

Kumari stormed in not long thereafter, the scent of stale jasmine trailing behind. Vimala retched again, then fell back onto her thin straw mattress.

"How could you be so stupid?" was all Kumari had to say.

That was the first time. It happened a second and then a third. The healer would arrive with a strong brew of fennel infusion. Some wild carrot and a few other concoctions too. None of it smelled good, all of it bitter, searing down her throat unwanted. And then came the cramps, and her body was expelling what little bit of life she had inside her like dirt.

It had happened so often in their brothel, no one bothered to think about it. An occupational hazard for almost everyone but Surasa. At least Surasa was spared of that. Vimala tried to feign disinterest, pretend it did not matter, but each time she emptied her womb, she knew she was lying to herself. A piece of her was dead.

Vimala watched the family reunion with an ache of desolation. If she had been allowed a daughter—if she had been allowed just one—what would she not have done to keep her safe? She would have been a good mother, she would have followed in her own mother's footsteps, transferred the wisdom that had been transferred to her. She would have run away right at the start and built a life that could have made sense for them both. She could see it all in her mind's eye, the life that could have been. Vimala looked at the Gathering Women, the women who were watching the scene just as she was, and recognized the unspoken understanding between them all.

But then Vimala saw someone else.

She saw someone standing there who challenged every thought she had just had, every assumption she had just made about women and motherhood and loss. Standing at the far end of the Gathering, Vimala saw Vaddhamata in the circle of women. The mother of young Vaddha, the tribeswoman who wore a red beaded dress. They had met her on the road ages ago, when they had lost their way. She remembered the taste of that fresh crisp water drawn right out of the well. What was Vaddhamata doing here? She had a clan and a family and a son somewhere else.

But then Vimala recalled that far-away look Vaddhamata had had as she listened to the story of the Gathering Women. Her dedicated attention to every detail, her astonishment when she learned that all were welcome, that the Royal Women did not discriminate. And now here she was, still wearing her red beaded dress, but her head was bare. No heavy embroidered headscarf and no hair.

Vimala walked over to Vaddhamata and tapped her on the shoulder.

"Do you remember me?"

Vaddhamata took a moment to register her presence, and then her face opened with a wide smile.

"Of course!" she replied. "I'm so glad to see you!"

"What are you doing here?" Vimala asked. "Don't you have a son?"

It was more than impolite, but Vimala could not help herself. Vaddhamata looked startled for only a moment, but then her face softened. Vimala's anguish was written all over her face.

"You are my sister from another life," she began with her lilting accent as she took Vimala's hands into her own, "so I will answer your question as only a sister can. I do have a son. My beautiful Vaddha, whom you met, but I have left him."

Vimala reeled.

"You left him? But why?"

Vaddhamata did not even bristle.

"It was not an easy decision, that much I can tell you. But it was a question I'd been wrestling with for years. I just never saw a way out. Until, that is, I met the three of you. You changed my life."

"What do you mean?"

The tribeswoman in the red dress took a moment to think through her response.

"The thing is," she began, "I could never see myself married with children. My friends and cousins all used to dream of the day they would have a home of their own. It was all anyone talked about when we were kids, but I could never see it when I closed my eyes.

"On my wedding day, I cried but it was not because I was sad to leave home. My tears were not tears of joy either. I cried because I had never felt more alone in my life. I was agreeing to something that I didn't want, but I could see no alternative. What girl feels that way on her wedding day? I was sure something was wrong with me. It was supposed to be the happiest day of my life.

"What I wanted, what I secretly *always* wanted, was a life of contemplation. I imagined myself walking barefoot in the Himalayas, making a small home for myself in an isolated mountain cave. That's what I wanted, but how does a girl admit to wanting something like that when she lives in a small tribe by the sea? Girls are not supposed to want such things. Girls don't even *do* such things. We are supposed to want family, to pray for husbands, to become the mother of a hundred healthy sons."

"But . . . what about your son?"

"I love my son. Please don't misunderstand me. I love my family and my clan. I love them all, but I am not meant for that life. I never was. When I met the three of you, everything changed. You showed me that renunciation *was* possible, even for women. And once one sees a possibility like that, one can never un-see it. So, I gave my son to the elders and kissed him goodbye. He will have a good life and he will be well cared for, but my role is not to be his mother. It never was. My role is to be someone else."

Vimala staggered under the weight of Vaddhamata's honesty. Women were *supposed* to want motherhood. They were *supposed* to take delight in growing bellies and little newborn cries. They were supposed to want husbands. Courtesans were supposed to want patrons. Women were supposed to want men. And yet standing before her, without a shred of apology or a hint of shame, was a woman who wanted something else.

Vimala's mind reeled with the implications. Vaddhamata did not want to be a mother, even though she loved her child. Yasodhara had let her child go, and yet she was holding him right there in her arms. Gotami had watched her son become the Buddha and flicker like a flame. Kisa Gotami held her dead baby in her arms. How many versions of womanhood could there possibly be? What other kinds of desire might women have if given the liberty to try? Vimala thought of Sama, Queen Samavati's lover, who went mad when Samavati died. What was all this complexity? Sama had never even pretended to love a man.

Bhadda Kundalakesa had said that the details might be different, but their stories were the same. And yet Vimala was beginning to realize that their stories were also *not* the same. Each woman in the Gathering had her own desires and needs and aspirations. Each one had arrived with her own hopes of what she might one day become. The Gathering Women were all so very different. What they shared was their understanding that life rarely gives us what we want. And that it was worth the risk to try for something more.

Vimala watched Yasodhara rocking her long-lost son.

"How are you, my sweet thing?" Yasodhara was asking. "Are you getting enough to eat?"

"I'm fine," he mumbled. He wiped his runny nose with the back of his hand.

"You've gotten so tall," she said with admiration. He just kept sniffling, seemingly overwhelmed at finally having his mother again.

A monk approached and interrupted the scene.

"Good morning, Madam," the monk said with a slight nod. "I am Mogallana, one of the senior teachers in this community."

His head was cleanly shaved and his robes were immaculate. His skin was the color of a dark storm-cloud. He stood before the Gathering Women with such elegant confidence, Vimala felt herself flush.

Yasodhara, however, merely nodded her head in return, but stayed where she was, on her knees beside her son.

"The Teacher will receive your community soon," he said, "but I must return the young master to Peak Hall. He has studies to attend to."

Yasodhara got off the ground and rose to her full height.

"I have not seen my son in many moons," she replied with imperial habit. "You can surely make an exception this one time."

"My sincere apologies, Madam, but it is not possible."

Yasodhara was on the verge of arguing, but Gotami stepped forward.

"Of course," Gotami replied. "We understand."

The monk named Mogallana nodded deferentially, but he did not bow, even though he was in the presence of royalty.

"Come," he said as he put his hand on the boy's shoulder. "It's time to go back."

19

Ananda

Peak Hall was immersed in contemplative quiet. It was his favorite time of day.

Ananda was in the kitchen, looking over the greens that had been laid out on the table, checking each stem. He opened the rice jar and sifted through some of the grains with his fingers. Picked up the bowl of clarified butter and inhaled its rich scent. Everything was where it was supposed to be. Soon, the metal bell would be struck and the kitchen would come to life. The morning meal would be whisked together with rapidly choreographed movements and delivered to the monks in the courtyard—one heaping of rice per bowl, one pile of steaming greens.

Ananda examined the milk he had simmering over the fire. This was not part of the community meal, but was something special he prepared for the Teacher himself. Every morning, he received fresh buffalo milk from a neighboring farm. He poured it into the pot over the fire and brought it to a slow boil, then added a slice of ginger, a piece of cinnamon bark, and a few cloves. Lately, he had taken to adding a scraping of nutmeg too. All of these items he kept tucked away in a pouch for safekeeping, his personal reserve for the Teacher's morning brew.

Ananda could never quite get used to the number of demands the Teacher was expected to meet. He had been raised around the Royal Family, so he was accustomed to seeing long lines of petitioners at the king's door, but the requests made of the Teacher were of a different caliber. People came at all hours requesting advice or hoping for blessings. Many asked for magical intervention. The sick begged for healing, the poor begged for food, kings asked for tactical counsel, and hermits crawled out of their caves just to see if he was real. There was no end to the requests, no limit to what people imagined the Buddha could do. He had to be everything to everyone, respond to every need. People asked and asked and asked, and the Buddha delivered. Because that is what buddhas do.

Ananda would never forget the day he joined the community. He had known the Buddha all his life. They were cousins and had grown up together, played together, argued, battled, wrestled, and talked. The Buddha was Siddhattha then, the Prince of the Sakya Kingdom. He was supposed to take the throne. Ananda had always felt a kind of inexplicable awe around Siddhattha, as though he knew that his cousin was someone special, and this not just because he had the Royal Turban wrapped around his head. Siddhattha carried himself differently from the others, kept his eyes focused elsewhere, as though he was looking at something the rest of them could not see. When Ananda woke to the news that Siddhattha had fled, charging out of the palace gates, Ananda tried desperately hard not to cry. He tried to convince himself it was for the best. Everyone knew Siddhattha did not belong in the palace. Everyone had heard the prophecies announced at his birth and could see that the palace was not where the story would end. But try as he might, Ananda could not withhold his tears after the prince left. He wound up sobbing like a child. It was as though the sun had set on his life; darkness had descended. Who would guide him now that Siddhattha had gone?

But then Siddhattha came back. He returned to Kapilavatthu years after his departure, and he was as magnificent as the rumors said he would be. He was no longer his cousin, no longer the one Ananda could play, wrestle, and argue with. He had become the Buddha and he shone like the sun. Ananda rushed forward to greet him, lowered himself to the ground with flooding devotion, and then, before he even knew what he was saying, he made his own request. "Please, Teacher," Ananda begged, his whole body trembling with emotion, "take me with you to the forest. Let me shave my head." The Buddha nodded imperiously, still a king, but one who ruled over very different territory. He laid his hand on Ananda's shoulder and simply said, "come."

That was it. Ananda had permission to become a monk.

Ananda stirred the pot of spiced milk as he recalled that day. He would never forget the moment he felt the Teacher's hand on his shoulder, the weight of it, the paradoxical lightness at the same time. He was welcome to come forward, to leave the madness of the world behind. He would become a monk and practice until he became free.

Someone struck the bell, a signal that the morning sit was over. He could hear the almost instant commotion outside. Feet shuffling about, whispers growing louder, a few of the less seasoned monks were probably already play fighting even though they had been repeatedly instructed to carry themselves with more dignity. Ananda stirred the warm milk a few more times and then laid the wooden spoon down on the table. It was ready. He would bring it to the Teacher in the Perfumed Chamber, in a cup he kept reserved just for him.

"Did you see all those women out there?" he heard a member of the kitchen staff saying as two of them burst in. "What are they doing here?"

"Kind of rude of them to appear so early in the morning, don't you think? The least they could do is wait until after the meal," grumbled the other.

"Do you think they expect to eat here? We didn't pick enough greens this morning to feed them too," the first one said. "We'd have to go back to the garden and then the whole meal will be late."

"Or we serve everyone a bit less, which isn't great either."

The two of them had recently been appointed as kitchen staff, one of the highest honors a layperson could receive. Feeding a community required the highest level of care. One had to pick just enough vegetables. Not too little, or some would go hungry, and not too much or there would be waste. One had to remember those with ailments, and calculate the monks who might be away, always juggling changing numbers. Working in the kitchen required a kind of mindfulness few exhibited.

"What are the two of you jabbering about?" Ananda asked. "What women? Who's here?"

The two staff members jumped. They obviously had not realized he was standing right there.

"Apologies, Venerable Ananda," one muttered quickly. "We were talking about all the women outside. Didn't you see them?"

"There are loads of them," said the other. "And I heard that the Queen of Sakya is there among them. Did you know they were coming?"

Ananda's mind went temporarily blank. The Queen of Sakya was a title he had not heard referenced in a very long time. He scrambled internally to make sense of it all. Then he jumped at the realization.

"Don't let the milk boil over!" he called out as he rushed out the door.

The women were standing in the field in organized rows, right in front of Peak Hall. *Why have they been left unattended*, Ananda hollered to himself with a rush of concern. He hurried towards them, trying to hold his robe in place over his left shoulder, trying not to trip, trying not to run at the same time. He looked frantically for the queen as he stumbled forwards, scanning faces, most of whom he did not recognize. And then he let out a yelp of surprise. The Queen of Sakya was standing front row and center, but she did not have a hair left on her head.

"Your Highness!" he exclaimed as he neared her. He was on the verge of reaching out for her, but then drew back instantly. Before he became a monk, the Queen of Sakya had been his aunt. She was one of the most familiar and most beloved figures of his early life. When he was little, she would hold him in her arms.

But he was a monk now. She was no longer his aunt. Physical contact was not allowed.

Gotami, the Once Queen of Sakya, watched her nephew readjust his expectations with a knowing smile. She waited for him to compose himself. When she felt he was ready, she replied.

"How lovely to see you, Venerable Ananda."

Ananda smiled in return. How much he had missed her.

Right there beside her was Princess Yasodhara. She too had cut her hair. Childhood memories came flooding towards him, filling him with affection. How good it was to see them both.

"What brings you here, Your Highness?"

The one who was once a queen dabbed at the edges of her eyes, where tears had been falling.

"We have left home, my dear Ananda. We are here to ask the Teacher for ordination."

Ananda went temporarily blank again. He then shook his head, as though trying to get the pieces of his mind back into their rightful places.

"But . . . you already asked him for ordination in Banyan Grove," he mumbled. "I was there." The monks had all been there. "The Teacher said no."

Gotami did not hesitate. She stood in front of the young monk with her most regal demeanor.

"Venerable Ananda, he did not say no," she explained. "He suggested we not ask the question."

"But that's the same thing," he said, scratching his bald head.

"It is not the same thing," she replied.

Ananda cocked his head to the side, wondering what she could possibly have in mind. And then, ever so slowly, the subtlety of the situation began to register.

"Do you mean . . . ?"

"What I mean, is . . ." she continued for him, "he did not *actually* say no."

His face opened wide, like the dawn of a new day.

Ananda hurried away, the urgency of the matter now so obvious to him. He wanted to run, but he knew not to. Instead, he walked as quickly as monastic decorum permitted. He even stopped to direct the traffic of monks, ensuring everyone was where they should be, answering questions or providing the requested advice. Monastic life might be a contemplative experience for some people, but it had always been a full schedule of events for him.

He reached the courtyard that was bustling with early morning activity. Monks in a circle debating here, monks repairing a column there. A few monks were sweeping the floor, pushing the dust from one area to the other, creating swirls with every step. Ananda got through as efficiently as possible and then climbed the central staircase. He was going to make an appeal in the Perfumed Chamber, the Buddha's private residence. It was also the Meeting Hall and the Hall of Instruction. It was everything that was important and sacred at Peak Hall. It was the reason they were all there.

Ananda reached the top floor. He stopped before the doors of the Perfumed Chamber. He felt temporarily dwarfed. *How do I do this?* he wondered. How should he present the situation? And how might the Buddha respond? He wiped his brow repeatedly as he stared at the doors, trying to calm himself down. When he was ready, he took a deep breath and pushed one of the doors open. The Buddha was sitting in contemplation on a raised platform at the other end of the hall.

For a brief moment, Ananda marveled again at the room's majesty. The workmanship of this room was beyond compare. Ananda sometimes wondered if some of the visitors came not to see the Teacher, but to see his Perfumed Chamber. It had become the most famous hall in Vesali. He had heard people debate its history, many convinced that only Vissakamma, the architect of the Gods, could have been the one to build it.

The most arresting feature of the hall was its magnificent scent. He was never quite sure what the source of the scent was, but each time he entered, he found the experience almost intoxicating. At first, he thought it was from the flowers. Visitors brought flowers on a daily basis, filling the Perfumed Chamber in all directions. There were cut flowers in vases, flowering plants in pots, garlands of flowers tossed near the Teacher's feet. It could make your head spin, there was so much. Ananda often wondered if devotees thought it was their responsibility to keep the chamber perfumed with their gifts.

But with time, Ananda came to realize that the scent was not coming from the flowers. He was able to distinguish other, more subtle scents beneath the surface. A touch of sandalwood. Lingering camphor. Even a hint of cinnamon at times. These smells seemed to come right out of the walls, the floor, the ceiling, as though they were built into its foundation. Each time he was in the hall, Ananda would sniff discreetly in the hopes of locating the source, but he never quite figured it out. The Perfumed Chamber was a mystery, its scent reaching for him even in that moment, as he stood at the door, looking in.

Ananda pressed his palms together and lowered himself to the ground. He prostrated three times with his whole body. When he was done, he walked slowly to the front of the chamber where the Teacher sat in silent contemplation. His mind was racing, his worries pooling, but with each step, he worked to quiet the storm inside.

When he reached the front, Ananda bowed again. He could not help himself. He tended to the Buddha more than almost anyone else. He saw him multiple times a day, and yet still his devotion overwhelmed him. He could never bow often enough.

"What can I do for you, Ananda?" The Buddha asked as he opened his eyes.

Ananda moved to the Teacher's right side and sat down.

"My apologies for bothering you during your time of private contemplation," Ananda began.

The Buddha nodded.

"I hope you had a good sleep and that you are feeling healthy," he continued.

It was only then that Ananda realized that he had failed to bring the Teacher his morning cup of spiced milk! It was still sitting on the fire, possibly even burned at this point. He almost slapped his forehead. How could he have forgotten? Preparing the Teacher's morning brew was the reason he skipped the first meditation.

Ananda wanted to bolt out of the room and check on the drink he had left on the fire, but he knew he could not. He was so easily distracted! He made so many mistakes every single day. He was upset with himself.

But it was not the time for that. *You came here with an urgent issue,* he reminded himself. *Queen Gotami is waiting. All the women are.* He set his frustrations aside.

"I was hoping I might ask you a question," he said, also hoping the Buddha might not have noticed that he was without his morning brew.

The Buddha waited.

Ananda pressed on.

"A few weeks ago, we were in Banyan Grove when Mahapajapati Gotami came to see you. She asked if you would give women permission to join the order. You said that it was not a good idea for her to ask the question." Ananda paused. He wiped his sweating brow. "Have I recalled the event correctly?"

"You have, Ananda."

"I am relieved."

Ananda struggled more than most monks when it came to discipline. He was sometimes overwhelmed and he was so easily distracted (the morning milk was a case in point). But the Teacher was patient with him, reminded him regularly that he had faith in his abilities. He told him to ask as many questions as he needed to ask, until he was certain things were right.

"The thing is . . ." Ananda continued, as he rubbed his head, "Gotami is standing at the edge of the property with the women right now. She stands there in a dusty robe, with tears streaming down her face."

Ananda expected the Teacher to react to this news, but the Teacher remained as still as he was before. Not even a raised eyebrow.

"Is your answer the same as it was that day in Banyan Grove?"

The Buddha looked at his disciple quietly.

"My answer remains the same. It is not a good idea that they ask the question."

"Of course."

The answer had not changed.

Ananda looked up at the Buddha on his platform and noticed that the cloth he was sitting on had a slight tear at one of the corners. *I must get that fixed.*

Focus, he reprimanded himself.

Gotami said that he had not said no. *What does that mean?* He closed his eyes, almost squeezing them shut, as he tried to turn the situation around and look it at in a new way. Where was the opening?

And then . . .

"Bhante," he began again, "I have a second question."

The Buddha nodded.

"If women practice the discipline just as you have taught it, would they be able to achieve perfection of the mind? Just like men?"

The Buddha did not hesitate.

"Yes, Ananda. If women practice the discipline just as I have taught it, they will achieve perfection of the mind. Just like men."

"So, women have the same abilities as men when it comes to achieving awakening?"

The Buddha raised an eyebrow.

"I just want to be sure I understand, Bhante."

"Yes, Ananda," the Buddha replied. "Women have the same abilities and the same potential as men when it comes to achieving awakening. There is no difference."

Ananda wanted to jump up and cheer. If women were just as capable as men, then there could be no obstacle to their ordination. The Buddha could say, "come" to the women just as he said it to him when he himself was ordained. Simple as that. There was no difference.

"So then, why is it that Mahapajapati Gotami is waiting at the edge of the property for permission to join the order? If she can achieve awakening the same way a man can, if she has the ability and the potential, why is she denied the opportunity? She stands out there in her dusty robe and with a tear-stained face. She who took care of you, nursed you, raised you after your mother died . . ."

But before he could finish his sentence, he realized the mistake he had just made.

In a rush of emotion, he had just ruined everything. He could see it in the Teacher's face. He had broken the cardinal rule, invoking family bonds to the Buddha, when it was the Buddha who taught them to let those bonds go. Who taught them that family bonds, like all earthly bonds, cause suffering and that the path to freedom required that they leave all bonds behind. *How could he ask a question like that?*

Even worse, his question sounded more like an accusation than a question. He had just wagged his finger at the Teacher, asking him how he could leave Gotami waiting after all she had done for him. As though he owed her. *What have I done?*

"Ananda, you must be careful with your emotions," the Buddha instructed him.

Ananda dropped his head in shame.

"My apologies, Bhante. I meant no harm . . ."

"I know."

And then the Buddha did something that was strikingly out of character.

He sighed.

A deep sigh. As though the weight of the world was upon him.

"Ananda, you worry too much about others and then get caught up in your emotions. My debt to Gotami can never be repaid. She was my mother growing up and she took care of me. She loved me and nursed me and then she let me go. Such generosity cannot be bartered or measured or negotiated. It stands apart and must be respected as the gift that it was. I cannot give her ordination because she gave me the gift of motherhood. That's not how this works."

"But doesn't she deserve to have this request met?" Ananda asked, emotional despite himself.

"She deserves everything that I can give her. And she will rise to meet any challenge I present her with. She is more formidable than you realize, Ananda. But if I grant her this request, it will not go just to her. She stands at the clearing, speaking for all women. For the women behind her and for all the women that will come after her too. My debt to her is not what is at stake."

Ananda was devastated. He felt like he was lost inside a story that was so much bigger than he was capable of understanding.

"I know I'm not the sharpest monk in our community, Bhante. I wish I could see more clearly sometimes."

The Buddha smiled tenderly.

"Your sincerity makes up for whatever other faults you might have, Ananda."

Ananda lifted his head.

"Would you permit me one last question?"

"You are welcome to ask as many questions as you want."

Ananda bowed deeply again, his reverence palpable.

"Bhante, you have often said that you are not the first buddha in the cycle of our universe. That there have been countless buddhas that came before you and that there will be countless buddhas to come after. That every cycle in our mysterious universe reveals a new Teacher who teaches truth and sets the wheel in motion."

"You are correct."

"You have also said, Bhante, that there are many similarities between all of these buddhas. That they all have similar life stories and that they all teach the same truth, because the truth does not change."

"You are correct," the Buddha repeated with a slight nod.

"These previous buddhas—they had followers, just as you do, right?"

"Yes," the Buddha replied.

"And they had monastics too?"

"They did."

"Well . . ." and here Ananda hesitated just a moment, but then he pressed on. "Did the previous buddhas have male *and* female monastics? Did those previous buddhas give women permission to join their Orders? What did previous buddhas do?"

The Buddha looked at his devoted disciple . . .

And then he laughed. A great big, mighty laugh that bounced against the perfumed walls and thundered with Indra's strength.

"You are much sharper than you permit yourself to believe, my dear Ananda. What you lack at times is confidence, but you have insight in abundance. Every one of my predecessors gave women permission to join the Order. Every one of them had fully ordained nuns in their communities. *Every single one.*"

Ananda shook with emotion. Had he asked the right question?

"You have asked the right question," replied the all-seeing Buddha. "Well done, my dear friend."

Ananda swayed with delight.

"But you will have to pace yourself now," the Buddha warned. "The next part won't be easy. Not for anyone."

20

The Eight Heavies

The Gathering Women were summoned to the Perfumed Chamber.

Everyone raced about, trying to make themselves presentable. Faces and bald heads were rinsed in the nearby river. Dust was shaken off dirty robes. Satchels and carts and cooking pots were set aside for safe keeping. It was the moment they had all been waiting for.

Vimala was not sure what to do with herself. She had not prepared for this. She had convinced herself that they would never get this far, and yet here they were being summoned in. She had not cut off her hair and was not sure if she ever would. She could not even leave her satchel behind. She looked over at Bhadda Kundalakesa and envied her clarity. Bhadda Kundalakesa had always known where she was headed and why she was there. Vimala was still caught in her own personal limbo.

Patachara was standing beside her. She too still had her hair. And her cloak was a sullied mess. But . . . why were Patachara's feet so clean? They almost gleamed in comparison with the grime that covered the rest of her. Vimala was about to ask, but then was distracted by Kisa Gotami approaching, looking almost rabid. A look of crazed fear was in her eyes; her dead baby was still clutched tightly against her chest. She placed herself beside Patachara, who did not seem to mind.

Vimala looked around and realized that even more women had joined the Gathering. There were new faces in the crowd, as though the community reproduced a bit more each time she closed her eyes. She noted the infuriatingly joyful Bhadda Kapilani, the old beggar Chanda, and Mutta, the girl who once wore flowers in her hair, whose head was now bald like a newborn babe. Vaddhamata stood in her red beaded dress, and Sama smelled like smoke. Vimala scanned the community, her eyes landing on familiar faces and others she had never seen before. Neelima was adjusting her blue robe with trembling hands.

Then Vimala noticed a familiar figure that took her by surprise. With her hair shorn, Ambapali was almost unrecognizable. She had no makeup on, no kohl outlining her eyes. She was wearing a simple cotton robe. Vimala smiled despite her own ambivalence, nodded her head. Ambapali smiled and nodded in return. *How many more women would join?* Vimala wondered. If this continued, there would be no women left in Bharata. She imagined men waking up everywhere to closed brothels and empty homes.

Vimala scanned more faces, drinking in the activity, when her eyes landed on someone she never expected to see again. She thought she had seen the last of her when she walked out of Kumari's brothel in Kapilavatthu.

"Is that really you?" she asked as she rushed towards Surasa. "I feel like I'm seeing a ghost!"

"In the flesh!" Surasa replied, with her arms open wide.

"How did you get here? Why did you come? You didn't actually walk through the forest alone, did you?"

"No," Surasa laughed. "I certainly did not. That would have been reckless, even for me."

"But then, I don't understand. How did you get here? And why?"

"I heard about your escape from Kumari. Everyone did! Kumari tried bartering with the Royal Princess and failed. I couldn't believe it! I never imagined anyone could pull that off! I know that you always talked about it. You've been dreaming of a better life since the day you showed up on our doorstep, but I never imagined you would actually manage! And then you did, and I guess . . ." here, Surasa shrugged her seductive shoulders, "there was no turning back after that."

Vimala was stunned. She had never considered the possibility that her own departure would have an effect on anyone else. She thought she barely existed, was convinced that no one knew she was even there. And yet, here was Surasa standing before her, with her eyes shining bright, ready to take on a new life because Vimala had shown her how.

"But . . . how did you get away?"

"That's the funny thing. Once you decide something, it really isn't that complicated to make it happen. The hard part is deciding to do it. The rest happened almost as though the gods were lending a hand."

Surasa spent the better part of the following day pacing up and down, just as Vimala once had, trying to figure her way out. When her first client arrived, she realized she had found the answer she was looking for. This client was a wealthy landowner who had been visiting her for years. She led him to her mattress, dropped her robe to the floor, and gave the performance of her life. She sobbed dramatically with one hand laid across her forehead, words spilling out of her the way her clothing had spilled off her back. By the time she was done, he was a committed accomplice. Together, they hatched a plan to get her out of Kumari's clutches.

"What was the plan?" Vimala asked, fascinated.

"It took a few days, but my client eventually found out that Princess Sundarinanda was preparing to make her own trip from Kapilavatthu to Vesali. I don't know how he did it, but he managed to convince her to take me as an attendant. He bought me this new robe and that was it. I think the princess's head would have split in two if she realized I was a whore! And a *pandaka* at that!" Surasa busted out with another laugh.

"But who is Princess Sundarinanda?" Vimala asked, mesmerized. "I've never even heard of her."

"She's right over there," Surasa pointed to a young woman surrounded by devoted acolytes, tossing long (unshorn) hair, sparkling in royal attire. "She's a cousin to the throne. After the queen and Princess Yasodhara left, she apparently felt left out and decided to join the Gathering Women too. But Princess Sundarinanda refused to walk barefoot. We made the trip with carts and palanquins and even a chef. It was the most luxurious trip of my life!"

Now Vimala was the one laughing. She shook her head with wonder. Again, and again, and again.

"So here I am, a fellow pilgrim in the Gathering. A pandaka prostitute among princesses and queens. About to meet the Buddha, no less."

Vimala felt a wave of emotion. She pulled Surasa into her arms and squeezed her tight.

"I don't know how you pulled it off," she whispered over her shoulder, "but I am so glad you're here."

The great oak doors were flung open. The most elaborate doors Vimala had ever seen. She thought she had seen Vesali workmanship at its finest, but this was something else. Each door had a tremendous tree carved into it, the leaves spreading out far and wide. Birds floated in the sky, along with gentle guardian spirits watching from above. Vimala had never seen anything so beautiful.

But then the Gathering was ushered into the Perfumed Chamber and her heart quite literally skipped a beat. The hall was glittering in the morning light, rays of sunshine streaming through the open windows. The air was cool and soft, and . . . wondrously fragrant. *What was that scent?* she wondered. She could not place it, but it was the most delicious scent she had ever known.

The Buddha was seated on a raised platform at the front of the hall. His eyes were gently closed. His hands were resting lightly on his lap. Vimala wanted to stare, but she knew better. He was higher than the gods, they said. She looked away, focused on the women walking ahead of her, conscious of the women walking behind.

Gotami stopped when she stood directly in front of the Buddha. She raised her pressed palms over her head, then brought them back to her heart and bowed with reverence. Lowered herself onto her knees and touched the floor with her forehead. She then got up and moved to the right side of him to sit down. The women followed her example and did the same, one after another. The Gathering had grown so large, the women filled the center of the Perfumed Chamber with their many fascinating, varied selves.

Vimala settled on the smooth stone floor, crossed her legs, placed her satchel on her lap. She tried to keep her back as straight as possible and tried not to fidget. She would not dare look up at the Buddha, but she did not know where else to place her gaze. She looked down at her hands, picked at her cuticles, moved her satchel from her lap to the ground beside her, then placed it back on her lap again.

Incapable of settling down, she decided to look around the room and only then discovered that the monks were there too. They were seated along the edges of the chamber, one beside the next, with their backs rising up against the towering walls.

Their presence did nothing to appease her. The monks did not make her feel welcome or safe. On the contrary, she felt surrounded. Squashed by their masculine seniority. Did they even want her here?

The Buddha broke Vimala's inner spell.

"Gotami," he called out. His voice rang like a bell.

"Yes, Teacher," she replied gracefully as she bowed her head.

Vimala expected him to follow some of the traditional rules of social decorum. To ask about her health or how the journey had been. Perhaps ask if she had eaten or wanted something to drink. Anything that would have made the moment more familiar. Recognizable. Easier to engage with. But the Buddha was not interested in social niceties. The negotiations had begun in Banyan Grove. He was picking up the thread where they had left off.

"You would like to have permission to join the Order," he stated regally.

"Yes, Teacher."

Vimala realized that Gotami was similarly direct. She did not ask about his health or try to add words where none were required. The two of them were facing off publicly in a conversation they were both apparently prepared for.

"I suggested that you not ask the question."

"You did, Teacher."

"And yet you are still requesting permission."

Gotami took a moment. But then she answered, just as clearly as she had before. Not a quiver or a waver in her voice.

"Yes, Teacher."

Now it was the Buddha's turn to be silent. Sun pooled in his lap.

"And you understand that your request has ramifications? That it will be difficult?"

She did not hesitate.

"I understand."

The Buddha stared at Gotami and she stared at him. Two giants facing off in a public forum. Vimala held her breath.

"Very well, Gotami. I grant women ordination into the Order."

There was a moment of hesitation, as though no one was certain that they had heard the words correctly. And then the women erupted with cheers! After all that time, after all the sacrifices, the arguments, the risks. After being rejected too. After escaping, dreaming, hoping for a different life—the women had been granted formal permission to join the Order! The words had been spoken. They would not be abandoned anymore. They would receive the teachings and they would have a community to call home. Tears of joy were streaming down cheeks, hands were covering faces, arms were rocking bodies tight. It had really happened.

Gotami had been right all along.

But around the women, surrounding them, were the monks. And while some smiled, others did not.

The Buddha held up his hand for quiet.

"Permission is granted, but that is only the first step. The second step is this: you must be willing to accept eight important rules for ordination to be possible. Rules that will be yours, as nuns, to follow for the rest of your lives."

Gotami nodded.

"The first rule," he began without pausing, "and the most important rule, is this: a nun who has been ordained even for one hundred years will be junior to a monk who has been ordained only one day. This rule has to be honored, respected, revered, venerated, and never transgressed throughout a nun's life."

Vimala had not seen this part coming.

The Buddha on his golden platform kept going.

"Rule number two is that nuns may not live in retreat without a monk nearby, but monks may live without nuns.

"Rule number three . . ."

Vimala's head began to spin. She did not think she had the courage to listen to these restrictions. He kept talking, but they had become muffled sounds in her ears. She closed her eyes, rested her head in her hands. Tried not to hear the rest.

"Rule number four is that nuns must receive instruction from monks, but monks will not be instructed by nuns.

"Rule number five is that nuns will confess their transgressions in front of monks, but monks will not confess their transgressions in front of nuns.

"Rule number six is that a nun must be ordained by a community of monks and nuns, but monks will be ordained only by fellow monks.

"Rule number seven . . ."

He was doing it. The Buddha was going through every possible scenario to ensure that nuns never have the upper hand. The Gathering Women had come all this way to ask to sit alongside the monks. The Buddha, however, would only offer them the right to sit behind the monks instead.

"And finally, rule number eight: a nun is forbidden from criticizing a monk. A monk, however, may criticize a nun."

That was it. The eight heavy rules. He had said them all.

Vimala was devastated. She looked around and saw similar faces of confusion and distress. When she looked over at the monks, though, she found expressions of relief. Vimala crumbled into herself, her back folding, her head falling.

And then Bhadda Kundalakesa's hand was on her shoulder.

"Courage, Sister," she whispered from behind her. "We will find our way."

Vimala grabbed the hand that was on her shoulder and held on tight. She did not know why this was having such an effect on her. Moments earlier, she had expected to be dismissed. She thought the Gathering Women had come here to be rejected. He would say no again, and they would leave to create some kind of homeless existence among themselves. Now they *were* accepted. She was invited to join the illustrious Order of the Buddha's Teachings. He had said yes, but with so many strings attached, it was almost as though he was still saying no. *Did she want any of this?* Vimala looked around herself, at the faces she had grown accustomed to seeing every day. At the friendships she had formed, the teachers who stood at the helm. She felt the strength of Bhadda Kundalakesa's grip on her shoulder. Was she prepared to walk away? Did she want to stay? What would she do now?

"Gotami, I know that these rules are not easy," the Buddha instructed. "But they are necessary if a monastic order for women is to be established. If you can accept these eight rules and all that they entail, you will be ordained."

The Buddha then got up and walked out of the Perfumed Chamber. The rest of the male monastic community followed. They were leaving the women alone to debate their response.

The Buddha's warning filled the air. The women had the permission they had come for, but it came at a cost. They would never be equal. They would have to remain one step behind. Even in the realm of the Awakened Ones, women were to be kept apart.

For a long time, no one said a word. But then Patachara stood up.

Without explanation or invitation, she was on her feet, in a hall filled with seated women. Her hair was wilder than ever. She looked like she was wearing a nest on her head. Her cloak was barely fastened, the ribbon that kept it closed by her neck was half torn and hanging, her pendulous breasts peeking out from behind the dusty curtain. And yet she walked with a steady gait, clear and focused. When she reached the front, she lowered herself to the ground and prostrated before the Buddha's raised platform even though he was no longer there. Then she turned around to face the community of women.

"I lost everyone," she began. "Before the Gathering found me, I lost them all. Like a curse, one family member after another was swallowed by Mara's wrath. I lost my husband. I lost my first child. And then I lost my second. After that, I lost my parents. All of them were dead in the space of one single, horrible day."

The room had become still. Patachara was commanding her audience, laying herself bare, with a kind of resilience Vimala had never witnessed before.

"I have performed this pilgrimage with loss in my heart. Reciting the names of my loved ones with every step, remembering their faces, repeating the details."

She paused. Tilted her head back, as though trying to see the heavens within her mind.

"I still recite their names," she admitted as she looked again at the faces in the room. "I probably always will. But this morning, after watching the Teacher sit in contemplation, something changed. I walked to the river's edge and sat there for a long time. I am normally frightened of rivers," her voice caught in her throat. "Vimala can attest to that."

Patachara looked directly at Vimala, held her with her eyes. Then they smiled at each other, the depth of their friendship so very clear to them both.

"I have not approached a river since I lost my children. But this morning, I decided that it was time. I sat beside the river behind Peak Hall and listened to the sounds it made as it moved across its bed. I pictured the Goddess Ganga pouring out of the heavens through Shiva's long locks and landing right there at my feet. The river was moving quickly, but she wasn't trying to harm anyone. She was simply doing what rivers are supposed to do. Moving through the earth, bringing with her whatever falls into her lap.

"So, after some time of quietly sitting, I dipped my feet in. I have not felt the gushing waters of a river in such a long time. Not since that day when my children were swept away. And I was surprised by how cooling it felt. I laid my feet on the pebbles and watched the water glide over me. I watched for what felt like forever as the water flowed, as it swirled and moved and directed itself, without ever going back. It flowed always forward, flushing the earth, flooding the dryness, giving life to some creatures, bringing death to others. The river is the way of the world, I realized. It is the way of the Earth Goddess."

Patachara, with her wild hair, looked like the Earth Goddess herself as she spoke. Or the Great Woman Tree come to life. Patachara was transforming right before Vimala's eyes. She had reached some kind of insight just by washing her feet.

"The rules proposed by the Teacher are not for me to negotiate. I am here to learn how to flow forward, and how to let the past go. Our relationship to the monks is beside the point for me."

Patachara then bowed to Gotami, bowed to the community, and walked back to her seat.

Voices rose and fell progressively. The women of the Gathering had to decide if, like Patachara, they could accept the limitations proposed or if they would walk away.

"Those rules are like shackles," one woman declared.

"Why would he impose such restraint?" asked another.

"It's like we never left home."

Many of the women were fuming. The sting of betrayal all too familiar. All too sharp.

"We didn't seriously expect to be treated equally," was one of the answers.

"We *are* women, after all," said another.

The arguments were flying back and forth, reaching into old wounds, creating new ones, confirming insecurities. Gotami sat back and watched without commentary. Vimala would have given anything to hear her pronounce on the subject, but Gotami's lips were sealed. Yasodhara was the one to speak instead.

"Sisters," she called out with a strong voice, "please settle down."

Some stopped, but others were in the heat of argument and kept going. Yasodhara tried again.

"Sisters, that's enough!"

Everyone stopped. Caught in mid-sentence.

"This is not how we will proceed. We are women, here to ask for the greatest blessing, the most precious gift. We are sitting in the Perfumed Chamber of the Blessed One. Remember who you are and why you have come."

Vimala had not heard much from Yasodhara. It was nice to see the lioness emerge.

"Everyone will have a chance to speak. We will go through all the arguments, one at a time."

She looked over the congregation with her eyebrows raised in defiance, daring anyone to challenge her authority.

"All right. Let's arrange ourselves into a circle so that we can hear and see each other clearly."

Immediately, a circle took shape.

"Now," she said. "Who would like to speak first?"

"The thing is," one voice began, "some of us have come from very difficult circumstances. I ran from my husband. I can't go back. He'd kill me on sight. I'll take the rules."

"But didn't we come here for something better?" asked another. "We marched through the forest hoping that this teacher would be different, that he would see us as real human beings, with full potential to achieve awakening just like him. We came here with high hopes. If we accept these rules, we are going right back to the hierarchies we were trying to escape."

"But what if hierarchies *can't* be escaped? What if this is the way of the world?" asked the woman with blue-black skin.

"Hierarchy may be inevitable, but why must women always occupy the lowest rung?" Bhadda Kundalakesa asked in return, the disappointment on her face tangible. "What would be so terrible, what devastating disorder or profound injustice would be wrought, if women were actually granted equal footing just this once?"

"But it *would* be an injustice if we were made equal," replied Bhadda Kapilani. "All my life, I was told that rebirth as a woman was proof of bad karma. That we must have done something in a past life to deserve this existence. Otherwise, we would have been reborn as men. I don't think we have the right to ask for equality. We are not equal by birth and we should not be equal in the Order. I don't see why we are even arguing the point."

"Whoever told you that was a fool!" Bhadda Kundalakesa snapped. "Those are folktales men create to justify a hierarchy that they alone benefit from. Women's bodies do not represent a failed rebirth."

"How would you know?" Bhadda Kapilani countered.

"I know because women's bodies can do a lot more than a man's. Have you ever watched a woman give birth? Seen her use her body as food, create life where there was none before? Women are like trees and grass and sky. They are like monsoon clouds, filled with water that feed the world. When men try to convince us that we're inferior in our bodies, they're lying to themselves and they're lying to us. You should know better than to believe such stupidities."

Everyone clamped their mouths shut at that. Bhadda Kundalakesa was the most feared debater in all of Bharata. Vimala understood why.

From the corner of her eye, Vimala caught movement by the door. Little Rahula, Princess Yasodhara's son, was trying to sneak into the hall. He was on all fours, crawling silently towards his mother. Most of the women were locked in their thoughts following Bhadda's devastating blow and did not notice the child sneaking in.

He reached his mother and tapped her on the shoulder. Yasodhara turned around and found her son's face shining at her.

"Hello, my darling," she said as she reached for his sweet cheeks. "What are you doing here?"

"I finished with my studies," he answered with practiced dedication. Yasodhara smiled.

"I have a feeling you're not supposed to be here, though."

Everyone watched the interaction with a familiar smile. The energy in the room, that was a moment earlier tight with tension, had instantly loosened. Yasodhara turned to look at Gotami. Could he stay?

Gotami reached out for her grandson's little body. "You can stay," she declared, "but you have to keep quiet. Is that understood?"

Rahula nodded vigorously and then made himself at home on his grandmother's lap. Gotami seemed delighted.

"Perhaps we need to try to understand *why* the Teacher would want to keep women in a lower position here," Yasodhara offered. "Any thoughts?"

A bit of mumbling, considering.

"Maybe because the monks would revolt if he didn't?"

Everyone turned to look at the speaker. She had not spoken before. It was Mutta, the girl who once wore flowers in her hair.

"But that makes no sense," Bhadda Kundalakesa responded with frustration. "What kind of a teacher would he be if he was afraid of his own monks?"

"He would be a human one," was Princess Yasodhara's response.

He was once her husband, after all. She should know.

"Maybe he doesn't believe we're really capable of awakening," someone reflected. It was the thought they were all considering but too afraid to voice. Maybe he was granting them ordination, but he did not actually expect any of them to get very far.

"That's not true!" Rahula exclaimed.

"Rahula," Gotami reprimanded. "You are not permitted to speak at this meeting."

"But it's not true, Grandmother," Rahula answered back. "The Teacher *does* think women can achieve awakening. I heard Ananda explaining it to the others just now!"

Yasodhara took his hand into her own, the three of them bound in a bracelet of intimacy.

"What do you mean, my darling? What are you talking about?"

Rahula looked up at his grandmother whose lap he was still invading, silently asking for her permission. She nodded.

"Ananda told the others just now that he had asked the Teacher if women could achieve awakening and the Teacher said yes. Women can achieve awakening just like men. The monks are discussing all this in the main residence just as you are all discussing it here. I heard Ananda say it."

"Because you were hiding somewhere, listening to conversations that were not for you?" his mother replied.

Rahula looked down at his hands.

She smiled.

What a blessing it must have been for her to be with him after all that time.

"But he said it. I heard Ananda clearly. He said that women can achieve awakening just like men."

The repetition was helpful. Vimala needed to hear the words a second time.

"If that's the case," Bhadda Kundalakesa thought aloud, "if the Teacher believes we are capable, then why is he keeping us down? Why would we have to bow to a monk who was ordained that day, even if we've been ordained one hundred years?"

Because, Vimala decided, the men would never accept it otherwise.

Vimala needed air. She walked out of the room, leaving behind the arguments that would keep circling. She needed to think about it all for herself. *Was it as simple as that?* Were the rules there because the men could not live without them? Were women kept down just so that men could feel higher up? Was that all there was to this history of interminable hierarchy? And was a Buddha not even capable of changing the tides? Being reborn a woman might not be the result of bad karma, but it certainly didn't feel like good karma either.

Vimala climbed down the stairs and out into the fresh open air. She felt like a prisoner who had just been released from criminal confinement. A few monks were sweeping the courtyard again, moving the dust around themselves in a perpetual cycle of return. The moment she appeared they stopped sweeping. They eyed her without saying a word.

She needed to get away. She left the courtyard and circled Peak Hall, to see what lay on the other side.

A large residence stood behind the monastery, along with a series of small huts that looked like personal rooms. This must be the living quarters, Vimala concluded, where the monks had been discussing the women, just as the women were upstairs discussing them. Laundry was hanging outside to dry. Old robes in different shades of orange fluttering in the hot wind. A few monks were chatting together on the steps of the main residence. Others flitted about in pairs, absorbed in conversation.

She could see the problem the Buddha would have to reckon with if the women joined the community. Where would the women live? How would the men react? How would the Buddha manage to keep the two sexes apart, and yet still consider them as two parts of a larger whole? And where would someone like Surasa fit?

The further Vimala wandered into the men's private space, the more aware of her own intrusion she became. The rules were not just about keeping women down, she was forced to realize. They were attempts at keeping the peace too. The men were already here. They had staked out the Buddha as their territory, the teachings as their home. The women would make for a complicated addition. Some of the monks might have joined the Buddha's Order to get away from women, just as some of the women had come to the Gathering to get away from men. Putting them all back together was bound to be complicated. She did not want to admit it, but she could see why he might put the reins on them all.

Vimala was on the verge of turning around, of leaving the men to their private communion, when one of the monks came charging at her.

"What do you think you're doing here?" he barked aggressively. "You can't be here. It's forbidden."

Vimala flustered.

"This is our sleeping quarters. Women are not permitted!" he barked again.

She was indeed a creature of trespass.

"I didn't know," she stammered. "I will go."

"But you won't," accused another. "That's the problem. You're all here to stay. And then what will happen to us?" His anger was frightening.

She started backpedaling, stumbling on her feet in reverse, when the first monk struck again.

"Women ruin everything. You're like mould on a rice field, killing a good crop with your presence. Everything we've built will be destroyed because of you."

Other monks started approaching. Robes of orange moving against her. Bald heads piercing against the sharp light. They looked like a mob more than the peaceful monks she had come here expecting to find. She moved backwards more quickly, rushing without seeing where she was stepping. Then she tripped and she was on the ground, the men all around her.

"That's enough," she heard someone command from behind.

The monk from earlier, the monk with skin like a storm cloud called Mogallana, was by her side. He gave her his hand and helped her back to her feet.

"You will have to confess this behavior to the Teacher, Nandaka," he admonished the first monk. "And you too," he pointed to the second. "Your anger is inappropriate. You should know better by now. Both of you."

Vimala looked up at the men, feeling more frightened than she was willing to admit.

"My apologies on behalf of the community," Mogallana offered graciously. "These monks will be reprimanded. This is not the type of behavior monks are meant to exhibit."

Vimala was disoriented. She had no words with which to respond. She dusted off her robe.

"The community is a bit rattled by the changes being negotiated," Mogallana continued. "It will not be easy for the community, but we will do as the Teacher recommends. We will adapt."

The monks dissipated, as though a magical command had sent them scattering. She was standing alone with Mogallana now. Unbidden anger rose to the surface before she could see it coming.

"I thought monks were supposed to be examples to the community," she retaliated, a bit too late.

"I'm sorry they frightened you," Mogallana answered calmly. "Truth be told, most of them are harmless. I think they were just caught off guard by the turn of events this morning. But they were out of line. They will be reprimanded."

"You call that *harmless?*" She spit the word at him with surprising force. "Where I come from, their behavior is called by other names."

Mogallana dropped his shoulders in resignation.

"I cannot pretend to know what it's like to be a woman in a world of men," he replied with sincerity. "All I can offer are my apologies. Let me escort you back to the Perfumed Chamber."

His response was so calm, she felt disarmed despite herself. He had not flinched or cowered before her anger. He just moved past it, as though it was not even there. She took in a long breath, tried to calm her frightened heart. When he began walking, she followed.

"I didn't expect the monks to be so harsh," she admitted. "I'm not sure what I expected, but I didn't expect that they would be . . . like men from anywhere else."

"Well, in some ways, they *are* like men from anywhere else. Some of them come from loving families and are encouraged to follow their dreams of liberation, but others have dragged themselves here with great burdens tied to their feet. They come here not because they are perfect, but precisely because they aren't."

Mogallana stopped walking and looked directly at her. He seemed to be staring into her, as though he could see her from the inside. Seeing her from behind the curtain of veils she had grown accustomed to armoring herself with.

"Many men are afraid of women, Vimala."

He looked right into her eyes, undaunted.

She took a step back.

"I suspect that you have learned to guard yourself from all men, Vimala, because some of them have been unspeakably cruel, because the world has so often disappointed you. But the point of this community is to free ourselves of all these wrong views. Everyone here is a work in progress."

Who was he to know so much about her? How did he even know her name?

"The difference between men and women that you are so concerned about will not exist here. Not in any fundamental way. The only important thing here is the awakening Mind."

She was standing in the middle of the men's private quarters. The doors of most huts were hanging uncomfortably open. This was a world she did not belong to.

"You can't pretend the differences don't matter," she countered. "The differences are everywhere. The rules the Teacher just proclaimed will *make* those differences matter."

Mogallana looked up at the huts with open doors.

"Perhaps you are right. There will indeed be differences between men and women here. Monks will ordain nuns, but nuns will not ordain monks. Monks will instruct nuns, but nuns will not do the same for monks. The difference between the sexes will be just as glaring here as it is everywhere else in the world. And perhaps this is as it must be. I don't think our world is ready for men and women to be the same. Socially, we are not likely to survive that way. Maybe in another time, in a different place, men and women *can* live side-by-side with shared equality, and maybe then the extra rules will no longer be required. But that is not who we are as a society today. Not now.

"My point is that the social world is not as important as you think it is. It is the realm of the mind that matters. The realm of the imagination. And there, Vimala, where awakening thrives and transforms, the differences don't mean a thing. Remember that the Buddha declared this too: women can achieve awakening just as men can. Fundamentally, there is no difference between us. That is our teaching too."

Vimala looked at the monk standing before her, at his earnestness, at his faith that the hierarchy would dissolve the moment she let it go, but she just could not agree. The hierarchy *would* matter. It always does. Only those who stood at the top of the ladder would condescend to say otherwise.

Mogallana led her back to the courtyard.

"I will leave you here to consider your decision."

Vimala remained as unconvinced as she had been before.

Vimala had planned on returning to the Perfumed Chamber, but she put one foot on the stairs and then sat down instead. She was not ready to fold herself into the masses yet.

She heard someone coming down from behind her. She got up to make room.

"Surasa!" she exclaimed as she watched her old friend reach her. "What's going on?"

Surasa wiped the sweat from her brow, readjusted her new robe and tightened the sash.

"I thought I was up for this," she said, "but I don't think I am. I just freed myself from Kumari after a lifetime of servitude. I have had to deal with men on top of me since I was old enough to bear their weight. I didn't come here to start that all over again."

"Don't tell me you're leaving," she begged. "You just got here."

"I know, but this isn't for me."

Vimala stared at her old friend. Surasa was fiddling with her sash again, trying to find a way to let it sit on her waist more comfortably. A few other women were now coming down the stairs too. Apparently, she was not the only one leaving. Surasa and Vimala stepped aside to let the others pass.

"Where will you go?" Vimala asked.

Surasa shrugged.

"I don't know. Maybe I'll try to find work in Vesali. With this new outfit, I can pass as a house-servant or something."

"But you won't become a nun?" Vimala asked.

Surasa laughed.

"I think we both know the answer to that."

Surasa gave Vimala a hug. She then turned around and walked away, following the others who had done the same.

Vimala stayed behind at the foot of the stairs. Wondering again, for the one hundred and eighth time, where she might belong.

Many Years Later:
The Great Immensity

"I guess the rest is history," I concluded. The sun was just beginning to set. We had talked through the entire day.

Darshani was staring at the sky, her knees tucked into her chest. She seemed older to me now than she had that morning.

"But what made you decide to join the Order?" she asked, looking perplexed. "If we have to live with all those rules now, if the monks will always be above us, why did you stay?"

It was the question I had been sitting with for a very long time. The question I knew I would have to answer once the story was all laid out.

"When I spoke with Venerable Mogallana that day," I replied, "he said one thing in particular that stayed with me. He said that men don't join the monastic life because they're perfect. They join the monastic life because they aren't. They join because it is their aspiration. More than anything else, I think he was right about that.

"These walls are not for Awakened Ones. Buddhas do not need community or rules. They don't even need rituals to perform. They are awake, the work is done. A monastery is for those who are not awakened yet. It is a place for the aspiring, for those who hope they can do more with themselves than ordinary life permits. We all come here because we are looking for something. We don't come here if we have already found it."

"I can understand that," Darshani answered, "but the Teacher was a Buddha! He was awake. Why would he make rules that he knew were unfair? He said that women have the same capacities as men and that we can reach awakening just as they can, so why would he then tell us to always stay one step behind? He didn't have to do that! He

could have made us equal right from the start, inside the walls of the monastery. Why make the monastery as unfair as everywhere else in the world?"

I had answers. I could hear myself shaping them as she battled with the story as I had presented it to her.

And yet at the same time, I knew that my answers would not suffice. These were questions she would have to wrestle with herself.

But she was looking to me for help.

"I cannot tell you what he was thinking, Little One. No one can. And some of us may even believe that the Buddha was wrong to institute those rules."

"So, you accepted the rules even though you thought they were wrong?" she asked with her eyebrows raised right into her forehead. She could not shake her frustration. I could not blame her.

"Truthfully?"

She nodded.

"Yes. I accepted them, but I never agreed."

Her emotions now bubbled over like a pot of hot buffalo milk.

"Then why didn't you all just leave and make up your own rules somewhere else?" she demanded.

"Who would have shown us the way? We had the Teacher right there in front of us. He was awake. I knew he was the Buddha with every fiber of my being. He shone like the sun. That's not something I was prepared to throw away.

"I learned long ago how important teachers are in a lifetime. We of course need friends, equal partners we can exchange with and debate. But we also need teachers. We should never be so arrogant as to believe that we don't. We all need guidance, and then when we are ready, we guide others in return. There is no desolation quite like being left without a teacher."

A herd of elephants emerged from beneath the trees at the bottom of the hill. Every afternoon, they made their way across the field to bathe in the mudbanks. They were on their way home. They walked in a line, one following another, with thick mud caked on their backs. The little ones held the tails of the larger ones with their trunks.

"Is that how you felt when you were at Kumari's?"

Darshani seemed reluctant to ask her question, looking elsewhere as she spoke, as though embarrassed to bring up that part of my life.

She probably never imagined she would be talking about brothels and prostitution inside the safety of our monastic walls. I laid my hand on her shoulder.

"Those years were a wasteland to me. I don't think I even knew at the time how alone I felt. But when I found the Gathering, it was like I could breathe again. After years of holding my breath. I remembered that I still existed, that I wasn't just a wandering, hungry ghost. My friends healed me and Gotami led the way. And then when I found the Teacher, I knew I could never turn back, even if I struggled with the limits I would have to face."

I thought back to all the extraordinary people I have had the blessing of sharing my life with. So many of them were gone now. I watched Gotami take her last breath years ago. Bhadda and Patachara too. When the Buddha died, it was as though Surya the Sun God had put out all the lights.

But none of those deaths felt like the desolation I had known in my younger years. It is the difference between loneliness and being alone that I was trying to articulate.

"I still think you could have created your own community, with just women. Then none of these rules would have had to exist," *Darshani argued.*

I understood her hurt so well.

"I wondered the same thing for a long time, but I don't think you're right. Even if we had started our own community in some idealized way, we would eventually have made our own mess. We are not immune to it just because we are women. It happens to everyone, every system, every organization and worldview."

Darshani brought her knees in tighter, frustrated. Disappointed. She looked away.

"There is no perfection out here in this samsaric world, Darshani. That is one thing I am sure of."

"So then, what? We just leave the world as it is?" *she whipped her head back to face me.* "We don't even try to make a difference? If women keep accepting inequality, nothing will ever change!"

She was right. Of course she was.

And yet . . .

The world had always been this way. If it is not women's inequality, it is something else, but it is always something. An injustice healed here becomes a new injustice elsewhere. We might make thirty-six million efforts, but we will only ever manage to move injustice around. We can never heal all of it.

But I knew the counterarguments too. I could hear Bhadda's answer in my head. If we accept the imperfections of the world too quickly, then we justify leaving injustice alone. We justify leaving widows by the roadside, prostitutes shackled to their brothels, queens set on fire in their homes.

And then I remembered watching Patachara quietly retrieving Chanda the widow out of her misery. Patachara did not even argue the point. She just found a way to help, to respond to the hurt of the world with kindness somehow. Regardless of heady arguments that go round and round.

I leaned back and wondered where my own answer to these questions lay. I had wavered for such a long time. I had heard so many stories of hardship, had absorbed them all like oil on dry skin. How could I look at Kisa Gotami's hurt, the battle scars she carried in the shape of a dead baby she kept in her arms, and not feel the urgency to participate? Everywhere I turned, I saw suffering. Every person I met had it written all over their face.

But in time, I also came to understand something else. That, of all the stories I heard as I walked with the Gathering Women, it was my own that I was being called to face. Just as others were being called to face theirs.

I had been drowning for most of my life. I had to find the root of my own suffering if I had any hope of reaching the other shore. The urgency I came to feel was not about the madness of the great big world we live in. It was not about rules or hierarchies or social injustices. It was about my own mind. I shaved my head because I wanted to free myself of the stories that were weighing me down, the sorrow and disappointment that had been my home for far too long. I did not want to drown anymore. I had an inner vastness to find.

"Do you remember the story about Markandeya?" I asked Darshani, changing course.

"The flying sage and the Cosmic Ocean?"

She was so quick. We would have to go through the story of the Gathering a few more times, but I knew she would be able to carry it.

"Can I tell it to you again?"

She looked uncertain, not sure why, but she nodded.

"Listen carefully, Little One."

It was a story that needed telling over and over again. She leaned back and closed her eyes. A crow landed on a branch overhead and cawed.

"There was once a great sage named Markandeya," I began, seeing the words from that piece of parchment from my childhood dancing before my eyes. They were as clear to me as they had been all those years ago. "Like many others, Markandeya had mastered the power of flight. He spent his time flying all over the cosmos, exploring every part of it that he could find. But one day, Markandeya flew so far and for so long, he thought he had reached the edge. It became dark and he started to feel scared. He was disoriented and did not know which way to go, but then he saw a bright light and he raced towards it. And then he was falling out of the darkness and he landed somewhere else.

"He had landed in the waters of the Cosmic Ocean. He had never seen anything like it before. It stretched out before him in every direction, a great immensity that terrified him. It was all so very big, so impossible to understand. He began to panic, and then he was flailing in the water, about to drown.

"That's when Lord Vishnu noticed him. It turns out that Markandeya had not been flying through the cosmos. He thought he had been, but in fact he was flying through Lord Vishnu's body, and when Vishnu yawned, it created a burst of bright light. Markandeya raced for the light and fell right out of Vishnu's mouth, which is how he found himself in the Cosmic Ocean. Markandeya, the great wisdom sage, was flapping his arms like a terrified bird and screaming for help.

"Vishnu saw the little screaming sage in the water beneath him and picked him up in his giant hands. He didn't want Markandeya to hurt himself, so he popped him back into his mouth and swallowed him, returning him to the inside of his body where he would be safe."

Darshani was listening attentively with her eyes closed, her knees still tucked under her chin.

"When I was a child, I thought that was the whole story," I explained. "I had found it on a piece of torn parchment in a corner of my mother's library. I didn't know that the story went further, but I always struggled with the ending, wondering what it could mean. Then one day, Venerable Gotami told me the story the way she had learned it. And it was as though the missing piece I had been searching for all my life had finally landed in my hands."

"There's more?" Darshani asked, her eyes flying open.

I smiled.

"According to Venerable Gotami, Vishnu sent Markandeya back to the inside of his body. Markandeya should have headed back home after that, but he couldn't stop thinking about the Cosmic Ocean. It was scary and he hadn't been prepared for it at the time, but he kept wondering what it would be like to see it again. He knew it was out there, and he knew he was stuck inside something much more limited."

This had become my favorite part of the story.

"So, Markandeya decided not to go home. Instead, he went back to where the opening was and waited for the bright light to show up again. Sure enough, one day Lord Vishnu yawned again and Markandeya launched himself at the light. He fell out of Vishnu's mouth and landed in the Cosmic Ocean, just like the last time."

Darshani gasped. She was on the edge of her seat, perhaps hoping that Vishnu would do something dramatic this time. Throw his discus or summon a lightning bolt.

I waited too, taking my time with this perfect story. A story I loved so very much.

"So, what happened?" Darshani finally asked.

"Nothing."

She stared at me, not understanding.

"Markandeya just looked out at the Great Immensity this time. He was no longer afraid of the vastness."

Notes

Many Years Later: Vimala Remembers the Gathering Women

The notes for this book are the result of many years of research. They are not exhaustive, but hopefully they will provide readers with some background to the material this book describes. I could have gone further, but I thought I should restrain myself a little bit.

First, a comment about the use of diacritics: since this book is aimed at a general audience, I avoid using diacritics wherever possible. This means that I discuss the *Therigatha* in-text without diacritics, but when making reference to a specific passage, I include diacritics (for example, *Therīgāthā* 11). I hope this is not too confusing.

I have focused on the main body of the book—the material between moments of Vimala's remembering. As an introduction to the notes and to the material, however, I will say a few things about the opening section.

Vimala refers to **songs of accomplishment**. This is a reference to the *Therigatha*, a collection of poems by some of the first Buddhist nuns in which they declare their awakening. I discuss the *Therigatha* in the introduction to this book. See Hallisey (2015) for a beautiful translation.

Vimala describes her process of transcribing and preserving these poems. Most of the literature was probably passed down orally in the first centuries of Buddhist history. We do not have any manuscripts from the time of the Buddha's life. But it *is* possible that some things were written down earlier than evidence suggests. And if this was the case, **the material used could well have been birch bark.** In the 1990s, a large collection of Gandharan scrolls was discovered that proved to be about 2000 years old, and the material used was none other than birch bark. The fact that the bark remained intact after such a long period is astonishing (prior to the 1990s, we had access to a few other birch bark scrolls, but they all disintegrated almost immediately upon contact). For an introduction to these scrolls, see Richard Salomon's book, *Ancient Buddhist Scrolls from Gandhāra* (1999). See also his translation of some of these fragments (Salomon 2018).

1. The Buddha Said No

Today, the Buddha is often presented as a secular character, but classical writings paint a very different picture. In traditional Buddhist storytelling, **the Buddha can read minds, fly through the air, even chase the fog away. And he might even "know everything"** (or just about, which is a topic often debated in Pali commentaries). Gotami here gives voice to this almost omniscient portrait of the Buddha. For an example of the Buddha's fantastical nature, consider the famous miracle at Sravasti, when he creates a jeweled walkway in the sky. It stretches from one end of the cosmos to the other. The Buddha struts across it while transforming his body into fire and water (*Buddhavamsa* 1.1*ff*). A pretty fantastical display, if ever there was one.

The Buddha's birth story is another beautifully fantastical scene. It is celebrated with earthquakes that set all ten thousand worlds shaking and giant flowers raining from the sky. Gods shower the mother and newborn with celestial waters while other gods descend to catch the newborn in their arms. This extraordinary scene is regularly depicted on temple walls, carved into stone, and described in almost every text that tells the Buddha's life story. For textual examples, see *Lalitavistara* (1:123*ff*); *Buddhacarita* (1.6*ff*); *Jatakanidana* (52*ff*). For academic discussions of his birth story, see Bareau (1987); Sasson (2007); Langenberg (2017).

The classical sources do not place **Mahapajapati Gotami at the birthing scene.** It is reasonable to assume, however, that as Maya's sister, she would have been among the first to attend. This is a point Garling makes in her book (2021). A Cambodian folksong translated by Trent Walker, entitled "Māyā's Guidance for Gotamī," provides a beautiful imagining of the sisters together under the tree in Lumbini, and I have taken my inspiration from him. See Walker's website: www.trentwalker.org for the songs in Cambodian and in translation.

The lullaby that Maya is described as singing to her newborn is borrowed from the *Pujavaliya*. I have Charlie Hallisey to thank for the translation (which is unfortunately not published). He is also the one who alerted me to Trent Walker's translations.

According to many sources, **Maya has prophetic dreams** when she conceives the future Buddha. She does not, however, have prophetic dreams about her death. But according to many sources, just before the future Buddha takes rebirth in her womb, he sees that she will only have seven days left to live after delivering him. So, while the texts do not have Maya foreseeing her own death in a dream, it made sense to me that she would. I therefore added it to the story. For a discussion about dreams in Buddhist hagiography, see Young (1995).

Gotami's request for ordination is at the heart of this book. It begins in Nigrodha Arama, which can be translated as Banyan Forest or **Banyan Grove**. Banyan trees are majestic beings with roots that fall from branches and anchor themselves back into the earth to form new trunks. The biggest banyan tree in the world is in the botanical garden of Kolkata and spans almost 1900 square meters in diameter, spreading out into a wide circle. For a Canadian like me, such trees completely overwhelm the imagination. In Canada, we have vast green spaces filled with trees, but our trees do not usually have aerial roots or span further than their original trunks.

In the Indian imagination, banyan trees are active beings that have roles to play in the larger cosmos. They can be haunts for ancestors or sites of pilgrimage and are often lovingly decorated with silk cloth and garlands of flowers. See Haberman for more (2013). Banyan Grove is described as being just outside the city of Kapilavatthu, the Buddha's hometown. For a reference, see *Sekhasutta* (*Majjhima Nikāya* 53).

This first request for ordination can be found in the Vinaya of the Pali Canon (*Cullavagga* 10.252). Parallel passages appear in other Vinaya collections, each of which has the Buddha responding to Gotami's request with a slightly different formulation (see Analayo (2016a) for comparative study). In all of them, the Buddha ultimately says no. Or at the very least, he does not say yes. His vague but unenthusiastic response has had commentators debating for centuries. Why didn't he say yes? Why did she have to ask three times, only to meet the same disappointing response? Was the Buddha succumbing to social pressure? Or did he just not want women in the community? Why did he predict that there would be a fourfold assembly, with monks, nuns, laymen, and laywomen, if he was averse to the idea of monastic women?

No matter how one answers these questions, at the end of the day we are left with a narrative that, if at all historically accurate, leaves women seemingly less than welcome. For a quick and efficient overview of monasticism and women's request for ordination, see Ann Heirman's chapters in Harris (2021). For a more in-depth discussion of the ordination request and its many facets, see the edited volume,

Dignity and Discipline (eds. Mohr and Tsedroen, 2010). Also, Analayo (2011 and 2016b) for textual variants.

There is a world of difference between asking for access to the teachings and asking for full ordination. When Gotami approaches the Buddha in this scene, she is not just asking to study his methods. According to Tibetan interpretations of the story, this had in fact already happened when he visited Kapilavatthu earlier. The Buddha had already met with the men upon arrival. Gotami then asked for permission on behalf of the women to meet with him too (Rockhill 1992 and Finnegan 2009). What she was asking for, according to these texts, was a seat at the table—not just access to the teachings. For a contemporary example of a similar request, see Makley (2005).

The name 'Mahapajapati' is often deemed interchangeable with 'Gotami'. It is not clear what the name 'Mahapajapati' means, nor is it clear why she is sometimes referred to only as Gotami. Garling explores some possible answers in her book (2021). My own inclination is to follow Jonathan Walters' (1994) suggestion: namely, that because Gotami is the feminine form of Gotama, and because the Buddha is often identified as Gotama (his clan name), calling her Gotami is a way of identifying her as the Buddha's female counterpart (he being the leader of the male community and she being the leader of the female one).

In many early sources, Gotami approaches the Buddha with 500 Sakyan ladies walking behind her. I must admit that this number has always seemed artificial to me—more of a narrative device than an attempt at recording history. I have therefore allowed myself to stray from this number, opting for a more modest gathering of women instead. As we shall see, I have also decided that her followers were not all Sakyan ladies, but that they come from different backgrounds and social levels. This is more akin to the *Therigatha's* structure and its cacophonous diversity than what the Vinaya records. As noted in the introduction to this book, the *Therigatha* is a collection of poems by the early nuns, and it reads like a chorus of different voices all at once. We have prostitutes and high caste women, poor widows, courtesans, and queens all sharing space together in the pages of the same book. Inspired by the *Therigatha's* diversity, I have imagined **a community of women from all kinds of backgrounds waiting for Gotami at the gates.**

The silence of the monks in the grove as they bear witness to the exchange between Gotami and the Buddha is a detail pulled from a different story. In the *Sāmaññaphalasutta*, a king is brought to the forest to meet the Buddha and his 1250 monks. When he arrives, the king's hair stands on end because it is so eerily quiet. He fears that he is being deceived, that he is about to be murdered by his enemies hiding in the silence. But as the king moves further in, he finds the entire monastic community sitting together in perfect stillness, "like a clear lake" (*Dīgha Nikāya* 2; Walsh 1995) and he is astonished. I borrowed this imagery and wove this quiet into the scene.

2. Vimala's Story Begins

When I first began imagining this book, I wrestled with the question of who the narrator or principal character should be. I considered a number of possibilities. Both Yasodhara (who was the narrator in my last book) and Gotami were obvious contenders. But I wanted this book to be focused on someone less prominent. I was looking for a character who lived on the margins, who was not famous or central, and who could therefore tell this story with a bit of distance. I spent a long time leafing through the *Therigatha*, looking for the one who would catch my attention. When I came upon **Vimala**, she told me unequivocally that she was the one I had been looking for. I had no choice but to do as she said.

The early sources do not tell us much about Vimala. She has one short poem in the *Therigatha* and only one scene elsewhere (that scene will appear later in the book). She does not even feature in the *Apadana*. Her *Therigatha* poem goes as follows:

Intoxicated by my good looks,
By my body, my beauty, and my reputation,
Haughty because of my youth, I looked down on other
women.

I decorated this body, decked out it made fools mutter,
A prostitute at the door, like a hunter spreading out the snare.

I flashed my ornaments as if I was showing my hidden parts,
I created illusions for people, all the while sneering at them.

Today I collected alms,
Head shaved, covered with the outer robe,

Now seated at the foot of the tree,
What I get has nothing to with schemes.

All ties are cut, whether divine or human,
I have thrown away all that fouls the heart,
*I have become cool, free (*Therīgāthā 72–76; Hallisey 2015)

This poem tells us a few things about Vimala. It tells us that she was once a common prostitute (*vesī*). It tells us that she was good at it (and she knew it). Most importantly, though, it tells us that she became free.

From Dhammapala's commentary to the *Therigatha*, we learn two other important details about Vimala's life: that she was from Vesali and that her mother also made her living "from her beauty" (*Therīgāthā-Aṭṭhakathā* 76–77; Pruitt 1999). What Vimala's life was like, though, how she was raised, how she eventually joined the order—none of this is part of the textual tradition. Which means that I was free to imagine it all for myself. We will learn more about her (as I have imagined her) as the book progresses.

As for Vimala's companion, **Surasa:** she does not belong to the early literature. She is a character I created. Surasa is described here as a *pandaka*, someone of "ambiguous sex." We find references to *pandakas* throughout early Indian literature (see Zwilling 2000) and the definition is consistently evasive. José Cabezón's *Sexuality in Classical South Asian Buddhism* (2017) provides the most detailed discussion on the subject. According to Cabezón, a *pandaka* has meant different things at different points in history, but ultimately refers to a third sex category (what he translates as queer) that may include those who have both male and female genitals, those without obvious male or female genitals, and even those who can magically change their genitals. A *pandaka* may also refer to those with non-heteronormative sexual desires, to impotent men, and to women who do not menstruate. In other words, the *pandaka* category is an umbrella term for everything that stands outside the Buddhist understanding of the norm where bodies, gender, and sexual desires are concerned.

Buddhist literature has much to say about *pandakas*. It therefore seemed natural to me that a *pandaka* would feature in this book too. The *pandaka* is, unfortunately, often vilified in Buddhist literature. They are prohibited from receiving Buddhist ordination and are sometimes even prohibited from receiving teachings as a lay person.

In a few surprising instances, however, the *pandaka* represents the "middle way" and is associated with bodhisattva status (see Gyatso 2003). Given the fact that *pandakas* are often portrayed as deviant, though, it seemed reasonable to me that a *pandaka* would suffer in most social contexts and might well wind up in a brothel, which is precisely where Surasa has landed.

Kumari, the brothel owner, is a character I created.

The early literature makes an important distinction between **the life of a common prostitute** (*vesī*) and the **life of a courtesan** (*gaṇikā*). Although the Pali and Sanskrit terms shift in emphasis over time, *vesī* usually refers to a prostitute (often of low birth), while *gaṇikā* is often associated with accomplished courtesans (women who belong to the clan, or the *gaṇa*). We shall hear more about courtesans later, but for now it is important to highlight some of the literature on prostitution in ancient India.

The *Kamasutra* recognizes a wide range of women sex workers, including:

> "the servant woman who carries water, the servant girl, the promiscuous woman, the loose woman, the dancer, the artist, the openly ruined woman, the woman who lives on her beauty, and the courtesan *de luxe*: those are the types of courtesan. All of them must choose appropriate lovers and helpers and consider ways to please them, get money from them, to get rid of them and to get back together with them . . ." (6.6.50–51; Doniger and Kakar 2002)

A prostitute (*vesī*) is generally understood as a woman of low birth who might sell her services from home or a small brothel (Perera 1993 and Cabezon 2017), whereas a courtesan operates at the highest echelons of society. Both prostitutes and courtesans appear throughout Buddhist literature. Although they are often disparaged, Buddhist sources also insist that they are capable of virtue, making gifts to the monastic community for merit and supporting the sangha in various ways (Collins 2007). There is therefore an ambivalence where sex work is concerned. Indeed, sometimes monastics are depicted as safe mediators between sex workers and their potential clients, with the sex workers trusting the monks for their input where unknown clients are concerned (Bailey and Mabbett 2003). We therefore find connections made to sex work throughout Buddhist literature, and not always in anticipated ways.

According to the *Arthasastra*, when a courtesan becomes less desirable (translation: when she gets old), she can be afforded protection by the king with employment in the kitchen (*Arthaśāstra* 2.27). She otherwise risks abandonment, violence, and untold miseries as she loses access to her primary source of income (Bhattacharji 1987). I used this detail as justification for **the old hags in Kumari's kitchen**. What is good for the goose (king) may also work for the gander (brothel owner).

Vimala's brothel is located at the outer edge of Kapilavatthu because it was not a place the town would have wanted to highlight. According to the *Mahabharata*, a prostitute's quarters should be kept to the south of the city because that is Yama's realm, the god of death (Bhattacharji 1987). This changes with the development of courtesan culture. Courtesans are described as living in the heart of great cities, but prostitution houses were kept further away.

Ambapali is one of the most famous courtesans of the early Buddhist period. We will hear more about her later.

The **mud-baked homes** described here are not based on research of early building materials, but are the types of houses I knew when I lived in Nepal in the mid-90s. I spent the better part of a year in a small village in Sindhupalchowk, and most homes at that time were built as I have described them (things have since changed, particularly after the 2015 earthquake). Every few weeks, a fresh mixture of water, mud, and animal dung was slapped onto the floors and walls.

I still remember the first time I learned what my hut was made of. I was standing on the mountain edge early one morning enjoying the view, when a woman walked over to a fresh pile of buffalo shit not far from where I stood. Without a word of warning, she bent down and shoved her hand right in there. I jumped back and yelped. Then she yelped too. Then we both laughed. It became a story to tell for a while, for her as much as for me.

The story of **Siddhattha** is referenced here as a way of bridging the previous book with this one (Sasson 2021). I cannot go over all the details (or the research) of that story here, but suffice to say that Siddhattha was the crown prince of the Sakya Kingdom and that he left home (abandoning everyone who depended on him) to look for the answer to suffering. He eventually became the Buddha, the teacher the women are following in this book. Siddhattha's hometown was **Kapilavatthu**, the city where Vimala now lives as a prostitute.

Lord Rama is the mythical king at the heart of the *Ramayana*. Rama is famous for many reasons, but above all for his moral rectitude and unwavering commitment to his royal obligations. Of course, too much "moral rectitude" is never a good thing, and Rama eventually makes a fateful mistake that costs him his marriage to Sita. Suddhodana is not so different, protecting his son to the point of virtually imprisoning him. There are countless studies on the *Ramayana*, but perhaps most useful in this context (if the reader is unfamiliar with the narrative) is the popular retelling by Divakaruni (2019).

Neelima is Princess Yasodhara's servant in *Yasodhara and the Buddha* (Sasson 2021). She is a character I invented for the purposes of narrative flow, and she has followed me here into this book.

3. The Leap

Bharata is the term used in classical sources for the land we now call India. Bharata is not a nation-state, but a united and sacred landscape. The *Mahabharata* ("Great Bharata") defines it as "the land north of the seas and south of the Himalayas" (Eck 64, 2012). In other words, Bharata is the entire subcontinent. It is, as Diana Eck argues, also a land united by pilgrimage, ritual, and mythology. It is a sacred landscape rather than a political entity. It is the term I imagine the characters of this book using when referencing the land.

Vimala walks through the brothel and finds the women in different positions, fast asleep. Some readers will recognize this as a reference to the *Buddhacarita* (5.45*ff*) After the future Buddha experiences the Four Sights (old age, sickness, death, and renunciation), he returns to the palace and is entertained by the harem women. He watches their performance without interest. Afterwards, they fall asleep in various positions. The gods are behind this deep sleep, providing the future Buddha with a chance to escape. Vimala has had three of the Four Sights parading before her for years (as we shall see). **Neelima is her fourth sight.** Then, like the experience of the future Buddha, the women fall fast asleep and she is finally free to escape.

It should be noted, however, that in the *Buddhacarita*, there is a strong misogynistic flavor to the scene of the sleeping women. When they were awake, the women were seductive and beautiful, but once they fall asleep, they look like broken instruments. The future Buddha is disgusted with the pleasure senses which further inspires him to leave the worldly life. He thinks to himself, "dirty and distorted lies here exposed the true nature of women in this world" (5.64; Olivelle 2008). **Vimala is *not* disgusted by her fellow prostitutes, but she is disgusted by the world they share**—a nod to the *Buddhacarita*, but without the concomitant misogyny. For discussion of this scene in the Buddha's biography, see Wilson (1996).

4. The Gathering

Bhaddha Kundalakesa is one of the nuns of the early tradition whose verses are preserved in the *Therigatha*. I imagine her as a feisty, strong-willed older woman who walked the length and breadth of Bharata on her own. I will not reveal the details of her story here (her story will come later), but I will share her verses from the *Therigatha* as Hallisey has translated them. From these verses, so much can be gleaned.

> *Once I wandered with hair cut off,*
> *Covered with dirt, wearing only one cloth,*
> *I thought there was a fault where there was none,*
> *and I saw no fault where there were.*
>
> *I went out from the day-shelter up Gijjhakuta mountain*
> *Where I saw the spotless Buddha honored by his monks.*
>
> *I bent my knees and worshiped,*
> *Facing him I joined my hands in honor.*
> *He said to me, "Come, Bhadda."*
> *That was my ordination.*
>
> *Chinna, Anga, Magadha, Vajji, Kasi, and Kosala–*
> *For fifty years I enjoyed the alms of these places,*
> *Never incurring a debt.*
>
> *The name I was called means good fortune,*
> *It now becomes me.*
>
> *That wise lay Buddhist made a lot of merit*
> *When he gave a robe to me,*

This Bhadda, who is quite free from all ties (Therīgāthā
  107–111; Hallisey 2015).

According to these verses, Bhadda was ordained by the Buddha
(with his standard invitation, "Come") directly after meeting her. She
was therefore not part of Gotami's march to Vesali. For narrative purposes, however, I have arranged Bhadda Kundalakesa's story differently. Here, she joins the Gathering first, walks to Vesali with the
women, and only afterwards is she ordained. For stories about Bhadda
Kundalakesa, see the commentary to the *Therigatha* (*Therīgāthā-
Aṭṭhakathā* 99–108); the medieval Sinhalese *Saddharmaratnavaliya*
(Obeyesekere 2001), and Bhikkhu Sujato's novella, *Dreams of Bhadda*
(2012).

One of the first things one discovers when immersing oneself in
these early Buddhist stories is that an agreed upon timeline rarely presents itself. One source tells the story this way, another tells it that
way. Sometimes multiple characters are conflated into one, and at
other times we have multiple versions of the same character floating
through the narrative at once. Buddhist storytelling does not happen
in a straight line. What we have instead is a wide range of voices
ringing out together, each in their own way. In this book, Bhadda
Kundalakesa joins the Gathering first and meets the Buddha afterwards. But elsewhere, the lineup of events is different. One story does
not cancel out the other. The stories work together. More like a flower
arrangement. Not like a race.

The Gathering is a term I created for this book. To my knowledge,
the sources do not provide us with a specific word for this early movement of women. I was initially tempted to call it a Women's March,
inspired by Pema Khandro Rimpoche (2019), but it sounded much
too contemporary to me. The annual Women Marches of today do
not, however, seem so different from the march the women in this
story are making. The women of this book are marching through the
forest to ask the patriarchal gatekeepers to let them in. They are asking for access and recognition, which is what women today continue
to ask for. This makes me wonder, at times, how much progress we
have really made.

**The mysterious woman with the blue-black skin is a veiled refer-
ence to one of the Buddha's two chief female disciples, Uppalavanna.**
She is one of the most important women characters of early Buddhist

literature and she takes a leading position as a teacher in the early community. We find references to her throughout the early sources (see Collett 2016 for an overview). She is described as having blue-black skin because her name stems from *uppala* (either a blue lotus or a blue waterlily).

Uppalavanna's story is almost unbearably haunting. I had diffi-culty imagining a way of bringing it into this book—perhaps in part because it is difficult for me to relate to. According to the com-mentary to the *Therigatha*, Uppalavanna's mother had a son (before Uppalavanna was born) and her son was eventually taken from her (long story). She was then captured by the king of thieves in the forest who made her his wife (probably without much consent). She then birthed a girl (the future Uppalavanna), and one day her husband threw his daughter against some furniture and cracked her head, cre-ating a scar. The mother ran away and left her child behind.

Now it starts to get complicated, so bear with me. The mother met another man and married him. She did not realize it, but the man she married was actually the son she had lost years earlier. *Uppalavanna's mother therefore married her own son.*

Years later still, the man (Uppalavanna's mother's son, who was now also her husband) met a young woman and married her too. Uppalavanna's mother and this young woman became co-wives. And then Uppalavanna's mother noticed the scar on the back of the young woman's head and realized it was the daughter she had left behind. In this way, Upalavanna had become co-wives with her mother. They were married to the same man. *Uppalavanna was married to her brother and her mother was married to her own son (Therīgāthā-Aṭṭhakathā 196ff).*

While the purpose of this book is to tell a story of the first Buddhist women (to which Uppalavanna rightfully belongs), and this book cer-tainly does not shy away from stories of suffering, I did not know how to negotiate my way through Uppalavanna's story here. I therefore left her in the background. She has a striking presence, but I could not bring her closer in.

5. The Past Comes Charging In

When Vimala is discovered by Kumari, she gets dejected and realizes that her hopes were nothing more than **a lump of foam on Ganga's shores**.

This is a reference to one of my favorite Pali suttas, the *Phenasutta* (*Saṃyutta Nikāya* 22.95), which teaches that all things are hollow and without substance, like a lump of foam, a mirage, or a water bubble.

Vimala's debt to Kumari is a form of enslavement. Like everywhere else in the world, people were bought and sold in early India. We find reference to slaves in the early narratives (like the *Mahabharata*), in legal codes (like the *Arthasastra*), and in Buddhist sources. One of the first Buddhist nuns, Punna, describes herself as having been a slave, fetching water in freezing cold temperatures and fearing the wrath of her mistress (*Therīgāthā* 236–251).

We find evidence of slaves being used for labor (agricultural, domestic, sexual). Slaves were gifted as commodities and they were included in large dowries. Slaves were won in bets (Yudhisthira and the dice game serves as an obvious example), captured in war, and exchanged for bad debts. With the development of institutional Buddhism, slaves may have even belonged to monasteries as objects of property (Schopen 2004). Slavery in a variety of forms was, in other words, a regular feature of early Indian life. But as Basham (2004) notes, slavery as an institution never took on the magnitude seen elsewhere (such as ancient Greece). Indeed, it may be for this reason that the ancient Greek historian Megasthenes believed that slavery did not exist in India when he visited.

Slavery in a variety of forms was practiced for most of Indian history, but we must not mistake this to mean that every manifestation of it reached the levels of cruelty we often associate with it (particularly given American slave history). For further discussion of slavery in ancient India, see Chanana (1960) and Thapar (1984).

The golden tent, along with the guardian tribeswomen, are details I have added in the hopes of creating some of the tension I imagine the community experiencing about the Royal Women. Although the Royal Women may have been prepared to abandon their own regal status, the surrounding women could not have bypassed it as easily. Royalty in ancient India was a gift bestowed by the gods, a divine right, a status that was inscribed onto the very beings of those who carried it. It was bound by ritual and it served to balance cosmic forces. The Royal Women might have been prepared to abandon their status, but everyone else must have still struggled with the question of it. Deeply engrained communal habits are not so easily shed. For discussion of kingship in ancient India, see Jan Gonda's work (Jan. 1956, April 1956, and 1957), along with Heesterman (1957).

Most of the literature on ancient Indian royalty is, however, focused on kings. Queens (and princesses) do not often feature in the discussion. Female members of royal families would have been high caste (*khattiya*), which assumes a level of inherited birth status, but it is not clear how much divinity would have been associated with them. Nevertheless, I think we can assume some level of embodied status.

6. The Walking Begins

Kisa Gotami is an important character in the early Buddhist community of women. Her story of loss and subsequent awakening (with the help of the famous mustard seed) is a beloved Buddhist teaching. We will learn more about her later in the book.

Vimala tells Bhadda **the story of creation, with courtesans emerging from the wrist of the Primordial Man.** The story of the Primordial Man's sacrifice can be found in the *Rig Veda* (10.90). In that story, the Primordial Man is sacrificed by the gods, with each part of his body generating a piece of the cosmos. His mythical sacrifice is at the heart of creation with "all the varieties of being from the inanimate to the living" (Eliade 18, 1954) finding their purpose. Although courtesans are not formally included in this creation narrative, it seemed to me that they should be. I have therefore added them to this myth.

Shining like a crazy diamond in the sky is an homage to Pink Floyd (1975). Because this is creative writing, I decided I could.

There is no textual evidence that Vimala's mother was a courtesan. All the commentaries tell us is that Vimala's mother made her living from her beauty, just as Vimala later did (*Therīgāthā-Aṭṭhakathā* 77). Perera (1992), however, assumed that Vimala's mother was Ambapali. It is not clear why he made this assumption, as I have not come across it elsewhere, but perhaps he was merely connecting some of the dots: Vimala was a sex worker of some kind, her mother was also a sex worker of some kind, and they were from Vesali, which is where Ambapali lived. Therefore, Vimala must have been Ambapali's daughter.

This is an interesting train of thought, but to my knowledge, the texts do not link the characters in this way. The other possibility is that Perera confused two Vimala characters: Ambapali had a son named Vimala-Kondanna (*Therīgāthā-Aṭṭhakathā* 207), so perhaps Perera confused the male Vimala with the female one?

Regardless of how Perera came to his conclusion, I have followed a different storyline here: Vimala's mother was a courtesan, but her mother was *not* Ambapali. Vimala later became an ordinary prostitute (*vesī*) as the *Therigatha* describes her.

Choosing this direction provided me with an important creative opportunity: by giving Vimala an illustrious birth among the courtesans but having her fall from that position to become an ordinary prostitute, Vimala could embody a wider range of experiences. The risk with focusing on one experience or the other is that I could have unintentionally participated in an age-old tradition of orientalist exoticism (Daud 2011) where sex workers are concerned. By giving her access to a range of experiences, Vimala emerges as a more complex character—and hopefully so does the history.

As discussed in the notes to chapter 2, **ordinary prostitutes were very different from high-class courtesans.** Women fell into prostitution for all kinds of (often unfortunate) reasons, whereas courtesans belonged to illustrious lineages that were passed down from mother to daughter. We do not know what courtesan life might have been like in the time of the Buddha, but we do see early evidence in Buddhist literature of courtesans having substantial means and independence (Ambapali being the most famous example). By the first millennium, Indian texts like the *Kamasutra* go into detail about the "man about town" (*nagaraka*) who was an expert in all pleasure senses (not just sexual) and enjoyed these with aesthetic and intellectual refinement (Doniger 2016). Courtesans became the anchors of this pleasure world, just as kings anchored the political one, each one sovereign in their respective domains (Gautam 2014). Courtesan culture eventually became so elaborate, Gautam credits them with the development and spread of the arts in ancient India. Perera describes the courtesan as having been "a woman of accomplishment" (Perera 215, 1992), who mastered a variety of cultural arts and served the elite not just sexually, but equally as performer, artist, and companion.

I must credit one book, in particular, that helped me imagine **the life of a courtesan:** an ethnography by Saba Dewan entitled, *Tawaifnama* (2019). Although *Tawaifnama* is focused on interviews with contemporary *tawaifs* (courtesans of Northern India today), their experiences may reflect earlier traditions. Indeed, Davesh Soneji (2012), whose research focuses on the *devadasi* traditions of South India, argues that we are likely to find echoes of ancient courtesan culture among the *tawaifs* more than anywhere else.

The Great Goddess dominating the battlefield is an obvious reference to Durga (she has many incarnations and many names, but Durga suffices for our purposes here). The story of Durga slaying the Buffalo Demon is one of the most celebrated stories of early Indian mythology, but the story only appears in written form around the fifth or sixth century CE (almost one thousand years after the Buddha's period). There is therefore something historically askew here by bringing Durga's battle into conversation with the characters of the Buddha's life. The timing clearly does not work.

And yet . . . we know that stories can circulate for centuries before they are committed to writing, particularly foundational narratives like Durga's. It is therefore within the realm of possibility that the characters in the Buddha's story engaged with stories about Durga (even if Durga's story was only written down centuries later). See Kinsley's chapter on Durga in his book *Hindu Goddesses* (1988) for an overview. See Parpola's book, *The Roots of Hinduism* (2015) for an argument that some form of Durga's story might even reach back as far as Harappan civilization.

I spent quite a bit of time wondering about **the kinds of oil Vimala would have used to massage her mother's feet**. Early ayurvedic texts regularly cite the importance of oil massage for its health benefits (with foot massage being a specific recommendation). What is unclear is what *type* of oil was used. Sometimes ghee is suggested, but most often it is oil—I just could not identify which oil was meant. For an overview of some of these early references, see Gode (1955). **Almond oil** was readily available at the time, so I chose to use almond oil in this scene.

But almond oil on its own seems rather plain to me—especially for courtesans who were so aesthetically refined. I therefore chose to add a scent. **Camphor oil** is not indigenous to India, but it has a long history on the subcontinent (McHugh 2014). Camphor would have been an expensive and exotic item in ancient India, imported from lands far away (often as far as Borneo). Courtesans had resources and therefore could have had access to camphor as a purchased product, but they would have used it sparingly, each drop a tiny fortune. It is for this reason that camphor is summoned into this scene: camphor is an ingredient Vimala and her mother could afford and take delight in.

The squirrel with a brightly colored tail is a reference to one of the most extraordinary animals native to India (in my view): the **Indian Giant Squirrel**. As a Canadian, I am quite accustomed to squirrels. They invade our cities, trampling our gardens and raiding our garbage bins. They make our house pets wild with anxiety as they parade in front of glass patio doors with twitchy tails. Canadian squirrels are small acrobatic wizards, but also frustrating urban rodents. In India, by contrast, the squirrel can take on a majestic quality (as things in India often do), with a long body and a swirl of color in its fur.

7. Patachara

Cultures in every part of the world have at one time or another practiced child marriage. In many regions, the practice continues still, but legislation (both local and international) has certainly put an end to much of it. Where child marriage does persist, a litany of medical, economic, and social ills invariably follows. Obstetric fistula is one of the most common problems child pregnancies produce, which is what I am referring to here with the **leaking urine**.

Writing this book has had me consider all kinds of experiences that women in ancient India might have encountered, including what we call "child marriage" today. To my knowledge, **child marriage in ancient India** has not received much academic attention. We have, of course, many studies on ancient India; we have studies on marriage in ancient India, and we have studies on child marriage in colonial and post-colonial India, but we do not have much on child marriage in ancient India specifically. Kapadia's study (1966) of marriage in India includes a chapter on the question of age at marriage, and sources indicate that girls were often married around puberty. But the discussion is ultimately vague, and this may be because clear ideas of childhood versus adulthood (to follow Ariès's now famous argument) were not fully articulated in the early literature.

In her study of child marriage in contemporary India, Mary E. John (2021) argues that it is almost impossible to study child marriage in India prior to the colonial period; the idea of child marriage, according to John, only becomes a nameable problem under colonial rule (thereby coloring the lens with which the colonial period examined it). Girls (and boys) were married young, which is a nameable problem now, but may not have been so earlier.

Gotami's reaction to child marriage here admittedly appears modern, but I cannot accept the idea that contemporary thinkers were the first to recognize the difficulties a girl is forced to endure when she becomes pregnant too young.

Mutta is a nun from the *Therigatha*. Two sets of verses are associated with a character named Mutta. This means either that these belonged to two different nuns by the same name (which is how Dhammapala's commentary interprets it), or that the two sets of verses belong to one and the same character. I have decided to bring the two collections together and conflate them into one character.

The first set of verses associated with Mutta in the *Therigatha* is spoken by the Buddha to Mutta. He counsels her to live up to her name, to free herself from whatever holds her back (*Therīgāthā* 2). Mutta's own verses (potentially the second Mutta) are quite different.

According to the commentary, Mutta's family was poor and could only afford an old and hunchbacked husband (*Therīgāthā-Aṭṭhakathā* 14). As I describe in this book, Mutta begs for her freedom and her husband eventually grants it. In her second set of verses, Mutta declares herself free of three crooked things: "mortar, pestle, and husband with his own crooked thing" (*Therīgāthā* 11; Hallisey 2015). Her husband was, apparently, crooked in more ways than one.

Unlike Mutta, who is a marginal character (or set of characters?), **Patachara** is one of the most famous nuns of the early Buddhist community. Her story is known throughout the Buddhist world. Early tellings are, however, mostly found in Pali sources (Collett 2016), although we do find a version in the *Saddharmaratnavaliya* (Obeyesekere 2001).

We will hear more about what happened to **Patachara** later in the book (I don't want to spoil the story for those unfamiliar with her tale). What is important to note is that the Buddha is usually the one to name her the Cloak-Walker (Patachara). In this case, I have given Gotami the privilege of naming her instead.

As mentioned above, the *Therigatha* gives some of Mutta's verses to the Buddha to recite. He is the one to counsel Mutta, but in this book, I have given Gotami the role of counselling her.

Giving Gotami a role the Buddha normally plays (either by naming Patachara or counselling Mutta) is a decision influenced by Walters's now famous argument. As noted above (notes to chapter 1), Walters argues that Mahapajapati Gotami is presented in the *Apadana* as the Buddha's counterpart. Calling her Gotami (the feminine form of Gotama) places her in direct apposition to the Buddha. She leads the women just as he leads the men. She is, in other words, **"the Buddha for women"** (Walters 375, 1994). She can therefore (I believe) safely assume certain roles that the Buddha normally plays in the literature. In my view, she has every right.

8. Beads and Mirrors

According to Google Maps, **the distance between Kapilavatthu and Vesali is about 400 kilometers.** With a quick and steady pace, the distance could be covered in ten days, but these women would not have moved so quickly. The Gathering Women were not wearing sneakers, they were not athletes, and many of the women were elderly. Combined with regular interruptions of local hospitality, I imagine the journey would have taken quite a bit longer—a question of weeks more than days.

There is nothing quite like a **child ascetic.** They are certainly endearing with their bald heads and long robes, and they are photographed with adoring enthusiasm by tourists all over the world. Many child ascetics grow up in loving environments, doted on by the senior monastics who care for them. Elijah Ary provides an intimate picture of his own monastic education as a child ascetic, which is worth reading (2013). The opening section of this book includes a loving representation of child asceticism, with Darshani cared for by her elders.

But it should come as no surprise that not all child ascetics are so protected. The past few years have seen a deluge of scandals emerging from Buddhist communities **on the subject of sexual abuse,** and while most stories do not involve children, it is surely only a question of time before more of them do. The Catholic Church is not the only tradition guilty of child abuse. Kalu Rimpoche's revelation of the abuse he experienced as a child monk is one of the most famous contemporary examples. For a discussion of this case and its context, see Wilde-Blavatsky (2013).

Research on child ascetics in early India is still in its infancy (no pun intended), but it is developing. Laurie L. Patton's chapter on children in Hinduism (2009) considers some of the ways children participate in the tradition or are represented by it. For evidence of **child abandonment by unwed mothers,** see Jonathan Silk's article (2007). Some Buddhist temples continue to play this role of accepting unwanted children (Lindberg Falk 2013), and Buddhist temples throughout the Buddhist world care for children in a variety of ways. Temples often run schools, do community outreach, and provide temporary ordination for children (almost like religious summer camp). See Boisvert's article on temporary ordination in Burma (2000). For further discussion on the roles children can play in Buddhist texts and traditions, see Sasson 2013a.

Bringing child asceticism into this book was a way of introducing the reader to the most famous child monk in Buddhist history: **Rahula, the Buddha's son.** We will meet him later in the book. Readers may be familiar with him from *Yasodhara and the Buddha* (Sasson 2021) which opens with the scene of his departure (his mother saying goodbye to her son as he prepares to follow his father into the forest). He was, according to some sources, only seven or eight years old when he left home.

The tribeswomen were created as a way of introducing the reader to a fascinating character from the *Therigatha*: **Vaddhamata** (literally, Vaddha's mother). We will hear more about her later in the book, but for now I will simply note that, according to the commentary, Vaddhamata was from **Bharukacchaka** (*Therīgāthā-Aṭṭhakathā* 171) which is today the city of Bharuch in the coastal province of Gujarat. To bring Vaddhamata from Bharukacchaka all the way to the Gathering (near Vesali), I created a backstory of war and displacement, something that is as familiar to us today as it must have been then.

The clothing and jewelry of these Bharukacchaka tribeswomen is inspired by traditional Gujarati costume. Vimala is awed by all the jewelry and wonders if the **women are wearing their family fortunes on their backs.** To wear one's fortune was in fact a custom in many parts of the ancient world. See Wendy Doniger (2017) for a discussion.

The wedding ritual of accompanying the bride to the groom's village is a practice that continues in South Asia to this day. During my time in Nepal in the 1990s, wedding rituals were performed this way, with villagers spilling out of their homes to accompany the bride to her new home. It is one of my most vivid memories of my time there.

Bhadda Kundalakesa wonders if the tribeswomen understand the local language, which is referred to here as **Magadhi.** We know that ancient India (like India today), could boast of tremendous linguistic diversity. Every region included a variety of languages and local dialects. The Buddha is described in the literature as spending most of his time in the Magadha region. He is therefore often associated with the Magadhi language. He may have used other dialects when required, but Magadhi was probably his mother tongue (although there is some debate about this). For a discussion of the Magadhi language (and the Buddha's relationship to it), see Bhikkhu Bodhi's introduction to his book, *Reading the Buddha's Discourses in Pali* (2020). Also, Norman's excellent book, *A Philological Approach to Buddhism* (1997). For the role of Magadhi as a primordial language, see Heim (2018).

9. The Long Road

Bhadda Kundalakesa identifies as **the most feared debater in all of Bharata**. While I don't want to divulge Bhadda's story yet, her debating skills are an important feature of her character. According to the commentary to the *Therigatha*, each time she entered a new town, she would build a small sand heap and place a rose-apple branch in it. Then she would declare, "if anyone is able to enter debate with me, let him trample down this branch" (*Therīgāthā-Aṭṭhakathā*, 101; Pruitt 1999). She waited, and if the branch was trampled, she would present herself for public debate.

Naturally, Bhadda Kundalakesa won every public debate. But one day, she met a disciple of the Buddha. He trampled her branch, engaged her in debate, and *he* was the one to win. She decided then and there to join the Buddhist Order.

Vimala's self-defence lesson comes out of my own experience with training in Kyokushin Karate. In practice sessions, we are careful to avoid hitting any of the "middle parts," but teachers always remind us that if we ever find ourselves in danger in the outside world, that's precisely where you aim—right through the middle. And you start with the groin.

10. Flying Horses

Assavata is a horse I invented, but is inspired by other horses of Indian literature. Most notably, Assavata is modeled on the Future Buddha's brilliant steed, Kanthaka. When the Future Buddha escapes his palace and makes his Great Departure, Kanthaka is the one to carry him. Kanthaka is said to have soared across three kingdoms in one night.

According to the *Jatakanidana*, he could have soared even further (he could have travelled the entire span of the cosmos had he wanted to), but he was impeded by all the flowers the gods were raining over them in celebration of their journey (64). For a translation of the *Jatakanidana*, see Jayawickrama (1990). For more on Kanthaka, see Ohnuma (2017).

The name of Vimala's horse, Assavata, is inspired by the famous Tibetan **Windhorse**. In Tibetan tradition, the Windhorse is often understood as an indigenous symbol of luck and good fortune. Its image is depicted on prayer flags and planted in high places for the wind to carry. Windhorse seemed to be a fitting name for Vimala's steed.

The story of the churning of the ocean is one of the most beloved stories of early Indian literature. As described here, the gods and demons churn the ocean together to reach the nectar of immortality that is buried at the bottom. All kinds of treasures emerge from this churning, including the mythical horse **Ucchaihshravas**. This story appears in a number of early sources, most notably the *Mahabharata* (1.17).

Horses make appearances throughout Indian literature (starting as far back as the *Rig Veda*), but domestic horses only seem to take root in India in the first millennium (van der Geer 2008). **For most people, horses represented an almost prohibitive expense**, which is why Vimala's mother is never quite convinced that Assavata will stay. Although horses were part of the landscape, Doniger argues that they were never fully incorporated into village traditions in India: "throughout Indian history, horses have belonged only to people who were not merely economically 'other' than the Hindu villagers—aristocrats—but politically and religiously other. The horse represented political power, military power, economic power . . ." (Doniger 443, 2014). See also Doniger's most recent book, *Winged Stallions and Wicked Mares: Horses in Indian Myth and History* (2021).

Vimala's music and dance training is not just the result of textual research. Every visit I have been privileged to make to South Asia over the years has included at least one musical performance (if not many). The performing arts continue to delight audiences, whether they take place on stages in great halls, on TV, or in small temples. Often these performances include a moment of recognition to the responsible deities of the region, along with an apology to the earth goddess for the stomping about to take place.

As mentioned earlier in these notes, I was influenced by Saba Dewan's descriptions of tawaif training in her book *Tawaifnama* (2019). Also noteworthy was Davesh Soneji's work (2010 and 2012) and David Shulman's many lavish descriptions that I have had the pleasure of hearing about over the years. See also Shulman (2012). The performing arts suffered terribly under colonial rule in South Asia; some practices have disappeared entirely as a result.

Courtesan history involves a delicate balance between the performing arts and sexual trade. In this scene, **Vimala acknowledges some of her sexual training,** making reference to techniques that are cited in the earliest literature. The *Kamasutra,* for example, includes an entire sub-chapter on **nail scratching,** introducing the practice with the statement that when passion mounts, "lovers scratch one another with their nails in the spirit of erotic friction" (2.4.1; Doniger and Kakar 2002). The text then proceeds to outline the kinds of scratches that can be performed on the body and different ways of caring for the nails. Buddhist monastic law is apparently aware of this connection between long nails and eroticism, as it records an episode in which a monk with long nails is propositioned by a woman. She threatens to scratch herself if he does not accept. The Buddha reprimands the monk for having long nails and declares it a rule that, in the future, any monastic with long nails would be found guilty of wrongdoing (*Cullavagga* 5.26). The assumption here is that the woman interpreted the monk's long nails as an invitation.

Dildos make an appearance in the Vinaya (the monastic code), but discussion does not always distinguish the use of dildos from masturbation. See Derrett (2006). We also find reference to dildos in the *Kamasutra* in a discussion about how women might keep themselves occupied while sealed up in a harem. Women are described as giving each other pleasure "with dildos or with bulbs, roots, or fruits that have that form." The women are also described as lying on statues of men "that have distinct sexual characteristics." And while women are mostly described as being the ones to use these sex toys on each other, the text adds that "kings too, if they are sympathetic to their women even when their passion does not stir, make use of dildos until they achieve their goal . . ." (5.6.2–4; Doniger and Kakar 2002). For a discussion of theses passages (and their subsequent Western translation hiccups), see Doniger's essay, "The 'Kamasutra': It Isn't All About Sex," (2003). She argues that some of the *Kamasutra's* history is focused specifically on women, their needs, and their desires (and that courtesans may have even commissioned parts of the text themselves), providing women with more agency and sexual freedom than later commentators were (and even later contemporary puritanism is) willing to recognize. For a discussion of this resurging puritanism, see Doniger's 2011 essay.

The idea that **a courtesan's life was like a spiderweb** (to the spider it was home, but to others it was a trap) is a metaphor I borrowed from Ocean Vuong. He turns to this idea repeatedly in his book, *On Earth We're Briefly Gorgeous* (2019).

References to **the use of cosmetics in ancient India** can be found throughout the early literature. Poets and storytellers often drop hints of the various types of products men and women might have used to beautify themselves. For a contemporary look back at some of these practices, see Chandra's almost encyclopedic volume, *Costumes, Textiles, Cosmetics and Coiffure in Ancient and Mediaeval India* (1973).

11. The Flying Sage

The story of Markandeya was first introduced to me through one of Wendy Doniger's writings. In a beautiful essay entitled, "Inside and Outside the Mouth of God" (1980), Doniger considers the theme of cosmic vision, and includes the story of Markandeya when he falls from Vishnu's mouth. I have kept this story close to me from the day I first encountered it and was glad to have an opportunity to share it here. Vimala has not, however, learned the whole story about Markandeya. There is more to Markandeya's experience, which she will discover closer to the end of this book. For a translation of the story, see *Classical Hindu Mythology* (Dimmitt and Van Buitenen, eds. 1978). See also Zimmer (1946) for discussion.

Bhadda Kundalakesa has never heard the story of Markandeya, which may seem strange given how worldly she is. This was an intentional decision on my part. One of the most extraordinary features of Indian storytelling is how much of it there actually is. Some stories span the length and breadth of India with three hundred and thirty million variations, while others are entirely regional concoctions. Storytelling in India is a like a great big tapestry (to use a familiar metaphor), with dozens of colors and different types of thread. There is just so much of it all. I wanted Bhadda Kundalakesa to have a vast repertoire of knowledge, but I also wanted her to be in a process of discovery at the same time. Because no one can know every story. Not even her.

12. River Mud

Vimala jumps into the river to bathe while remembering what it was like to have to bathe behind the brothel at Kumari's. The question of where one can or cannot bathe is an important public concern. The Buddhist monastic code includes a few episodes of nuns bathing near prostitutes and the situation always ends badly. In one case, the prostitutes tease the nuns and try to seduce them back to the world of the senses, saying things like "why are you living the life of a renunciant when you are so young?" (Vinaya iv 279; Horner 1997). Monastic writers were obviously uncomfortable with the idea of prostitutes and nuns interacting. And while the Buddha does not forbid nuns from bathing with prostitutes explicitly, the rules he does establish make it more difficult for prostitutes to get close.

Such passages suggest that prostitutes were probably kept apart. It therefore makes sense that **Vimala would have been forced to bathe in private,** far from the "respectable women" who bathed in the river. I also suspect, however, that prostitutes risked abuse if they bathed in public, so the concern might well have gone both ways.

The beauty-clay Vimala washes with is a piece of my childhood. I used to wash with "beauty-clay" at my aunt's pond in the countryside whenever we visited as children. My cousins and I would cover ourselves with the grey slop and massage it into our hair and throw clumps of it at each other as we laughed. Years later, I had a similar experience at the Dead Sea just outside of Jerusalem, covering myself with Dead Sea mud. Reference to the use of clay as a beauty product can be found throughout the early literature, including in the Buddhist monastic code where rules outline how much clay can be used and how. For a list of early references in Indian literature, see *Costumes, Textiles, Cosmetics and Coiffure in Ancient and Mediaeval India* (Chandra 1973).

Patachara's story is one of the most famous stories of early Buddhism. While it is never wise to compare suffering, her experiences with suffering are among the most pronounced. I will not reveal much here (for those readers unfamiliar with her tale), but I do want to provide a bit of background.

According to the commentary to the *Therigatha*, Patachara is born into a wealthy family in the city of Savatthi. She eventually falls in love with a man her family disapproves of, and from there everything falls apart. According to the commentary, the man she marries is a house servant (108). According to the *Apadana* (616), he is a country boy. I have followed the commentary to the *Therigatha* here, by having her fall in love with a servant instead of a country boy.

The fact that she chooses her own husband (instead of accepting an arranged marriage) speaks to her independence. As Collett notes (2016), the *Therigatha* provides us with stories about women from all types of backgrounds, but only two choose their own spouses (more on this later). In every other case, the women are married off by their families. Patachara fell in love and ran away with her beloved. This might be interpreted as stubbornness (or something to that effect), but her choice can also be admired for its agency and freedom. According to the commentary to the *Dhammapada*, Patachara's parents try to stop her by imprisoning her in a tower (Rapunzel?), but Patachara finds a way out (*Buddhist Legends* 8.12). She races off with her beloved . . . and the rest is devastating history.

The story of the ladder and the mango tree is not part of the tradition, but one that I created to give voice to Patachara's privileged background and her strength of character. The **Stairway to Heaven** reference is from Led Zeppelin (1971). It was impossible to resist.

The detail about her being so wealthy that **she had different kinds of rice to eat** is inspired by a passage that I thought was in the *Buddhacarita*, but that is in fact not there . . . In my head, the *Buddhacarita* describes the Future Buddha as having been raised with such extravagant wealth, he even had different kinds of rice to eat. I have made reference to this passage in talks and interviews and even in my classes, but when I returned to the text to jot down the reference, I could not find it. Stumped, I looked elsewhere, in other texts that describe his opulent life, but nowhere did it appear.

And so here we have a genuine example of storytelling birthing itself into something new. I have discussed this detail so many times, I have convinced myself (and probably many others) that it was true. But the detail is not in the *Buddhacarita* or anywhere else that I can think of. I am not sure what happened in my head—where the details of other stories collided to create something new—but the story is so entrenched in my mind, I cannot shake it. The detail therefore remains.

I did, however, find one reference to rice that might have inspired this mutation: in the *Sukhamalasutta*, the Future Buddha is described as having been so wealthy, even his servants ate rice and meat (*Anguttara Nikāya* 3.38). It's not multiple kinds of rice, but it's as close as I can get.

The red rice that her father sometimes has brought in from the Himalayas is a reference to Bhutan's famous red rice, which does indeed have a delicious nutty flavor. I had the privilege of visiting Bhutan a few years ago with my family, and the red rice quickly became one of our favorite side dishes.

13. Vesali

In the early sources, **Vesali** is described as having been a beautiful city. Archaeological remains agree. The city was fortified with a strong wall and surrounded by a moat. It was also elegantly arranged and crafted (Schlingloff 2013). The city itself was small, but the literature describes an extensive kingdom that went well beyond the boundaries of the city itself (Cunningham 1871).

The Licchavis (sometimes also called the Vajjians) are associated with this kingdom and the Buddha is described as having been impressed with their organizational habits. In the *Mahaparinibbana-sutta*, a king asks the Buddha if he thinks he would be successful in an attack against the Vajjians. The Buddha explains that the Vajjians are well organized, meet together in assemblies, and listen to each other. He therefore counsels the king *not* to attack, because he would not win against such a harmonious community (*Dīgha Nikāya* 16). For further discussion of the Licchavis and their guilds, see Law (1922) and Singh (2009).

Vimala's backstory (like much of Patachara's) is a story I invented, made from pieces picked up in various places. As noted earlier, all we know about Vimala's childhood is that her mother made her living "with her beauty," just as Vimala later did, and that they were from Vesali. The *Therigatha* is filled with stories of loss—a reflection of the fundamental Buddhist insight that everyone experiences suffering. I therefore created a story of suffering for Vimala that I thought would have made sense given her context.

Vimala's mother was not cremated because she died of the Skin Disease. Cremation is important not just as a means of body disposal; it is also infused with ritual and symbolic meaning, not the least being that fire acts as a source of purification. Some people are therefore *not* cremated: renunciants, for example, are often not cremated because they have already burned away their own impurities. Children are likewise not always cremated (presumably because they have no impurities yet to speak of), along with those who die of snakebite. Jonathan Parry (1994) also includes those who die of smallpox, because the Goddess of Smallpox, Sitala, inhabits the corpse and therefore cannot be burned. In all of these cases, bodies are traditionally immersed in a river instead.

Early Buddhist writings also make reference to **charnel grounds** as spaces where the dead would be "dumped" and left to rot. It is not clear why some bodies were dumped (as opposed to being cremated or immersed), but I think it is safe to assume that some of these bodies were deemed too polluting to deal with (such as someone who has died of the Skin Disease). Charnel grounds become important imaginative spaces in Buddhist lore. They become meditation spaces for monks to develop awareness of impermanence. They also become the haunts of great masters (like Padmasambhava and the Dakinis). In some accounts, the Buddha uses the robe of a rotting corpse that he found in a charnel ground soon after making his Great Departure (Schopen 2006).

I was not sure, at first, that I could introduce such lavish **blue paint** into Ambapali's courtyard, but a bit of research confirmed that the color blue was well established as a natural dye long before the Buddha's period. Lapis Lazuli was mined in what is today's Afghanistan, and the Indigo plant (in its many varieties) has been harvested and transformed into dye from as early as the Indus Valley Civilization.

For an accessible discussion of the history of color, see Finlay's travelogue entitled *Colour* (2003). Perkin provides a step-by-step description of how Indigo is harvested and transformed into dye in his article, "The Indian Indigo Industry" (1915). While Perkin describes the process as he witnessed it in 1915, Mira Roy argues that the dyeing process remained mostly unchanged until the synthetic process overtook it (1977).

I realize, of course, that these details are not crucial to a reader's understanding of the story, but I fell down the rabbit hole of blue dye and its history, and I need to share some of the results.

14. Hollowed-Out Mess

Vesali was famous for its organizational structure, with guilds and city taxes and elected governing bodies. **Courtesans were part of this institutional setup: not only did they pay taxes, but their fees were set** by the city (*Arthaśāstra* 2.27). The rise of courtesan culture is directly tied to the rise of urbanism, with courtesans being proudly described as "ornaments of the city" (*nagaramandana*; see Saxena 2006). Unlike prostitutes who were often relegated to the outskirts, **courtesans lived in city centres, proudly and without apology.**

The Gathering Women are hosted by Ambapali. Early Buddhist sources do not tell us where the women went when they first arrived in the city, nor do they tell us who took care of them, fed them, and hosted them throughout their time there. Presumably, however, a large gathering of women would have had to go somewhere. I thought that Ambapali, with her extensive resources and her developing interest in the Buddha's teaching (see below) was an obvious solution.

One of the questions scholars have wrestled with more generally is, **where did the female followers of the Buddha actually live?** The Buddha and his monks are regularly described as being housed in beautiful monasteries (*vihara*) provided by wealthy donors (often kings) in forests outside the city gates. But nuns are forbidden from living in the forest. According to Schopen, all the Vinaya traditions forbid nuns from living in the forest (the Pali Vinaya is an exception here, but Schopen notes that even in Pali sources, indirect evidence for this rule can be found). Instead, nuns are required to set up monastic residences in urban settings. Nuns would therefore not have had the privilege of living in isolation (as the monks did in forest monasteries), retreating from the mundane complications of a busy world, but would have been quite literally "embedded in their local urban environment."

This fact alone may "turn out to be the single most important difference between Buddhist nuns and Buddhist monks" (Schopen 6, 2014). The rules concerning where nuns might be allowed to live are therefore quite contentious, and many nuns today challenge the interpretation that they cannot live in isolated retreat. There are strong legal arguments on both sides of the equation. I have therefore decided to have Ambapali host **the Gathering Women inside the city, as per Schopen's conclusion,** but where they will establish themselves afterwards remains unclear. Hopefully some of the women managed to live in isolation, if that is what they wanted.

Ambapali is the most famous courtesan of Buddhist literature, but she is certainly not the only one. Addhakasi, for example, describes herself as having been such an expensive courtesan, her nightly fee was equivalent to the income of the whole land of Kasi (*Therīgāthā* 25). As she aged, however, she was worth only half the amount (hence her name, Half-Kasi). An alternative reading provided by the commentary is that she charged half the amount for half a day (instead of a whole night) for those customers who could not afford a whole night (*Therīgāthā-Aṭṭhakathā* 31). Either way, Addhakasi is known to have been an extremely expensive courtesan and her fees were institutionally set. Ambapali is said to have been so expensive, she was the primary reason for Vesali's exceptional wealth (*Mahāvagga* 8.1).

Ambapali becomes a nun later in her life and her poem in the *Therigatha*, where she reflects on her fading beauty, is especially touching. She says that her hair was once black and curly, but now has become coarse. Her body that was once "like a polished slab of gold" (*Therīgāthā* 266; Hallisey 2015) is covered with wrinkles. Every aspect of her once radiant beauty has faded.

When Vimala notes how much Ambapali has aged, it is a nod to her poem. Ageing is impermanence made manifest. Nothing personal, as she repeats in her poem at every refrain. "Nothing different than that" (*Therigatha* 270, Hallisey 2015).

Patachara's story is one of devastating loss. We met Patachara for the first time in chapter 6, but it is only now, in this chapter, that we finally hear the story that she has been holding.

Patachara has many verses in the *Therigatha*. Not only does she share her story of accomplishment, but she also gives teachings. Consider this section, which she speaks to a group of nuns:

> *You keep crying out, "My son!"*
> *To that being who was coming or going somewhere else*
> *And who came from somewhere else,*
> *None of which you know . . .*
>
> *He came from there uninvited, he went from here without*
>   *permission,*
> *He came from somewhere or other, he stayed a bit.*
>
> *From here he went one way, from there he will go another,*
> *A hungry ghost will be reborn as a human.*
> *He went the way he came, what is there to grieve about?*
>   (Therīgāthā *127–130; Hallisey 2015).*

For a mother who lost both children to ask, "what is there to grieve about?" speaks volumes of her accomplishment. She knows things most of us cannot even whisper in the dark.

Patachara's story is also recorded in the commentary to the *Therigatha* (108–118), in the *Apadana* (409–434), and in the Sinhala *Saddharmaratnavaliya* (Obeyesekere 2001). In all of these accounts, Patachara first loses her husband while she is giving birth in the forest. Then she loses both of her children, and then when she finally makes it to Savatthi, she discovers that she has also lost her parents in a fire (caused by the storm). Patachara's story is an extraordinary story of loss. She goes mad for a while, walking barefoot and naked in grief, until she discovers the Buddha's teachings and becomes free.

For studies on Patachara, see Collett (2016). See also Fonseka (2017) who compares Patachara's story with Sonali Deraniyagala who lost her two children, her parents, and her husband all at once during the tsunami of 2004. As extreme as Patachara's story might seem to many of us today, it does not belong exclusively to ancient history.

I have changed **the order of events in Patachara's story**. Normally, Patachara emerges from the forest and encounters the Buddha directly. Then, in one dramatic moment of public revelation, she falls at the Buddha's feet and becomes free. But in this story, I wanted to give Patachara space to slowly unfold. I could not imagine her walking out of the forest naked and mad, meeting the Buddha and transforming instantly. While I understand that the early writers were referencing the Buddha's power by telling the story this way (he was so impressive that one moment with him could eliminate lifetimes of pain), I think a contemporary reader might better relate to her story if she goes through stages, peeling off one layer of grief at a time. Readers who are familiar with the traditional story of Patachara's conversion will be surprised by the order of events here, but if there is one thing I have learned about Buddhist storytelling, it is this: Buddhist stories shift and change, expand and contract with every new telling. This book offers a new telling, allowing Patachara's story to change again.

15. The Great Woman Tree

We encounter a passing reference to the mysterious **blue-black woman** again here. As noted earlier (notes to chapter 4), this is Uppalavanna, one of the Buddha's future chief female disciples.

Ambapali is said to have been discovered at the foot of a mango tree. The most logical explanation for this is that she was abandoned at birth, but Buddhist storytelling rarely operates on such a mundane level. Ambapali was therefore not abandoned. The story is, rather, that as a result of accumulated merit from her past lives, Ambapali was granted the *privilege* of being born outside a mother's womb. She was therefore born spontaneously at the foot of a mango tree (*Therīgāthā-Aṭṭhakathā* 207).

Celebrating birth outside the womb has an obviously misogynistic flavor. Early Indian literature regularly describes the mother's womb as a dark, smelly, and even violent place. Spontaneous birth outside the womb liberates one from having to undergo what would otherwise be a traumatizing (and unhygienic) experience. Many characters are granted miraculous births that separate them from their mother's disgusting insides (not the least being the Buddha himself). For a Buddhist description of life in the womb, see the *Visudhimagga* (499–502). For discussion of these issues, see Sasson (2009), Kritzer (2009), and Langenberg (2017).

Ambapali's mango grove is the setting for her most famous scene in the Buddha's life story: after hearing him teach, Ambapali asks the Buddha for the privilege of hosting him for a meal in her mango grove. This is a common practice in Buddhist narrative, with community members vying for the honor of hosting him. The Buddha, however, never went to these meals alone. He brought his five hundred monks with him. Whoever invited him had to therefore have the means (and the space) to receive them all. The fact that Ambapali asks to host the Buddha speaks to her extensive resources.

The fact that the Buddha accepts her offer speaks to his openness (an obvious Jesus and Mary Magdalene parallel here). What is wonderful, however, is what comes next in the story: some Vesali princes meet Ambapali on the road in their fancy chariots. She is in her fancy chariot and there is some jostling for space between them on the road. Ambapali informs them that she is in a hurry because she has invited the Buddha and his monks to her grove for a meal. The princes are offended and go to the Buddha to complain. They ask him to come to *their* residence for a meal instead. The Buddha refuses because he has made a commitment to Ambapali. Their (fabulously revealing) response is: "we are beaten by this mango-girl" (*Mahāvagga* 6.4).

The Great Woman Tree does not belong to the early sources. She is a tree I created for this book, but she is built on narratives about other "people trees" (to borrow Haberman's language; see his book, *People Trees*, 2013) of the Indian imagination. As noted in chapter 1, trees in South Asia are often worshiped. They have personal characteristics and have ways of interacting with the local community. One book in particular inspired me for this chapter (one of the most majestic books I have ever read actually): *The Overstory* by Richard Powers (2018).

Gotami's hair cutting scene is likewise not part of the traditional story. When Gotami makes her first request in Banyan Grove, the texts do not suggest that she has cut her hair. But when she arrives in Vesali with the Gathering Women, the Pali Vinaya explicitly mentions her shaved head (*Cullavagga* 10.1).

The fact that she arrives with a shaved head means that, at some point between the first request in Banyan Grove and this second request in Vesali, Gotami must have taken a moment to cut her hair. But when did she do it? And why? And did she have permission?

While the question of permission might seem unusual (it is *her* head, after all, so her choice), a shaved head in this context is an obvious symbol of Buddhist monasticism. But the Buddha did not give her permission to join the Order. She was *not* a Buddhist monastic. So how could she justify shaving her head as though she were one?

If she did shave her head between his initial refusal and her arrival in Vesali, then one might interpret her head shaving as an act of defiance. This is tempting. After all, how else do women break the glass ceiling? It is not usually by following the rules or accepting the status quo.

But having Gotami break the rules and defiantly going her own way is its own interpretive risk. If we decide that Gotami defied the Buddha and shaved her head *despite* his rejection, then we are saying that one of the most important characters of the Buddhist tradition defied the Buddha himself. Religious readers may find this conclusion difficult to accept.

I can appreciate the reluctance many may feel if Gotami is interpreted as defying the Buddha. On the other hand, if women do not defy the limitations they are presented with, nothing changes. I am quite certain that monastic women to this day defy rules they believe are unjust. I therefore propose a middle way with this narrative: Gotami cuts her hair even though he never said yes, but precisely because he did not say no. The very obscurity of the Buddha's response is the grey zone she uses to make the call herself.

Alternative Vinaya accounts do, however, provide us with a different window of opportunity here. In a few of these, after Gotami makes her request for ordination and after the Buddha refuses, he suggests that she shave her head *as a householder*, a kind of "celibate holy life, presumably in the protected environment of her home" (Analayo 2016a, 52). Perhaps this is its own middle ground of the time, and Gotami shaved her head not as an act of defiance, but in proper accordance with her status as a practicing householder. I am inclined, however, to imagine Gotami as having been more radical than that. After all, she was not asking for permission to practice as a householder. She was asking to become a nun.

As for *how* I created Gotami's hair-cutting scene: it is modeled on the Future Buddha's own hair-cutting scene. According to many early sources, the Future Buddha makes his Great Departure dressed in royal regalia, with princely clothes and a tremendous jewel-studded turban (according to the *Jatakanidana*, the turban has no less than ten thousand layers!). When he reaches the edge of the forest, he removes his turban and slices off his hair with his jeweled sword. The hair (and the turban, according to most accounts) is caught by Serpent Deities and carried into the sky. The earth rumbles and shakes, expressing its enthusiasm for this moment of extraordinary renunciation. See Sasson (2021b) for further discussion.

Most early Buddhist writings were likely produced (and preserved) by male writers. If women had been invited to preserve more of their stories (perhaps during the first council, where their input is notably absent, as Bhikkhuni Vimalanyani insightfully noted during one of our talks together), they would have surely provided us with a story of how Gotami had cut her hair. Since they did not, I thought I would offer one.

As we have already noted, one interpretation of these early narratives is that Gotami functioned as the Buddha's female counterpart. This is, at least, Walters' conclusion in his study (1994) and I have relied on it throughout this book. If Gotami is the leader of the women as the Buddha is the leader of the men, then her hair-cutting scene must be just as significant. The cosmos therefore rumbles with pleasure as Gotami slices off her hair. But instead of Serpent Deities catching the hair as in the Buddha's narrative (which are symbolically male), **she is greeted by a tree goddess (symbolically female).**

16. Bhadda Kundalakesa

Bhadda Kundalakesa's story can be found in the commentary to the *Therigatha* (99–108). A similar version can be found in the *Saddharmaratnavaliya* (Obeyesekere 2001). In both of these accounts, Bhadda Kundalakesa is raised in the lap of luxury by overly indulgent parents. She sees a thief walking to his execution and asks to have him as her husband. Her parents accept her proposal and everything falls apart from there.

Bhadda Kundalakesa joins the Nigantha sect after killing her husband. The Niganthas of early Buddhist writing are today known as the Jain tradition. We unfortunately do not know much about the first Jain nuns. We do know that women were included in the Jain monastic order from very early on (probably before Buddhists ever formed a female monastic community of their own), but we know very little about how the first monastic Jain women lived, how they came to join the community, and what rules they were asked to follow. This may be because the early literature was quickly consumed by the schism it experienced between two competing sects (the Digambaras and the Svetamabaras). Whenever the issue of women's participation in the community is raised, it is usually in connection to this schism.

One of the main issues behind this schism is the issue of clothing. Some Jains believed that to truly renounce, one must renounce everything, including one's clothing, and thus live "sky-clad" (naked). The other sect believed that everything should be renounced, *with the exception* of clothing. Since many did not believe that women could live safely as sky-clad renunciants, their status in the community was negotiated separately. For an excellent overview of women in Jainism, see Jaini's contribution, *Gender and Salvation* (1991).

The main teacher of the Jain community, Mahavira, was probably a sky-clad monk. I considered depicting him naked, but since his clothing is far from the point in this scene (and I did not want to *make* a point of it), I decided to avoid the issue.

Bhadda Kundalakesa kills her husband by throwing him off a cliff. In the account provided by the commentary (*Therīgāthā-Aṭṭhakathā* 100), her husband first asks her to take off her jewels and make a pile on the ground, after which he says that he will kill her. She removes her jewels and then pushes him off the cliff from behind. In the *Saddharmaratnavaliya*, he does not ask her to remove her jewels. He simply announces that he will kill her. While circumambulating him, she manages to kill him first (Obeyesekere 2001).

Surprisingly, this entire scenario is played out a second time with a second character in early Buddhist storytelling: in the *Sulasa Jataka* (419), a courtesan named Sulasa sees a thief from her window walking to his execution. She bribes the executioner and marries the thief. They eventually go to a mountain top to thank the deities for his reprieve and, as with Bhadda Kundalakesa, Sulasa pushes her husband off the cliff once she realizes he was preparing to kill her.

The detail of **Bhadda throwing her necklace down after him** is not part of any of these accounts. I borrowed it from Bhikkhu Sujato's novella, *Dreams of Bhadda* (2012). I thought the detail was so good, it deserved a second iteration.

As Collett notes (2016), Bhadda Kundalakesa is one of the few women from the *Therigatha* who chooses her own husband (she unfortunately chooses very badly). She shows remarkable independence and strength of character throughout her life. I hope I have captured some of her personality here.

The temple Bhadda Kundalakesa and her husband visit is inspired by one of my favourite temples in South Asia. In the beautiful Himalayan region of Mustang, there is an important pilgrimage site known as Muktinath. The Muktinath temple sits on a mountain top overlooking a sea of neighboring cliffs. It has a wood roof with bronze trim, and natural spring waters that pour out of one hundred and eight waterspouts. It is, however, dedicated to Lord Vishnu (not a mountain goddess). I used the image of Muktinath, but placed a goddess in the shrine. For a discussion of Muktinath, see Poudel (2000).

Last time I visited Muktinath, I offered a coconut. I smashed it on the stone floor and watched as its juices poured out. **Coconut offerings take place in temples all over South Asia.** People will tell you that it serves as a replacement for human sacrifice, that it represents a human head, or that it is your ego that you are smashing apart (a more modern interpretation, I suspect). Whatever it means to whoever is doing the explaining, coconut smashing is a tradition with a long history. I am sure Bhadda smashed a few coconuts in her time too.

17. Muttering and Mad

I had not noticed **Chanda** before reading Charlie Hallisey's translation of the *Therigatha*. But in his introduction, he points out how the *Therigatha* pays special attention to the social realities of the time, and to the suffering that women in particular were forced to experience. Chanda is one such example. She ordains "not out of any spiritual aspiration, but as a way of getting food" (Hallisey xxx, 2015).

Chanda suffers in particular because of **the stigma widows have often been made to suffer.** Widowhood is a challenging issue in South Asia and has been discussed by many. See Nagarajan (2018) for a discussion of women and auspiciousness (and by extension, the loss of auspiciousness in widowhood). The difficulty for widows has sometimes led to a particular kind of suicide known as *sati*. This tradition has a long history, but is at the heart of devastating orientalist exaggerations, so I would caution readers not to jump to conclusions too quickly. For a discussion, see *Ashes of Immortality: Widow Burning in India* by Catherine Weinberger-Thomas (1991). For a different take on widowhood, see Shanti Mishra's novel, *A Widow's Gift* (2008).

The *Therigatha* preserves two characters by the name of **Sama** and in both cases, they are described in the commentary as having been friends with someone called Samavati (37–38 & 39–41). Both Sama characters are likely one and the same. In the first version, Sama has to hear the teachings multiple times before understanding them. In the second version, Sama is described as having struggled as a nun for twenty-five years before she finally became free. In the commentary to the *Therigatha* (44-46) we learn that Sama was devastated after her friend Samavati died. While we are not told more about who Samavati was, it is possible that she was one of King Udena's wives who was murdered by a competing wife. Queen Samavati was barricaded in her palace and burned alive (*Buddhist Legends* 2.1). I imagine Sama watching her friend die in the flames.

If Sama's friend was in fact Queen Samavati, it is possible (given Sama's devastation after losing Samavati) that they were lovers. The *Therigatha* does not explicitly identify any of the characters as having been queer. It is, in fact, a surprisingly heteronormative text (surprising given all the diversity it otherwise represents). But same-sex love must have been present among the Gathering Women, even if the texts themselves do not reveal more. Monastic codes, by contrast, provide us with many rules that take the question of same-sex desire seriously. For an overview, see Cabezón (2017).

Peak Hall is a monastery located in the forest, just outside of Vesali. In Pali it is called Kutagarasala, which means a building with a great hall and a peaked roof. Kutagarasala is often translated as Gabled Hall, but I have chosen to translate it as Peak Hall here.

Bhadda Kapilani is an important teacher in the early Buddhist community. She annoys Vimala and Bhadda Kundalakesa with her chirpy joyfulness, but I have not chosen this depiction out of disrespect.

Bhadda Kapilani's story is lighter than most. She does not have to fight, stumble, negotiate, or run away as so many other women did. People with easy life journeys are sometimes annoying to others. This is just the way human relationships go. And while I realize that the women of these stories all become exceptionally accomplished, they are also human. They must have gotten on each other's nerves at times. When we read the sources carefully, we find that the early community was constantly negotiating conflict. The Vinaya alone provides more than enough evidence.

According to the sources, Bhadda Kapilani married the one who came to be known as Mahakassapa. They both yearned for a life of renunciation, so when they heard about the Buddha, they left together. Eventually, they decided that it would be more appropriate if they separated. **Bhadda Kapilani joins the women and Mahakasspa finds the men.** Her story can be found in the *Therīgāthā-Aṭṭhakathā* (67–75), as well as in the *Apadana* (882–951).

Kisa Gotami is one of the most familiar characters of the *Therigatha*. Her story is specifically associated with devastated motherhood and serves as a warning to others (if you don't let your child go, you will be like Kisa Gotami, crazed with grief and a dead baby in your arms). In the commentary to the *Therigatha*, Kisa Gotami's child is a few years old when he dies. He is described as running in all directions, and then "he died" (*Therīgāthā-Aṭṭhakathā* 174; Pruitt 1999). I have chosen to shorten the timespan here, so that the child is born and dies almost immediately thereafter.

We do not follow Kisa Gotami's story to the finish line in this book, but her story is well known. When Kisa Gotami appears before the Buddha with her dead baby still in her arms, the Buddha asks her to fetch a mustard seed from a home that has never known loss. She knocks on one door after another, asking for a mustard seed and asking if there has been loss. Every house has mustard, but every house also has loss. She eventually comes to realize that loss is universal, that it is not personal, and she lets her dead baby go. Her verses can be found in the *Therigatha* (213–223) and her story is narrated in the commentary (*Therīgāthā-Aṭṭhakathā* 175). For a discussion of Kisa Gotami and motherhood, see Ohnuma (2007) and Collett (2016).

18. Motherhood Lost and Found

We learn a bit more about **Bhadda Kundalakesa's journey** in this chapter. She remains with the Niganthas for a period of time, but eventually realizes that she needs more. Their teachings do not satisfy her. According to the commentary to the *Therigatha*, she walks from village to village, listening to teachers, debating them, but no one impresses her. One day, she encounters Sariputta (one of the Buddha's chief disciples). He debates her and she loses. She asks Sariputta for permission to join the Buddhist Order. He brings her to see the Buddha and she receives ordination (*Therīgāthā-Aṭṭhakathā* 101ff).

Bhadda Kundalakesa does not join the Gathering Women on their collective march in most renditions. On the contrary, she is ordained independently. According to her verses in the *Therigatha*, she goes to see the Buddha and he replies with the simple formula, "come, Bhadda" (*ehi bhadda*). She then states, "That was my ordination" (*Therīgāthā* 109).

Because she does not mention the dual ordination procedure outlined in the *Cullavagga*, some have argued that Bhadda Kundalakesa was ordained *before* Gotami made her request with the Gathering Women. She may have therefore been the first Buddhist nun. While I do love this possibility, I chose to include her in the Gathering so that she could participate in the story right through (am calling upon creative licence as justification). For the argument that she was ordained individually, see Williams (2000) and Krey (2010).

The female Jain teacher referenced here, **Candana**, appears in a number of early Jain sources. See Jaini (1991) for references.

The Buddha is described as having renounced his worldly life as though it were nothing more than "a ball of spit." This expression is taken from Pali sources that describe his Great Departure precisely in these terms (*Jātakanidāna* 63). The future Buddha had the best of all possible worlds, the most beautiful home, a loving family. And yet, it was nothing more than a ball of spit to him when compared with the spiritual life he was hoping to find. For further discussion, see Sasson (2021b).

The monks are sitting in meditation when the Gathering Women arrive. At first, they appear to be perfectly still and perfectly uniform. But as Vimala looks more closely, she notices small differences. Their hair is not all the same, nor are their robes. These differences are important. Throughout this book, I have worked to humanize the women. They are not perfect, they do not all renounce with pure intentions. They are layered and complicated and real. The monks must have been just as complicated. Their hair is therefore not all the same, their robes are all a bit different. Some of the monks are asleep in the back row. This is monastic life as I have witnessed it over the years (in a number of settings). No monastery is perfect. Monks do not float on clouds and speak with perfect wisdom (only Shantideva does that). Monasteries are messy expressions of real human life. To pretend otherwise is to create a pedestal from which they will invariably fall.

Some of the monks do not have shaved heads but instead have long dreadlocks. This is a practice that continues to this day, particularly in Himalayan traditions (most notably, among Ngagpas). Hindu renunciants (*samnyasi*) often grow out their hair as well. The hair is abandoned as a sign of renunciation (instead of shaving it). While I do not have evidence of any of the early monks practicing this tradition (indeed, Ngagpas are not strictly speaking monks), I think it is fair to assume that such differences existed even during the Buddha's lifetime. Mahakasspa, for example (Bhadda Kapilani's former husband), was famous for his ascetic disposition. He wore rag robes and kept apart. Perhaps he let his hair grow during periods of intense isolation? It is surely reasonable to expect variety among the first Buddhists (just as there is variety today). Human beings never last long in organizations that require militant sameness. See Hiltebeitel and Miller (1998) for discussions about the significance of hair in South Asia.

Yasodhara's experience of loss is at the heart of my last book, *Yasodhara and the Buddha* (2021a). See also Sasson (2020) for the academic argument behind the book. A number of early sources give voice to this experience of loss. See the *Buddhacarita*, the *Bhadrakalpavadana*, and the *Sugata Saurabha* (among many others). The scene of Yasodhara watching the Buddha's return from a window and refusing to come down to greet him can be found in the *Jatakanidana* (90). She thinks to herself that if she has any virtue, he will come find her in her room (and he does). Many sources describe her telling her son to ask his father about his inheritance. See the *Jatakanidana* (91) and the *Mahavastu* (3:262). See also Crosby (2013) for a discussion.

The king requests a moment of *darshan* with his son. *Darshan* comes from the verbal root "to see" in Sanskrit and refers to the experience of reciprocal sight one might have with a deity when going to the temple. One sees the deity and the deity sees them. That is *darshan*. See Diana Eck's book, *Darśan* (1998), for more on this. But the experience of *darshan* is not limited to deities in temples. One can also have *darshan* (sight) of an important teacher. In this case, the king hopes to have *darshan* of the Buddha, who has become a great being. *Darshan* is a very dear term to me, and I always look for ways of including it in my writing. It is name we gave our son.

Vimala watches the mother-son reunion and suddenly wonders, *who is who in this story*. Are they renunciants asking for permission to join the order, or are they family members looking to reunite? This question is important to consider. Because renunciation is often imagined in its most abstract form, we expect renunciants to feel nothing about the families they have left behind. But recent scholarship on family in Buddhism has made it much clearer that such absolute notions are unrealistic (and in most cases, undesirable too). Renunciants may renounce their families, but renunciants are still human beings with personal histories.

The Buddha himself is surrounded by family members in the forest. Most of the early community is related to him in some way. When Gotami sings her final verses in the *Apadana* and performs her feats of accomplishment, the Buddha tells Ananda to announce that his mother has reached Nibbana (*Apadāna* 155). The Buddha still calls Gotami his "mother;" he does not speak about her with neutrality. He does not pretend she is just a random individual he barely knows. Family remains family, even in awakening. The quality of the relationships might change, but the relationships themselves are undeniable. For discussion of these themes, see Shayne Clarke's book, *Family Matters in Indian Buddhist Monasticisms* (2014). Also, Liz Wilson's edited volume, *Family in Buddhism* (2013).

Vimala thinks back to the miscarriages and abortions she was forced to endure. Students often ask me if abortion could have existed in "ancient times." It is a fair question, given that we associate abortion with modern technology and medication, but abortion is far from modern. When I lived in Sindhupalchowk (a rural area of Nepal) in the mid-1990's, a student told me that couples often snuck into the forest to "be together." When I asked him what happened if the girl became pregnant, he shrugged and replied, "we have herbs for that." I never learned what those herbs were.

The early sources do not provide us with much technical information about how one might rid oneself of an unwanted pregnancy, but the fact that texts regularly condemn abortion tells us that abortion was in fact practiced. The details were probably passed down in oral traditions that are now lost to us. For discussion, see Riddle (1994) and Lipner (1989). For a discussion of abortion in Buddhism, see Damien Keown's edited volume, *Buddhism and Abortion* (1999).

Vimala has a fantasy that she could have raised a daughter the way her mother raised her. Courtesan culture was matriarchal, with the lineage passed down from mother to daughter. See Saxena (2006) and Bhattarcharji (1987); the *Arthasastra* likewise makes reference to an inherited lineage between mothers and daughters (2.27). In the South Indian epic, *Manimekhalai*, the protagonist Manimekhalai is the daughter of a courtesan, and her mother was the daughter of a courtesan too. See the translation by Daniélou (1989). For discussion of the *Manimekhalai*, see Paula Richman (1986).

Vaddhamata is a fascinating character from the *Therigatha*. We met her in chapter 8. Mothers are often represented in Buddhist literature as being desperately tied to their children and incapable of achieving awakening as a result. It is only when they lose their children that mothers are described as finally free to pursue awakening for themselves. For a discussion of this recurring theme, see Ohnuma (2012) and Sasson (2013b).

Vaddhamata, however, represents an interesting challenge to this worldview. She does not lose her child before she dons the robes. Instead, she chooses a life of renunciation while her son is still alive (and young enough to need her). Like the Buddha, **Vaddhamata leaves her son behind.** A few years later, her son joins her in the forest and becomes a monk (also like the Buddha), crediting his mother with the inspiration.

Vaddha's verses of accomplishment (as a monk) can be found in the *Therigatha*, alongside his mother's. He recognizes her wisdom and then gives her credit for his own realization: "urged on by my mother, I reached the highest peace" (*Therīgāthā* 211–212; Hallisey 2015).

Along with Sariputta, **Mogallana** is one of the Buddha's two chief disciples. Unlike many other characters in the Buddha's story, Mogallana is not a member of the Buddha's family. He would therefore not be personally acquainted with the Royal Women, which is why Mogallana is so formal when he meets them. In the *Buddhavamsa* (1.58), **Mogallana is described as having dark skin** (like Uppalavanna) and psychic powers that made him thunder like a storm cloud. I have combined these images in my description of him. For a biography of Mogallana, see *Great Disciples of the Buddha* by Nyanaponika Thera and Hecker (1997).

19. Ananda

Ananda is known throughout the Buddhist world for being the Buddha's chief attendant, but he receives this position late in life. The story of the Gathering Women occurs earlier in the Buddhist story, which means Ananda has not yet been appointed as chief attendant. It seemed natural, however, that even before he is appointed, he reveals some of the qualities that he later becomes famous for.

According to the early sources, once Ananda does become chief attendant, he ensures that the Buddha is always comfortable, that he has his meals at the right time, that he is not disturbed at the wrong time. He fields visitors and takes care of the Buddha's sleeping quarters. According to Malalasekera, he would circle the Buddha's chambers at night repeatedly to ensure the Buddha's sleep was not disturbed (1:251, 1997). For a general discussion of his character as it appears in the Pali Canon, see Nyanaponika and Hecker (1997).

Ananda is described as having cried when the Future Buddha left home. This is not part of the story insofar as any of the traditional sources claim, but it is familiar behavior for Ananda. When the Buddha dies, Ananda is described as being utterly inconsolable. Despite having spent more time with the Buddha than almost anyone else, he does not achieve awakening during the Buddha's life (presumably because he was too busy to work on his attachment issues). At the funeral, Ananda therefore sobs (unmonastically) while other monks sit with mindful awareness.

In Ananda's defense, he does achieve awakening soon afterwards . . .

Ananda is working in a kitchen, making the Buddha's morning brew. As some readers are surely aware, the Vinaya declares that monks are supposed to be wandering and homeless, unattached to any one particular space. They are not permitted to work the land like farmers or cook in a kitchen. For a discussion of some of these rules, see the article by Aleksandrova and Rusanov (2021).

But Vinaya regulations are regularly negotiated to fit local contexts and needs. Ananda should not strictly speaking be working in the kitchen, but the Vinaya is not always followed to the letter. Most monasteries today (if not all of them) have busy kitchens with monastic members moving in and out of them. The rules around food production and distribution in particular have faced significant reinterpretation throughout the Buddhist world.

One may argue, however, that Vinaya rules were not being renegotiated so early on (during the Buddha's very lifetime), but given how elaborate the Vinaya is, the Buddhist monastic community must have been in perpetual legal transformation. What the Vinaya declares and how those first Buddhist monks actually lived are two different questions. I therefore conclude that Ananda may well have been working in the kitchen.

Ananda's dedication to the Buddha's morning brew was inspired by the book, *From the Zen Kitchen to Enlightenment* (Dōgen and Uchiyama 1983), where **kitchen work is described as requiring the highest level of mindfulness.** This scene also provided me with the opportunity to acknowledge kitchen (traditionally women's) labor which so often goes unnoticed.

Unlike Mogallana, who would have had no personal relationship with the Royal Women, Ananda was the Buddha's cousin. The Buddha and Ananda grew up together, and so the Queen of Sakya was his aunt. It is for this reason that **Ananda and Gotami greet each other with easy recognition.**

When speaking with the Buddha, Ananda often addresses him as **"Bhante."** This term is regularly used in Pali sources and means something to the effect of "Venerable." It can therefore be used as a term of address for any monastic, but in Pali literature it is generally reserved for the Buddha.

The Perfumed Chamber (*gandhakuti*) is a curious feature of the Buddha's story. In a number of sources, the Buddha is said to reside in what has come to be known as a Perfumed Chamber. The Jetavana monastery in Savatthi was the first to have had a *gandhakuti*, but eventually every monastery built one. It is not clear whether the

Buddha is responsible for the scent, or whether the chamber is itself scented, but either way the literature is clear: wherever the Buddha resides, perfume follows. The most important article on this subject remains John Strong's piece, "Gandhakuti" (1977).

Ananda's role in the story of the women's request for ordination is well known. According to the Pali Vinaya, he is the one to have noticed Gotami standing by the gate, "her feet swollen, her limbs covered with dust, with tearful face and crying" (*Cullavagga* 10.2; Horner 1997). He therefore approaches the Buddha to ask if women might be allowed to receive "the going-forth from home to homelessness." Because he intervened on their behalf, Ananda is beloved by nuns throughout the Buddhist world. See for example, Paula Arai's work (2000).

However, Ananda is reprimanded by the monks during the first council *precisely* because he intervened on the women's behalf. So the *Cullavagga* claims, the monks accuse Ananda, saying: "This too is an offense of wrong-doing for you, revered Ananda, in that you made an effort for the going forth of the women in the dhamma and discipline proclaimed by the Truth-Finder" (*Cullavagga* 11.9; Horner 1997). Ananda defends himself and says, "I do not see that as an offense of wrong-doing," but because he had faith in the community, he agreed to confess it anyway. In other words, Ananda apologized for helping the women, but he did not think he should have to. It is no surprise that Buddhist nuns everywhere still express their gratitude to him.

According to the account preserved by the *Cullavagga*, Ananda asks the Buddha three times for women to receive "the going-forth" and three times the Buddha responds as he did when Gotami made the same request ("it is not a good idea to ask the question").

After the third rejection, Ananda changes tactic. **Ananda asks if women are capable of achieving awakening (perfection of the mind).** The Buddha says yes. Ananda then asks why Gotami, who was his stepmother, who nursed him and cared for him, is standing at the gate. The Buddha finally agrees to give Gotami ordination (with conditions attached, as we shall see in the following chapter). For a comparative analysis of the different Vinaya accounts, see Analayo's *Foundation History* (2016a).

A number of questions arise from this dialogue. First and foremost, why does Ananda negotiate the request instead of Gotami? In the Vinaya, Ananda speaks on her behalf, but Gotami was there, just outside waiting to speak with the Buddha herself. She was the one to ask the first time. Why is she not the one making the request again?

Also pressing is the question of whether this request for ordination applies *only* to Gotami, or if it extends to the other Gathering Women as well. Ananda refers specifically to Gotami's ordination. If the ordination (and the subsequent conditions attached) applies only to Gotami, then where do the other women stand in all of this? Does the Buddha ordain Gotami and Gotami ordains the others? Do the conditions apply to everyone or just to Gotami? There are legal implications to each of these questions, depending on how one decides to answer them.

Most of all, why did the Buddha say yes? **Was it out of guilt? Ananda points to the Buddha's relationship with Gotami and references the fact that she raised him.** Does the Buddha owe her? Is that what women's ordination is ultimately about?

This last question troubles me most. If the Buddha ordains Gotami out of guilt (or to pay a personal debt), then what does that say about the Buddha's emotional range? And how does this translate for the other women who receive ordination? Would every Buddhist nun have to be understood as carrying the remains of the Buddha's personal debt to his mother? Are women monastics objects of guilt? Buddhism has a long history of filial piety and this may indeed be an interpretive venue to pursue (see Ohnuma 2006, for example), but what a devastating conclusion that would be. For a broader discussion of filial piety in Buddhism, see Cole (1998).

A counterargument to this concern can be found in the repeated reference to the "fourfold assembly." **Buddhist literature regularly proclaims the importance of the "fourfold assembly"—namely, the need for monks, nuns, laymen, and laywomen in the Buddhist Order.** According to the *Lakkhanasutta* (*Dīgha Nikāya* 30), the wheel-marks on the Buddha's feet (that he was born with) represent the fourfold assembly that he was destined to establish.

In the *Mahaparinibbanasutta* (*Digha Nikaya* 16) which takes place on the Buddha's deathbed, Mara (the rough equivalent of the devil) reminds the Buddha of a promise he made on the eve of his awakening (years earlier) that he would not die before successfully establishing the fourfold assembly. The Buddha confirms that he has indeed established the fourfold assembly, so he is free to die.

The point for our purposes is that this means the Buddha intended on establishing a nuns' order from the very beginning. Even before he became a Buddha, before he achieved awakening, *the Buddha had planned on having nuns in his community*. See Analayo (2015). Add to this the notion of the Buddha-life Blueprint (Strong 2001) whereby all Buddhas make similar (if not identical) decisions about the community's structure, *including establishing a fourfold assembly*, and there really is no question anymore: fully ordained nuns must be part of the Buddhist Order.

Ananda does not make this point about the fourfold assembly in the *Cullavagga*, but I added it to their discussion because it is an important point to highlight. I simply cannot imagine the Buddha agreeing to ordain women out of obligation. He could not have been guilted into it either. If this story has any internal logic, the Buddha must have ordained women because it was the right thing to do, because every previous Buddha had ordained women, because the markings on the soles of his feet predicted he would do the same, because the Buddhist community would be incomplete without them. Because a community without nuns would be like a table with only three legs (so the saying goes).

20. The Eight Heavies

Vimala looks around at the many Gathering Women and wonders if one day there would be no women left. In the *Temiya Jataka*, this in fact happens, with entire cities emptying out after everyone turns towards asceticism. In that story, renunciation seems to be almost contagious.

But I was primarily thinking about the biblical book of Esther when I wrote that there would be no women left. Queen Vashti publicly defies her royal husband in the book of Esther. The ministers warn the king that if he does not reprimand his disobedient wife, women everywhere will hear of it and they too will defy their husbands (Esther 1:18). Women everywhere will walk right out the door. The fear that women might one day just up and leave is obviously a fear that resonates across cultures.

We met **Sundarinanda** at the very beginning of the book. Translated, her name means "Beautiful Nanda." She may have been Gotami's daughter with her husband King Suddhodana. The literature, however, is confusing because several characters have the name Nanda. The most important article on Nanda is Collett's (2014).

I decided not to bring a sister named Nanda into *Yasodhara and the Buddha*, since her character is rather evasive, but I did want to include her here (I have, however, made her a cousin). In the commentary to the *Therigatha*, we learn that **Sundarinanda leaves the home life because everyone else did.** She watched as her brothers, her parents, her nephew, and even her sister-in-law all go forth. She asks herself, "'now what shall I do in the house? I shall go forth.' And she went to the bhikkhuni monastery. She went out of love for her relatives, not because of faith" (*Therīgāthā-Aṭṭhakathā* 81; Pruitt 1999). This is to me one of the most fascinating features of the early literature: it presents us with characters who renounce not out of spiritual aspiration, but for personal reasons (not all of which are particularly lofty). The commentary also describes **Sundarinanda as vain and self-centered.** It is for this reason that she refused to walk barefoot to Vesali. It is also why she is described at the beginning of the book as having such difficulty adjusting to monastic life.

The Eight Heavies (as Janet Gyatso once dubbed them at an American Academy of Religion meeting long ago) are known in Pali as the eight *garudhammas*. They can be translated as the "Eight Heavy Teachings" or "Eight Heavy Things," but I like "the Eight Heavies" best. According to Bhikkhu Sujato, they might also be translated as the "Eight Rules to be Respected" (Sujato 2007, 46).

However we choose to translate the term, the *garudhammas* are, without a doubt, the most contentious rules of the Vinaya. In an impassioned article on women's ordination, Gyatso describes the *garudhammas* as "a liability . . . to Buddhism as a whole." (Gyatso 14, 2010). Every Vinaya collection includes a similar formulation of these rules.

I wrestled with the question of including the *garudhammas* for a long time. Many feel that that Buddha could not possibly have been the one to institute them. Scholars have repeatedly raised questions about their historical validity, arguing that they are probably later additions.

The most convincing argument on this front is that Vinaya rules are usually articulated *after the fact*. A monk or nun does something they shouldn't and the Buddha creates a rule forbidding that behavior as a result. But the *garudhammas* are delivered in one fell swoop, before any of the relevant situations have generated a reason for delivering them. On this basis alone, we have reason to question their historical validity. See Bhikkhuni Kusuma (2000), Analayo (2010), Hüsken (2010).

In an online course, Venerable Vimalanyani made an argument that I found particularly compelling: in *Anguttara Nikaya* 8.53, Gotami approaches the Buddha with the request for instruction so that she might live in isolation (which is in itself fascinating, since most Vinayas explicitly forbid nuns from living in isolation). The Buddha responds with a list of eight practices she should remain mindful of.

Bhikkhuni Vimalanyani argued that the eight practices described in the *Anguttara Nikaya* might have been the original teaching associated with Gotami, and the *garudhammas* were created as a mirror text to replace them. In one set of eight, women monastics are instructed about the teachings so that they can practice independently, while the eight rules of the Vinaya do the exact opposite, ensuring women monastics are *never* independent. In other words, from this perspective, the earlier (and more inspiring) teaching would be the one that grants women monastics agency and independence. But with time, women monastics lost that agency and eventually found themselves with the *garudhammas* instead.

Whatever the historical truth of it all, the *garudhammas* are challenging (if not downright upsetting). For a detailed examination of each of the *garudhammas*, see Bhikkhu Sujato (2007).

The fact remains, however, that even if the Buddha never articulated the *garudhammas* himself, **the *garudhammas* now belong to the tradition.** Buddhist monastic women in most parts of the Buddhist world have to negotiate them. I first began exploring the *garudhammas* during my ethnographic work in Sri Lanka in 2004 and have continued to raise the topic at every possible juncture since—during Sakyadhita meetings, when visiting monasteries in different parts of the world, over coffee (or tea) with monastic friends.

Every argument presented in this chapter is an argument I have encountered from Buddhist nuns about whether one should or should not abide by these heavy rules (historical arguments aside). There is, unsurprisingly, no consensus.

The most pressing question is whether a senior nun should bow to a junior monk. Gotami raises this question herself almost immediately after accepting to live by the *garudhammas*. According to the *Cullavagga*, Gotami agrees to abide by the *garudhammas*, but then asks for an amendment. She says, "It were well, Lord, if the Lord would allow greeting, standing up for, salutation and the proper duties between monks and nuns according to seniority" (*Cullavagga* 10.2; Horner 1997). In other words, she would like monks and nuns to recognize each other by seniority, regardless of who is a monk and who is a nun.

Ananda takes this request for an amendment to the Buddha and the Buddha replies: "This is impossible Ananda, it cannot come to pass . . . Ananda, these followers of other sects, although liable to poor guardianship, will not carry out greeting, standing up for, salutation and proper duties towards women, so how should the Truth-finder allow . . . it?"

Translation: the first rule disturbed Gotami enough to have her challenge it, and the Buddha's concern (at least insofar as the *Cullavagga* tells it) is that the locals would never accept things otherwise. Locals would never accept the idea of monks bowing to nuns. Whether the Buddha makes this decision due to peer pressure (not a very charitable interpretation) or the Buddha was simply acting in accordance with the limitations of his time, the fact remains: the answer is no.

The Buddha and Gotami meet in person for the delivery of the *garudhammas*. Afterwards, the Buddha steps aside to let the women discuss the rules among themselves. But this is not how the story is traditionally told. I have called upon my creative license to justify the change.

According to the *Cullavagga* version of the events, the *garudhammas* are given to Ananda and Ananda delivers them to Gotami. The entire negotiation happens *through* Ananda. The Buddha and Gotami never face off in person. And then, according to the *Cullavagga*, Gotami agrees to the rules without consulting the women.

None of those details makes sense to me. I cannot imagine something so important as the delivery of the *garudhammas* happening through an intermediary. I also cannot imagine the Buddha giving his stepmother ordination from a distance. If nothing else, it seems rude. Gotami and the Buddha met in person in Banyan Grove when she made the request for ordination the first time. Why would he suddenly use an intermediary for this second scene? It makes no sense.

I also cannot imagine Gotami accepting such heavy rules without discussing them with the women first. The implications are significant. The rules require conversation. I therefore decided to change the story. I recognize, however, that the early sources do not tell the story this way.

Patachara's speech in the Perfumed Chamber follows the tradition to some extent, but as I noted earlier, the order I have created is different.

According to the commentary to the *Therigatha* (111) Patachara hears the Buddha preaching and falls at his feet in a moment of extraordinary public conversion. She tells her story and is subsequently ordained. In this book, I have changed the order of events and included her among the Gathering Women, so she encounters the Buddha along with everyone else (and not separately at another time). However, I still wanted her to have a moment of public declaration, so she stands before the community of women after having seen the Buddha and speaks to them instead.

The experience she describes about **washing her feet in the river** is taken directly from her verses in the *Therigatha*. Her story of awakening is described with the following:

While washing my feet, I made my mind useful in another way,
By concentrating on it move from the higher ground down.

Then I held back my mind,
As one would do with a thoroughbred horse,
And I took a lamp and went into the hut.

First I looked at the bed, then I sat at the couch,
I used a needle to pull out the lamp's wick.
Just as the lamp went out, my mind was free
    (Therīgāthā 114–116; Hallisey 2015).

This may be my favorite poem in the *Therigatha*. She achieves awakening by reflecting on ordinary reality. She watches the water move, she enters her hut and sits down, she pulls out the lamp's wick, and she becomes free. It is just as Ambapali said: nothing more than that.

I have incorporated Rahula into this scene, having him enter the Perfumed Chamber during the women's debate, and his grandmother Gotami happily welcomes him onto her lap. This detail is not part of the tradition, but it was an explicit decision on my part. While radical separation may be the theoretical goal of monastic life, I have not encountered it as a lived reality very often. Monastics continue (in most cases) to be in relationship with their families even after they ordain.

Even when radical separation of family ties does take place, it does not exclude monastics from expressing genuine affection and love. I have witnessed tender moments in almost every monastic setting I have visited over the years. I can well imagine Gotami inviting her grandson onto her lap, before *and* after attaining complete and perfect awakening.

Vimala wonders where Surasa, as someone of "ambiguous sex" (*pandaka*) would fit with strictly separate areas for monks and nuns. As we saw in the notes to chapter 2, *pandakas* represent a third sex, and the Buddha never even considered establishing an Order for them.

Pandakas pose a challenge to a binary system like Buddhist monasticism. It is therefore unsurprising that Buddhist rules rejected all *pandakas* as potential candidates. As Cabezón explains, "to this day, in ordination rituals in many Buddhist countries, one of the ordaining elders will ritually inquire of every candidate whether he or she is a non-paṇḍaka . . ." (Cabezon 2017, 383). If the answer is no, they are immediately denied access.

Nandaka is one of the bad guys of early Buddhist monasticism (at least in my view). In the *Nandakovadasutta*, Nandaka is described as having been reticent to teach the nuns when the Buddha requested it of him (*Majjhima Nikāya* 146). Analayo argues that this text (along with its many parallels) is a type of androcentric-narrative-distancing used by the sources to keep the nuns apart (2016a). Nandaka may or may not have been a misogynist in reality, but his character is used by these texts as a means of expressing some level of disdain towards nuns.

I have chosen to use Nandaka in a similar way here: according to the *Cullavagga*, after the women accept the *garudhammas*, the Buddha is described as lamenting the decision (which makes little sense—why would a perfectly awakened Buddha lament his own decision?) and claims that while the teachings would have lasted 1000 years, they will now only last 500 years because, **women are to the Order what mould is to a rice field** (*Cullavagga* 10.1).

This line of women being like mould on a rice field has haunted me since I first encountered it. This line is attributed to the Buddha, but I simply cannot have the Buddha say it here (I guess that's my personal limit). I have therefore given Nandaka the prestige of making the Awful Statement. I don't know if he actually deserves it, but he is the villain in this story and will have to carry the weight.

Perhaps I am being too easy on the Buddha, by giving this line to someone else, but it is the best I can do. If the Buddha really existed, and if the Buddha really once said that women are like mould on a rice field . . . well I am not quite sure where I go from there. For more on this prophecy, see Williams (2002).

According to the commentary on the *Therigatha*, **Vimala sees Mogallana** in Vesali during his alms round and falls in love with him. She follows him back to his hut and tries to seduce him. He replies with a stream of abuse: "You bag of dung, tied up with skin, you demoness with lumps on your breast . . . ," rejecting her as a disgusting creature whose body smells vile and emits liquid sewage, and whom anyone wishing to remain pure would stay away from as they would from human faeces or an overflowing public latrine (*Therīgāthā-Aṭṭhakathā* 77; Pruitt 1999)

Apparently, Vimala achieved a level of insight as a result of this tirade. She calls Mogallana a great hero for his teaching. Jonathan Silk has noted that this scene between Vimala and Mogallana has a parallel in the *Mulasarvastivada Vinaya*, but this time with Utpalavarna (Silk 2009).

Since this is my reading of the tradition and creative licence abounds, I have made the decision to change the quality of this encounter. I did not want to omit it, because it is Vimala's only scene outside of her verses in the *Therigatha*, but I could not accept that she tried to seduce Mogallana (the fact of her being a prostitute is not an argument). I also could not accept that a great monk like Mogallana would be so cruel. I imagine this scene being produced by later (and angrier) writers, who twisted the tale. *They* decided that her intentions were seductive and *they* decided that she deserved to be reviled.

I have no evidence to support my view. There is nothing in the literature that can directly point me away from the harshness of this scene, but history is replete with unfair accusations made against women. I therefore think my direction is reasonable, even if it is not textually anchored. I have given Vimala and Mogallana a moment to explore competing worldviews in a reasonable tone, without accusation or assault (from either one of them). I hope they both appreciate the adjustment.

Mogallana knows Vimala's name. This is not part of the story of their encounter, but I include it here because Mogallana is famous for his psychic powers. He can slip through a keyhole, read minds (*Aṅguttara Nikāya* 8.20), engage with invisible beings (*Udāna* 4.4). He would have known Vimala's name without requiring an introduction.

We have now reached the end of the notes. I could have written more, but I am sure this is enough material for most readers. For those interested in going further, I recommend digging into the bibliography. There is so much good scholarship on the early Buddhist community, so much to read and learn and wonder about. The Study Questions that follow might help launch the exploration. Enjoy!

Study Questions

1. In the notes to the book, the author claims that "Vimala . . . told me unequivocally that she was the one I had been looking for" as the main narrator of *The Gathering*. What does that mean to you?

2. Many of the women in this book have painful histories. Sasson explains in her introduction that this is a feature of the *Therigatha*, with women coming from all kinds of difficult circumstances. What is the relationship between women and suffering? Do you see suffering as intrinsically linked to women's lives?

3. Motherhood is an important theme in this book. Some women are devastated by the loss of motherhood (Patachara and Kisa Gotami), but others let their children go (most notably, Yasodhara and Gotami). One character, Vaddhamata, goes even further: she decides to leave her child behind. Can a mother lose her child or even let her child go, and still be a mother? What does motherhood mean to you?

4. Men do not feature much in this book. When they do, it is not often in the best light. Are men fairly treated here?

5. Ananda is a particularly beloved figure for Buddhist women. He intervened on their behalf, argued their case, and fought to help women receive ordination. After the Buddha's death, the monks reprimanded him for his advocacy (see the notes for more on this). He confessed his participation as a wrongdoing, but it is clear that he did not agree (he confessed out of respect, not out of conviction). How do you feel about Ananda's role in this story?

6. Women were welcome to practice Buddhism as lay people. So why did Gotami seek ordination for herself and her followers? If the point is liberation, and liberation can be achieved without ordination, what difference does monastic ordination make?

7. Why do you think the Buddha instituted the "Eight Heavies"? If the Buddha was an awakened being, why did he declare that nuns must always bow to monks, regardless of seniority?

8. According to the notes, the Buddhist scholar Janet Gyatso has expressed the view that the Eight Heavies are a liability to Buddhism

(Gyatso 14, 2010). Do you agree with Gyatso? Did you expect Buddhism as an institution to include rules like these?

9. This book tells the story of women who marched through the forest to ask for access to the tradition. More than 2000 years later, women are still marching for equal access in a variety of contexts. Is progress a figment of our imagination?

10. Last question—and perhaps the most important: the women of this story believed that renunciation would lead to liberation. Do you agree? Would you ever walk away from it all? Shave your head and disappear? Would that be liberation for you?

Bibliography

Primary Sources (in translation)

Appleton, Naomi and Sarah Shaw, trans. *The Ten Great Birth Stories of the Buddha: The Mahānipāta of the Jātakatthavaṇṇanā.* Chiang Mai: Silkworm, 2015.

Bays, Gwendolyn, trans. *The Lalitavistara Sūtra, Voice of the Buddha: The Beauty of Compassion*, 2 vols. Tibetan Translation Series. Berkeley: Dharma Publishing, 1983.

Bhikkhu Bodhi, trans. *The Connected Discourses of the Buddha: A New Translation of the Saṃyutta Nikāya.* Boston: Wisdom, 2000.

Bhikkhu Bodhi, trans. *The Numerical Discourses of the Buddha: A Translation of the Aṅguttara Nikāya.* Boston: Wisdom, 2012.

Bhikkhu Ñāṇamoli, trans. *Visudhimagga: The Path of Purification by Bhadantācariya Buddhaghosa.* Seattle: BPS Pariyatti Editions, 1975.

Bhikkhu Ñāṇamoli and Bhikkhu Bodhi, trans. *The Middle Length Discourse of the Buddha: A New Translation of the Majjhima Nikāya.* Boston: Wisdom, 1995.

Burlingame, Eugene Watson. *Buddhist Legends, Translated from the Original Pali Text of the Dhammapada Commentary*, 3 vols. Delhi: Munshiram Manoharlal Publishers, 1999 (1921).

Daniélou, Alain, trans. *Manimekhalaï (The Dancer with the Magic Bowl) by Merchant-Prince Shattan.* New York: New Directions, 1989.

Doniger, Wendy, trans. *The Rig Veda: An Anthology.* London: Penguin Classics, 2005.

Hallisey, Charles, trans. *Therigatha: Poems of the First Buddhist Women.* Murty Classical Library of India. Cambridge, MA: Harvard University Press, 2015.

Horner, I. B., trans. *The Minor Anthologies of the Pali Canon, Volume III: Buddhavaṃsa (Chronicle of the Buddhas) and Cariyāpiṭaka (Basket of Conduct).* London: Pali Text Society, 1975.

Horner, I. B., trans. *The Book of the Discipline: Vinaya-Piṭaka.* 6 volumes. Oxford: The Pali Text Society, 1997.

Hrdaya, Chittadhar. *Sugata Saurabha: An Epic Poem from Nepal on the Life of the Buddha*. Translated by Todd T. Lewis and Subarna Man Tuladhar. New York: Oxford University Press, 2010.

Jayawickrama, N. A., trans. *The Story of Gotama Buddha (Jātaka-nidāna)*. Oxford: The Pali Text Society, 1990.

Jones, J. J., trans. *The Mahāvastu*. 3 vols. London: The Pali Text Society. 1976–1987.

Olivelle, Patrick, trans. *Life of the Buddha (Buddhacarita) by Ashvaghosha*. Clay Sanskrit Library. New York: New York University Press, 2008.

Kautilya. *Arthashastra*. Translated by R. Shamasastry. Bangalore: The Government Press, 1915.

Obeyesekere, Ranjini, trans. *Portraits of Buddhist Women: Stories from the Saddharmaratnāvaliya*. New York: State University of New York Press, 2001.

Pruitt, William, trans. *Commentary on the Verses of the Therīs (Therīgathā-Aṭṭhakathā Paramatthadīpanī VI) by Acariya Dhammapāla*. Oxford: The Pali Text Society, 1999.

Rockhill, W. Woodville, trans. *The Life of the Buddha and the Early History of his Order, Derived from Tibetan Works in the Bkah-Hgyur and Bstan-Hgyur*. New Delhi: Asian Educational Services, 1992.

Tatelman, Joel. "The Trials of Yasodharā: A Translation of the *Bhadrakalpāvadāna* II & III." *Buddhist Literature* I (1998), 176–261.

Vatsyayana Mallanaga. *Kamasutra*. Translated and edited by Wendy Doniger and Sudhir Kakar. Oxford's World Classics. Oxford/New York: Oxford University Press, 2002.

Walsh, Maurice. *The Long Discourses of the Buddha: A Translation of the Dīgha Nikāya*. Boston: Wisdom, 1995.

Walters, Jonathan S., trans. "Legends of the Therīs." In *Legends of the Buddhist Saints: Apadānapāli*. http://apadanatranslation.org 2017.

Woodward, F. L., trans. *The Minor Anthologies of the Pali Canon, Volume II: Udāna, Verses of Uplift and Itivuttaka, As It Was Said*. Oxford: The Pali Text Society, 1996.

Secondary Sources

Anālayo. "Mahāpajāpatī's Going Forth in the Madhyama-āgama." *Journal of Buddhist Ethics* 18 (2011), 268–317.

Anālayo. "The Four Assemblies and Theravāda Buddhism." *Insight Journal*, Barre Center for Buddhist Studies, 2015.

Anālayo. *The Foundation History of the Nuns' Order*. Freiburg: Projekt Verlag, 2016a.

Anālayo. "The Going Forth of Mahāpajāpatī Gotamī in T60." *Journal of Buddhist Ethics* 23 (2016b), 1–31.

Arai, Paula. "Japanese Buddhist Nuns' Ritual of Gratitude and Empowerment." In *Women's Buddhism, Buddhism's Women: Tradition, Revision, Renewal*, edited by Ellison Findley, 119–130. Boston: Wisdom Publications, 2000.

Ariès, Philippe. *Centuries of Childhood: A Social History of Family Life*. Translated by Robert Baldick. New York: Vintage Books, 1965.

Ary, Elijah. "The Westernization of Tulkus." In *Little Buddhas: Children and Childhoods in Buddhist Texts and Traditions*, edited by Vanessa R. Sasson, 398–427. New York: Oxford University Press, 2013.

Bailey, Greg and Ian Mabbett. *The Sociology of Early Buddhism*. Cambridge: Cambridge University Press, 2006.

Bareau, André. "Lumbinī et la naissance du futur Buddha." *Bulletin de l'Ecole française d'Extrême-Orient* 76 (1987), 69–81.

Basham, A. L. *The Wonder That Was India: A Survey of the History and Culture of the Indian Sub-Continent Before the Coming of the Muslims*. Third Revised Edition. London: Picador, 2004.

Bhattacharji, Sukumari. "Prostitution in Ancient India." *Social Scientist* 15. 2 (1987), 32–61.

Bhikkhu Bodhi. *Reading the Buddha's Discourses in Pali: A Practical Guide to the Language of the Ancient Buddhist Canon*. Boston: Wisdom, 2020.

Bhikkhu Sujato. *Bhikkhunī Vinaya Studies: Research and Reflections on Monastic Discipline for Buddhist Nuns*. Santipada, 2007.

Bhikkhu Sujato. *Dreams of Bhadda: A Historical Novella*. Santipada, 2012.

Bhikkhunī Kusuma. "Inaccuracies in Buddhist Women's History." In *Innovative Buddhist Women: Swimming Against the Stream*, edited by Karma Lekshe Tsomo, 5–12. Richmond: Curzon, 2000.

Boisvert, Mathieu. "A Socio-Cultural Analysis of the Burmese *Shin Pyu* Ceremony." *Journal of Beliefs and Values* 21.2 (2000), 203–211.

Cabezón, José Ignacio. *Sexuality in Classical South Asian Buddhism*. Studies in Indian and Tibetan Buddhism. Somerville, MA: Wisdom, 2017.

Chanana, Dev Raj. *Slavery in Ancient India: As Depicted in Pali and Sanskrit Texts.* New Delhi: People's Publishing House, 1960.

Chandra, Moti, S.P. Gupta, K.N. Dikshit, Vinod P. Dwivedi and Shashi Asthana. *Costumes, Textiles, Cosmetics and Coiffure in Ancient and Mediaeval India.* Delhi: Oriental Publishers, 1973.

Clarke, Shayne. *Family Matters in Indian Buddhist Monasticisms.* Honolulu: University of Hawaii Press, 2014.

Cohen, Leonard. "Anthem." Song in the album *The Future.* Columbia (record label), 1992.

Collett, Alice. "Therīgāthā: Nandā, Female Sibling of Gotama Buddha." In *Women in Early Indian Buddhism: Comparative Textual Studies,* edited by Alice Collett, 140–160. South Asia Research. New York: Oxford University Press, 2014.

Collett, Alice. *Lives of Early Buddhist Nuns: Biographies as History.* New Delhi: Oxford University Press, 2016.

Collins, Steven. "Remarks on the Third Precept: Adultery and Prostitution in Pāli Texts." *The Journal of the Pali Text Society* 29 (2007), 263–284.

Crosby, Kate. "The Inheritance of Rāhula: Abandoned Child, Boy Monk, Ideal Son and Trainee." In *Little Buddhas: Children and Childhoods in Buddhist Texts and Traditions,* edited by Vanessa R. Sasson, 97–123. New York: Oxford University Press, 2013.

Cunningham, Alexander. *Ancient Geography of India: The Buddhist Period, Including The Campaigns of Alexander and the Travels of Hwen-Tsang.* London: Trubner and Co, 1871.

Daud, Ali. "Rethinking the History of the Kāma World in Early India." *Journal of Indian Philosophy* 39 (2011), 1–13.

Derrett, J. Duncan M. "Monastic Masturbation in Pāli Buddhist Texts." *Journal of the History of Sexuality* 15.1 (2006), 1–13.

Dewan, Saba. *Tawaifnama.* Chennai: Context, 2019.

Dimmitt, Cornelia and J. A. B. Van Buitenen, eds. *Classical Hindu Mythology: A Reader in the Sanskrit Purāṇas.* Philadelphia: Temple University Press, 1978.

Divakaruni, Chitra Lekha Bannerjee. *The Forest of Enchantments.* Delhi: HarperCollins, 2019.

Dōgen, Zen Master, and Kōshō Uchiyama. *From the Zen Kitchen to Enlightenment: Refining Your Life.* Translated by Thomas Wright. New York: Weatherhill, 1983.

Doniger, Wendy. "The 'Kamasutra': It Isn't All About Sex." The Kenyon Review 25.1 (2003), 18–37.

Doniger, Wendy. "From Kama to Karma: The Resurgence of Puritanism in Contemporary India." *Social Research* 78.1 (2011), 49–74.

Doniger, Wendy. *On Hinduism*. New York: Oxford University Press, 2014.

Doniger, Wendy. *Redeeming the Kamasutra*. New York: Oxford University Press, 2016.

Doniger, Wendy. *The Ring of Truth: And Other Myths of Sex and Jewelry*. New York: Oxford University Press, 2017.

Doniger, Wendy. *Winged Stallions and Wicked Mares: Horses in Indian Myth and History*. Charlottesville: University of Virginia Press, 2021.

Doniger O'Flaherty, Wendy. "Inside and Outside the Mouth of God: The Boundary Between Myth and Reality." *Daedalus* 109.2 Intellect and Imagination: The Limits and Presuppositions of Intellectual Inquiry (1980), 93–125.

Eck, Diana L. *India: A Sacred Geography*. New York: Three Rivers Press, 2012.

Eliade, Mircea. *Cosmos and History: The Myth of Eternal Return*. Translated by Willard R. Trask. New York: Harper Torchbooks, 1954.

Finlay, Victoria. *Colour: Travels Through the Paintbox*. London: Hodder & Stoughton, 2003.

Finnegan, Diana Damchö. *For the Sake of Women Too: Ethics and Gender in the Narratives of the Mūlasarvāstivāda Vinaya*. PhD diss. University of Wisconsin-Madison, 2009.

Fonseka, EA Gamini. "Female Resilience in the Face of Family Tragedy: A Comparative Study of Sonali Deraniyagala's Wave and the Buddhist Tale of 'Bhikkhuni Patachara.'" In *Avenues: Papers on Peace, Reconciliation and Development Challenges: Proceedings of the 2nd International Conference on Humanities & Social Sciences*, edited by Upali Pannilage, EA Gamini Fonseka and P.K.M. Dissanayak, 142–157. Matara, Sri Lanka: University of Ruhuna, 2017.

Garling, Wendy. *The Woman Who Raised the Buddha: The Extraordinary Life of Mahaprajapati*. Boulder: Shambhala, 2021.

Gautam, Sanjay K. "The Courtesan and the Birth of 'Ars Erotica' in the Kāmasūtra: A History of Erotics in the Wake of Foucault." *Journal of the History of Sexuality* 23.1 (2014), 1–20.

Gode, R. K. "History of the Practice of Massage in Ancient and Medieval India—Between B.C. 1000 and A.D. 1900." *Annals of the Bhandarkar Oriental Research Institute* 36. 1/2 (January-April 1955), 85–113.

Gonda, J. "Ancient Indian Kingship from the Religious Point of View." *Numen* 3.1 (Jan. 1956), 36–71.

Gonda, J. "Ancient Indian Kingship from the Religious Point of View (continued)." *Numen* 3.2 (April 1956), 122–155.

Gonda, J. "Ancient Indian Kingship from the Religious Point of View (continued and ended)." *Numen* 4.2 (April 1957), 127–164.

Govindraja, Radhika. *Animal Intimacies: Interspecies Relatedness in India's Central Himalayas.* Chicago: University of Chicago Press, 2018.

Gyatso, Janet. "Female Ordination in Buddhism: Looking into a Crystal Ball, Making a Future." In *Dignity and Discipline: Reviving Full Ordination for Buddhist Nuns,* edited by Thea Mohr and Jampa Tsedroen, 1–22. Boston: Wisdom, 2010.

Haberman, David. *People Trees: Worship of Trees in Northern India.* New York: Oxford University Press, 2013.

Harris, Elizabeth J., ed. *Buddhism in Five Minutes.* Sheffield, U.K.: Equinox, 2021.

Heesterman, J. C. *The Ancient Indian Royal Consecration: The Rājasūya Described According to the Yasju Texts and Annotated.* The Hague: Mouton, 1957.

Heim, Maria. *Voice of the Buddha: Buddhaghosa on the Immeasurable Words.* New York: Oxford University Press, 2018.

Hiltebeitel, Alf and Barbara D. Miller, eds. *Hair: Its Power and Meaning in Asian Cultures.* New York: State University of New York Press, 1998.

Hüsken, Ute. "The Eight Garudhammas." In *Dignity and Discipline: Reviving Full Ordination for Buddhist Nuns,* edited by Thea Mohr and Jampa Tsedroen, 143–148. Boston: Wisdom, 2010.

Jaini, Padmanabh S. *Gender and Salvation: Jaina Debates on the Spiritual Liberation of Women.* Berkeley: University of California Press, 2000.

John, Mary E. *Child Marriage in an International Frame: A Feminist Review from India.* London: Routledge, 2021.

Kapadia, K. M. *Marriage and Family in India.* Delhi: Oxford University Press, 1966.

Keown, Damien, editor. *Buddhism and Abortion*. Honolulu: University of Hawaii Press, 1999.

Kinsley, David. *Hindu Goddesses: Visions of the Divine Feminine in the Hindu Religious Tradition*. Berkeley: University of California Press, 1988.

Krey, Gisela. "Some Remarks on the Status of Nuns and Laywomen in Early Buddhism." In *Dignity and Discipline: Reviving Full Ordination for Buddhist Nuns*, edited by Thea Mohr and Jampa Tsedroen, 39–64. Boston: Wisdom, 2010.

Kritzer, Robert. "Life in the Womb: Conception and Gestation in Buddhist Scripture and Classical Indian Medical Literature." In *Imagining the Fetus: The Unborn in Myth, Religion, and Culture*, edited by Vanessa R. Sasson and Jane Marie Law, 73–90. New York: Oxford University Press, 2009.

Langenberg, Amy Paris. *Birth in Buddhism: The Suffering Fetus and Female Freedom*. Routledge Critical Studies in Buddhism. London: Routledge, 2017.

Law, Bimala Charan. *Ksatriya Clans in Buddhist India*. Calcutta: Thacker Spink, 1922.

Lindberg Falk, Monica. "Buddhism as a Vehicle for Girls' Safety and Education in Thailand." In *Little Buddhas: Children and Childhoods in Buddhist Texts and Traditions*, edited by Vanessa R. Sasson, 266–289. New York: Oxford University Press, 2013.

Lipner, Julius J. "The Classical Hindu View on Abortion and the Moral Status of the Unborn." In *Hindu Ethics: Purity, Abortion, and Euthanasia*, edited by Harold Coward, Julian J. Lipner, and Katherine K. Young, 41–69. Albany: State University of New York Press, 1989.

Makley, Charlene E. "The Body of a Nun: Nunhood and Gender in Contemporary Amdo." In *Women in Tibet: Past and Present*, edited by Janet Gyatso and Hanna Havnevik, 259–284. New York: Columbia University Press, 2005.

Malalasekera, G. P. *A Dictionary of Pāli Proper Names*. 3 vols. Oxford: The Pali Text Society, 1997.

McHugh, James. "From Precious to Polluting: Tracing the History of Camphor in Hinduism." *Material Religion* 10. 1 (2014), 30–53.

Mohr, Thea and Jampa Tsedroen, eds. *Dignity and Discipline: Reviving Full Ordination for Buddhist Nuns*. Boston: Wisdom, 2010.

Nagarajan, Vijaya. *Feeding a Thousand Souls: Women, Ritual and Ecology in India—An Exploration of the Kōlam*. New York: Oxford University Press, 2018.

Norman, K. R. *A Philological Approach to Buddhism: The Bukkyō Dendō Kyōkai Lectures 1994*. London: School of Oriental and African Studies (University of London), 1997.

Nyanaponika Thera and Helmuth Hecker. *Great Disciples of the Buddha: Their Lives, Their Works, Their Legacy*. Boston: Wisdom, 1997.

Ohnuma, Reiko. "Debt to the Mother: A Neglected Aspect of the Founding of the Nuns' Order." *Journal of the American Academy of Religion* 74.4 (2006), 861–901.

Ohnuma, Reiko. "Mother-Love and Mother-Grief: South-Asian Buddhist Variations on a Theme." *Journal of Feminist Studies in Religion* 23.1 (2007), 95–116.

Ohnuma, Reiko. *Ties That Bind: Maternal Imagery and Discourse in Indian Buddhism*. New York: Oxford University Press, 2012.

Ohnuma, Reiko. *Unfortunate Destiny: Animals in the Indian Buddhist Imagination*. New York: Oxford University Press, 2017.

Parpola, Asko. *The Roots of Hinduism: The Early Aryans and the Indus Civilization*. New York: Oxford University Press, 2015.

Parry, Jonathan P. *Death in Banares*. Cambridge: Cambridge University Press, 1994.

Patton, Laurie L. "Hinduism." In *Children and Childhood in World Religions: Primary Sources and Texts*, edited by Don S. Browning and Marcia J. Bunge, 217–276. New Jersey: Rutgers University Press, 2009.

Pema Khandro Rimpoche. "The First Women's March." *Lion's Roar*. January 2019.

Perera, L. P. N. *Sexuality in Ancient India: A Study Based on the Pali Vinayapitaka*. Kelaniya, Sri Lanka: The Postgraduate Institute of Pali and Buddhist Studies, University of Kelaniya, 1992.

Perkin, Mollwo. "The Indian Indigo Industry." *Journal of the Royal Asiatic Society of Arts* 63.3241 (1915), 117–129.

Pink Floyd. "Shine On You Crazy Diamond." Song composed by David Gilmour, Roger Waters, and Richard Wright, in the album *Wish You Were Here*. Pink Floyd Music Publishers, Ltd., 1975.

Poudel, P. C. "Muktinath, Nepal: Spiritual Magnetism and Complexity in Space." *Himalayan Review* 31 (2000), 37–59.

Powers, Richard. *The Overstory*. New York: W. W. Norton, 2018.

Richman, Paul. "The Portrayal of a Female Renouncer in a Tamil Buddhist Text." In *Gender and Religion: On the Complexity of Symbols*, edited by C. W. Bynum, S. Harrell, and P. Richman, 143–165. Boston: Beacon, 1986.

Riddle, John M. *Contraception and Abortion from the Ancient World to the Renaissance*. Cambridge, MA: Harvard University Press, 1994.

Roy, Mira. "Dyes in Ancient and Medieval India." *Indian Journal of History of Science* 13.2 (1977), 83–112.

Salomon, Richard. *Ancient Buddhist Scrolls from Gandhāra: The British Library Kharoṣṭhi Fragments*. University of Washington Press, 1999.

Salomon, Richard. *Buddhist Literature of Ancient Gandhāra: An Introduction with Selected Translations*. Somerville, MA: Wisdom, 2018.

Sasson, Vanessa R. *The Birth of Moses and the Buddha: A Paradigm for the Comparative Study of Religions*. Sheffield: Sheffield Phoenix University Press, 2007.

Sasson, Vanessa R. "A Womb with a View: The Buddha's Final Fetal Experience." In *Imagining the Fetus: The Unborn in Myth, Religion, and Culture*, edited by Vanessa R. Sasson and Jane Marie Law, 55–72. New York: Oxford University Press, 2009.

Sasson, Vanessa R. ed. *Little Buddhas: Children and Childhoods in Buddhist Texts and Traditions*. New York: Oxford University Press, 2013a.

Sasson, Vanessa R. "Maya's Disappearing Act: Motherhood in Early Buddhist Literature." In *Family in Buddhism*, edited by Liz Wilson, 147–168. New York: SUNY, 2013b.

Sasson, Vanessa R. "A Buddhist Love Story: The Buddha and Yaśodharā." *Buddhist Studies Review* 37.1 (2020), 53–72.

Sasson, Vanessa R. *Yasodhara and the Buddha*. London: Bloomsbury Academic, 2021a.

Sasson, Vanessa R. "Jeweled Renunciation: Reading the Buddha's Hagiography." In *Jewels, Jewelry, and Other Shiny Things in the Buddhist Imaginary*, edited by Vanessa R. Sasson, 65–85. Honolulu: University of Hawaii Press, 2021b.

Saxena, Monika. "Ganikas in Early India: Its Genesis and Dimensions." *Social Scientist* 34.11/12 (2006), 2–17.

Schopen, Gregory. "The Monastic Ownership of Servants or Slaves: Local and Legal Factors in the Redactional History of Two *Vinayas*." In *Buddhist Monks and Business Matters: Still More Papers on Monastic Buddhism in India*, 193–218. Honolulu: University of Hawaii Press, 2004.

Schopen, Gregory. "A Well-Sanitized Shroud: Asceticism and Institutional Values in the Middle Period of Buddhist Monasticism." In *Between the Empires: Society in India 300BCE to 400CE*, edited by Patrick Olivelle, 315–348. New York: Oxford University Pres, 2006.

Schopen, Gregory. "The Urban Nun and a Protective Rite for Children in Early North India." In *Buddhist Nuns, Monks, and Other Worldly Matters: Recent Papers on Monastic Buddhism in India*, 3–22. Honolulu: University of Hawaii Press, 2014.

Schlingloff, Dieter. *Fortified Cities of Ancient India: A Comparative Study*. London: Anthem Press, 2013.

Shulman, David. "Creating and Destroying the Universe in Twenty-Nine Nights." *The New York Review*. November 24, 2012.

Silk, Jonathan A. "Child Abandonment and Homes for Unwed Mothers in Ancient India: Buddhist Sources." *Journal of American Oriental Institute* 127.3 (2007), 297–314.

Silk, Jonathan A. *Riven by Lust: Incest and Schism in Buddhist Legend and Historiography*. Honolulu: University of Hawaii Press, 2008.

Singh, Upinder. *A History of Ancient and Early Medieval India: From the Stone Age to the 12ᵗʰ Century*. Delhi: Pearson, 2009.

Soneji, Davesh, ed. *Bharatnatyam: A Reader*. New York: Oxford University Press, 2010.

Soneji, Davesh. *Unfinished Gestures: Devadasis, Memory, and Modernity in South India*. Chicago: University of Chicago Press, 2012.

Strong, John S. *The Buddha: A Short Biography*. London: Oneworld, 2001.

Thapar, Romila. *From Lineage to State: Social Formations of the Mid-First Millennium BC in Ganga Valley*. Bombay: Oxford University Press, 1984.

van der Geer, Alexander. *Animals in Stone: Indian Mammals Sculptured Through Time*. Leiden: Brill, 2008.

Vuong, Ocean. *On Earth We're Briefly Gorgeous*. New York: Penguin, 2019.

Walters, Jonathan. "A Voice from the Silence: The Buddha's Mother's Story." *History of Religions* 33.4 (1994), 358–379.

Weinberger-Thomas, Catherine. *Ashes of Immortality: Widow Burning in India*. Translated by Jeffrey Melhman and David Gordon White. Chicago: University of Chicago Press, 1991.

Wilde-Blavatsky, Adele. "What Lies Beneath the Robes: Are Buddhist Monasteries Suitable Places for Children?" *Elephant Journal*, June 2013. https://www.elephantjournal.com/2013/06/what-lies-beneath-the-robes-are-buddhist-monasteries-suitable-places-for-children-adele-wilde-blavatsky/

Williams, Liz. "A Whisper in the Silence: Nuns Before Mahāpajāpatī?" *Buddhist Studies Review* 17.2 (2000), 167–173.

Williams, Liz. "Red Rust, Robbers, and Rice Fields: Women's Part in the Participation of the Decline of the Dhamma." *Buddhist Studies Review* 19.1 (2002), 41–47.

Wilson, Liz. *Charming Cadavers: Horrific Figurations of the Feminine in Indian Buddhist Hagiographic Literature*. Chicago: University of Chicago Press, 1996.

Wilson, Liz, ed. *Family in Buddhism*. New York: State University of New York Press, 2013.

Young, Serinity. *Dreaming the Lotus: Buddhist Dream Narrative, Imagery, and Power*. Boston: Wisdom Publications, 1995.

Zimmer, Heinrich. *Myths and Symbols in Indian Art and Civilization*. Princeton: Princeton University Press, 1946.

Acknowledgments

When everything has been written, when pages have been edited, when it is finally time to press send, only then do I allow myself the bittersweet experience of writing my acknowledgments. The "bitter" part is inevitable: I never really want the book-writing process to end. But it is so sweet, because I am perpetually amazed by the number of precious people I have in my life to thank.

I begin with Naomi Appleton, who has been a wonderful friend and colleague these past few years. She introduced me to the Equinox family, and they have steered this book towards the finish line with efficient grace. Pauline Burton, in particular, edited the bumpy bits and made this book so much better than it once was. What an extraordinary editor you are.

I thank also Wendy Doniger. Her writing has been with me for many years, but her personal support has made the most difference. She has encouraged me throughout this project with her generous kindness, never tiring of my questions and never failing me when my confidence wanes. She has taught me, more than anyone else, to remember that we do not write for our colleagues. We write for our students. We do this work for them.

Maria Heim, Kristin Scheible, and Amy Langenberg have been constant companions in the field of Buddhist Studies. I know I could not have survived the academic terrain without them. Each one has taken the time to read drafts of this book, provide feedback, and has encouraged me to keep exploring my creativity. Friendship with each of them is a precious gem.

Amy Langenberg, in particular, has been a rigorous partner in conversations around women's ordination. We have travelled the world together, attending conferences, sitting side-by-side at Sakyadhita meetings, debating and negotiating and wondering together. So many of the themes I have written about in this book are the result of that time with her. I hear Amy's voice in many of these pages.

This leads me to thank Sakyadhita as an organisation. While I cannot marry myself to every element of an institution, Sakaydhita has provided me with extraordinary opportunities to think through questions and appreciate diverse responses with regards to women's monasticism in the tradition. I am grateful for the many events I have been able to participate in and the many friendships I have enjoyed as a result. Karma Lekshe Tsomo and Jetsunma Tenzin Palmo have been fearless leaders.

I am deeply grateful to John Strong for his support. I hope he knows how important his mentorship has been for me over the years. I don't believe many of us are capable of taking a journey through the complicated maze of academic learning without the benefit of others showing us the way.

Charlie Hallisey is another teacher that I find myself deeply grateful for. His encouragement means more to me than I can articulate. I have chosen an unusual path with this type of writing, and Charlie keeps cheering me on. His translation of the *Therigatha* was with me throughout the process.

Heartfelt gratitude goes to Bhikkhuni Vimalanyani, who provided me with invaluable commentary and insight. Andy Rotman, Nancy Lin, Liz Wilson, and Kim Beek have each taken the time to think through questions with me or read sections of this book. I also thank Selena Liss, Holly Wheatcroft, Rachel Levine, Nancy Berman, and Kim Kujawski for supporting me in this work, for reading parts (or entire drafts), and for their enduring friendship. Selena in particular read two full drafts of this book, including the first messy disaster version (that alone deserves a prize!). Thanks also to my student, Kennedy Lalonde, for being a brilliant conversation partner and most enthusiastic interviewer. I can't wait to see where life takes you.

And finally, my enduring gratitude to my family: my little Egyptian (but sort-of Syrian) tribe of parents and sisters and aunts and uncles and cousins that are everywhere in my life, perpetually shouting, laughing, complaining, eating, and loving. And to Sebastien, my gentle husband (of 25 years!), who is so much nicer to me than I think I deserve (he staunchly disagrees with this statement, but I write it here anyway). And to our beautiful son, Darshan, who makes me laugh every single day. And of whom I am so very proud. I love you.